25 TO LIFE

25 TO LIFE

THE TRUTH, THE WHOLE TRUTH, AND NOTHING BUT THE TRUTH

LESLIE CROCKER SNYDER

WITH TOM SHACHTMAN

WARNER BOOKS

An AOL Time Warner Company

Warner Books, Inc., 1271 Avenue of the Americas, New York, NY 10020

Visit our Web site at www.twbookmark.com.

An AOL Time Warner Company

Printed in the United States of America

First Printing: September 2002

10 9 8 7 6 5 4 3 2 1

Library of Congress Cataloging-in-Publication Data

Snyder, Leslie Crocker
    25 to life : the truth, the whole truth, and nothing but the truth / Leslie Crocker Snyder
with Tom Shachtman.
        p. cm.
    ISBN 0-446-53020-4
    1. Snyder, Leslie Crocker 2. Women judges—New York (State)—New York—Biography.
3. Crime—New York (State)—New York. I. Title: Twenty-five to life. II. Shachtman, Tom.
III. Title.

KF373.S62 A3 2002
347.73'014'082092—dc21
[B]   2002069187

To my beloved family

and

to "the team": Alex, Teresa, and Rocco

CONTENTS

ACKNOWLEDGMENTS

I would never have written this book without the encouragement of the author Lorenzo Carcaterra. Although I had toyed with the idea for several years (after suggestions and encouragement from others), it was Lorenzo who made me feel I could and should go ahead and just *do* it. He is a great friend.

My agent, Suzanne Gluck at William Morris, was always helpful and is a truly dynamic woman. You are terrific!

Jamie Raab is a wonderful editor, guiding and assisting but never interfering; she is also a lovely person and I was truly fortunate to have her helping me.

Lou Pitt: Your constant encouragement and enthusiasm have been invaluable; I appreciate everything you have done, including helping me over a number of "bumps" in the road, as well as being a good friend.

Paul Sherman: I can't thank you enough for being a good friend and a fine lawyer.

Tom Shachtman: Your assistance was appreciated.

My deepest thanks go to my incredible legal team: Alex Calabrese and Teresa Matushaj, my former and present law clerks, and Rocco DeSantis, my court clerk. Alex is my surrogate kid brother and always will be; Teresa a surrogate daughter. I love them both and could never have accomplished my work on the bench without them. Rocco is simply the best court clerk in the business and one of the nicest human beings on earth.

To the friends and colleagues whom I value, you are too numerous to name.

To the men and women who have protected my family and me all these years, no words can ever express our appreciation. We literally might not be here without you and will forever be grateful to you.

Most important to me in life has been my wonderful family. My mother, father, and brother have always encouraged me, and my mother, in particular, inspired me.

Our kids—the best in every way—could not be discussed or described for security reasons, but they know how much they mean to me: They make my life worthwhile. I am sad that I could not talk about them more.

And, saving the very best for last: Nothing would be possible without my Fred, my inspiration for everything good and meaningful in life.

Thank you all.

Leslie Crocker Snyder
New York City, March 2002

The Goal

"Lives of great men all remind us
We can make our lives sublime,
And, departing, leave behind us
Footprints on the sands of time . . ."

from "A Psalm of Life" (1839)
by Henry Wadsworth Longfellow

25 TO LIFE

TARGET:
A VERY CREDIBLE
THREAT

"Judge, there's a hit team on its way here to kill you."
"What?"
*"I'm sorry, Judge, but we've just received information that
a hit team is on its way here from L.A.—with a contract to kill
you. . . ."*

It was a weekday, just before Christmas of 1988, and I was
working at the job I loved, being a judge on New York State's
highest criminal trial court, the supreme court. I'd been on the
bench for six years and on the supreme court since 1986, presiding over some of New York City's most serious drug and
drug-related murder cases. I was listening intently to testimony
about the neighborhood-enslaving tactics of the latest in a long
line of drug dealers when lunchtime rolled around. Usually I
spend the lunch recess at my home away from home, Forlini's
restaurant. But it was almost Christmas and I hadn't finished
shopping for my husband and kids; the weather was good, and
Barneys was a ten-minute cab ride away. I went for it.

It didn't take long to pick out some nice shirts, ties, and belts.
I was pleased at my efficiency, albeit exercised at the eleventh
hour. But I had to get back to court to set up for the afternoon

session; I like to be the first one in the courtroom. It took me a good ten minutes to find a cab. I had to wander along several blocks and turn on a little New York–style aggression.

My courtroom was empty when I arrived, until the ranking court officer burst in. A fat, older guy with a know-it-all attitude, this sergeant acted as though he ran the place. I found him quite annoying, and perhaps he felt the same way about me, because he seemed almost pleased when he delivered this message: "Judge, I'm sorry to have to tell you this, but there's a hit team on the way from Los Angeles to kill you. One black guy, one white guy."

My heart skipped a beat. "Is this a joke?"

"No, Judge. We have very credible information from a reliable source, and we checked with the L.A. police. They *are* missing a black-and-white hit team. In the last couple of days, the team hasn't been seen in L.A., and that conforms with the information we received."

I was almost certain this was another of the sergeant's bad jokes and was about to tell him off, but his expression conveyed that for once he wasn't joking. Now my heart began to race.

"You can't be serious. That's absurd!"

"I'm afraid it's all too serious, Judge."

The idea that anyone would want to kill me was unreal; I'd never confronted anything like it. Sure, there had been threats shouted at me in the courtroom by defendants to whom I'd given stiff sentences, the occasional "Go fuck yourself, bitch!" but those men were in handcuffs or at least surrounded by court officers. In my courtroom I'd always felt safe.

Now I didn't know exactly how I felt, but I certainly didn't feel safe. It suddenly struck me that there was no security to speak of in the building and none at all at the courtroom door. Anyone could walk in, up to the well—the partially fenced-off area in which the judge, jury, lawyers, and defendants sit—and get within fifteen feet of my bench without being challenged. At that distance, a hit man wouldn't have to be a very good shot.

Those ten minutes I'd spent wandering the streets, searching for a cab: how vulnerable I'd been. Anyone could have followed me. Maybe I'd never again be able to do something as spontaneous as last-minute Christmas shopping.

My mind flashed to when I had been eight and a half months pregnant and working as a special prosecutor out of an office high up in the World Trade Center. Information had come in that the FALN, a Puerto Rican extremist group, had planted a bomb in the building. This was a time of extremist attacks, and a number of buildings had been bombed, so the threat was taken seriously. The elevators had been stopped, and we couldn't get out. I hadn't wanted special treatment, but then I phoned Fred—my husband, my best friend, my rock. He's a pediatrician, and the parents he deals with invariably say he's the calmest person they've ever met. Fred insisted that the police would want to get me out of the World Trade Center right away because they wouldn't want to deliver a baby in the midst of the larger crisis. He was right; they took me down in an emergency elevator and put me in a cab to go home. In retrospect, of course, I can see that I was very fortunate, as were all my friends and co-workers, because it wasn't 2001 and the devastating terrorist attack that destroyed the World Trade Center; in fact, nothing happened.

On this pre-Christmas day in 1988, there was no easy or quick escape. The best I could manage was a one-hour recess while the court officers decided how to protect me. I tried to stay in control of my emotions even if I was not in control of the situation. Since I didn't have a robing room or my own bathroom, there was no private place where I could let my emotions hang out; I had no choice but to calm down, inwardly and outwardly.

A detective from the New York City Police Department's intelligence unit ("Intell") walked briskly into the courtroom. After identifying himself to me, he said he was appalled at how easily he was able to enter the court and come near me without being questioned. At the door he hadn't shown his shield or ID, and he was well dressed and didn't look like a skel—a low-life—but still. He could not believe there were no metal detectors in the building, no way to X-ray bags, no guards to prevent people from getting into the courtroom without having to identify themselves. After all, this was 111 Centre Street, an official courthouse.

"What cases are you handling?" he asked, on the obvious theory that the threat emanated from one of them. That was also a good guess because I was routinely being given cases with some of the most violent defendants in the system. Another detective tried to pry information from the court officers, who had deliberately kept some of what they knew from me, a standard law enforcement tactic (ignorance is bliss?).

At the end of the day I was driven home in a court car by a court officer assigned as my security and was told that a similar car would pick me up again the next morning. It was presumed that I'd be fine until then, since we lived in a reasonably secure apartment building with a doorman.

Despite my devotion to my work, my family is the most important part of my life. Virtually every moment I'm not at the courthouse I spend with my husband and kids. So that night, after the kids went to bed, Fred and I had quite a discussion. He was upset for me but calm about the rest of it: "The threat is real, but the protective measures are appropriate and adequate."

"My concern is the kids," I responded. "I think I can handle being in danger myself, but obviously I don't want you and the boys in jeopardy."

"The threat is against you, not against the family. We'll be okay."

Next morning we told the kids; we had to, because we were going to notify their schools. I was not totally reassured by the schools' responses. They seemed annoyed at the bother that our kids' security entailed, even though these schools had among their students a number of the sons and daughters of celebrities and the very wealthy, children who went to school with their own bodyguards.

The source of the threat was eventually traced to a drug gang, or "posse," made up of Jamaicans known for putting people's eyes out and for "ultimate torture," terrorizing people to obtain what they wanted. I'd never thought about what they might do to me. Or what some other drug lord might try to do. My judicial "calendar" (cases assigned to me) was full of drug cases; few other judges were handling as many serious ones.

The threat came specifically from a scary guy I'll call "Fitzgerald"—that's not his real name—a notorious drug dealer in Brooklyn. He was charged with dealing, an A-1 felony, the highest-level felony in New York, punishable by up to twenty-five years to life. Now things began to make sense. Fitzgerald and his lawyer had both been cocky and antagonistic to me and to everyone else in the courtroom, acting as though the system would never be able to do anything to them. And for a while, they had been right about that: I had attempted to remand Fitzgerald—send him to jail with no way to get out on bail—but his lawyer had, in effect, appealed my ruling and gotten it knocked down to $350,000 cash or bond, and soon Fitzgerald was out on the street again. Reports said that he was continuing his drug dealing.

A month or so later, the frightened bail bondsman appeared in my court, pleading to have the bond revoked and Fitzgerald returned to jail. Though terrified, he declined to share with us what had led him to this point, just saying shakily that his company now found the collateral insufficient to guarantee the defendant's return to court. He had a legitimate fear of Fitzgerald skipping to Jamaica and of his bond company's bail money being forfeited; I also suspect he had heard that Fitzgerald was continuing to run a highly profitable drug operation and was afraid to report it to the authorities (as the law required him to do). Never before had a bail bondsman made such a request in my court; I had no choice but to agree. The cops picked up Fitzgerald, who affected outrage at the indignity, and I remanded him again. Once Fitzgerald understood that he'd have to remain incarcerated without bail until his trial, which was months away, he apparently decided to have me killed.

An informant was planted near Fitzgerald in jail and, sure enough, Fitzgerald bragged about his plans for "blowing up" the judge. His cell was tossed—searched—and yielded instructions on how to make a bomb and a letter featuring stick-figure drawings of him killing me with it. If before then a part of me had been unwilling to believe the threat was real, all of me believed it now. I expected my protection to be beefed up.

"Sorry, Judge. There's only so much Intell can do. Ariel Sharon, the Israeli defense minister, is in town, and we have to deploy our resources to protect him first."*

How comforting! My security was haphazard at best.

My law clerk, Alex Calabrese, and I were warned to watch out for letter bombs. Knowing nothing about letter bombs, we were sent to watch a movie produced by various impressive law enforcement authorities. I'll never forget that experience. In the film, an ordinary letter arrives at a law office, a secretary goes to open it, and—boom!—everyone dies and the place is wiped out. It was the scariest film either of us had ever seen; we left the screening totally shaken. The NYPD was sifting our office mail for letter bombs, but Alex raised a logical question: "What good does it to do screen the office mail without also

---

*Intell, the intelligence unit of the NYPD, is charged with protection duties. Other than on this one occasion, it has always taken my security very seriously.

screening the judge's home mail?" Doing the home mail was cumbersome, since it had to be done by the feds because the state did not then have the equipment; I thought it was not being done at all, until a suspicious-looking package arrived at our building, wrapped in brown paper and not well marked. The NYPD bomb squad gingerly carried it away and put it through the scanner . . . which found in it the denim skirt I'd ordered while on vacation. What a relief—and a minor embarrassment—but it didn't lessen the pressure. I hesitated before opening packages or letters whose origin I wasn't sure of, and Fred and I wouldn't let the kids touch any mail or packages.

During the day I functioned pretty well, keeping at bay the idea of someone planning to kill me. I repressed things, as we all do when we're busy—focus on your work, then run home, make dinner, spend time with the kids. But at three in the morning I'd wake up in a cold sweat produced by moments of terror, not for myself but for my kids. I felt I could not live with myself if as a result of doing my job anything happened to *them*. Every parent has nightmares about their kid crossing the street and getting struck by a car; my nightmare felt far worse and had a very real chance of coming to pass, or so it seemed at 3:00 A.M.

"Any reports of a black-and-white hit team in New York City looking for me?" I'd ask each week.

"Nope, Judge. Nothing."

Was that a good sign or a bad one? If the hit team were professionals, wouldn't they know how to elude the authorities? The danger continued, unabated. And we had to decide what to do with the Fitzgerald case. I didn't want to recuse myself; if I did, the skels of the world might conclude that making threats against your judge—especially a female judge—was a great way to get a judge of your own choosing.

A key defense motion was due for a pretrial hearing: a motion to suppress the introduction into evidence of the drugs that the police had found in Fitzgerald's possession after executing a search warrant. If the drugs went into evidence, there would likely be a conviction; if they were not allowed in, there very well might be a different outcome.

Since the threats had been made against me personally, rather than against judges in general, and since the ruling on the motion to suppress would likely determine the result of the trial process, I decided to discuss the matter with my administrative judge. Appearances were the issue; a judge has not only to be fair but to give the appearance of being fair and of meeting the interests of justice. I knew I could be fair, but we agreed that in order not to give the appearance of bias, the motion to suppress should be reassigned to another judge. The administrator told me whom he had in mind; I respected that judge and was comfortable with having the matter sent to him for the hearing.

After that, the police believed that the threat against me eased. The protective measures were reduced, and gradually my family and I went back to our usual daily routine. But we could not completely forget the Fitzgerald episode. It left a feeling of uneasiness, even though I was able to push that feeling into the background.

The second judge ruled for Fitzgerald and suppressed the drugs, finding the officers' testimony not credible and the search warrant legally deficient. As a result, the case against Fitzgerald was dismissed. Had I examined the same evidence, I doubtless would have come to the same conclusion—even if I hadn't liked the probable result, which was that a heavy drug dealer would be released to go back to his drug dealing. My duty under the law is to evaluate everything in a fair manner, and I take that obligation very seriously. In any event, Fitzgerald did go right back to dealing.

A year later, I learned that the Immigration and Naturalization Service (INS) was trying to deport Fitzgerald. Still later, I heard that while INS was actually putting Fitzgerald on the plane to leave the country, the process was stopped, and he was taken off the plane and released from custody. I was outraged, but the story rang true: Fitzgerald had repeatedly boasted of his "contacts," by which he probably meant people he knew who were on his payroll. He had used some of these to conduct his drug business while he was in jail, and he'd evidently used them to buy his way out of deportation. Today, I'm told, he is still dealing in Brooklyn. Not exactly a vote of confidence for the criminal justice system.

After Fitzgerald, the feeling that I had to look over my shoulder never completely left me. I was happy to move across the street to 100 Centre, which had better security. My new courtroom was smaller than the previous one, but that was of no importance to me; what did matter was that everything felt better, safer.

What I did not realize in 1989 was that the Fitzgerald threat was only the first of many to come in my judicial career, some of which would be even more serious. I also did not realize that ultimately, as a result of those later threats, my entire family and I would be placed under full-time police protection.

The cases on my calendar continued to be among the most violent handled in the criminal justice system (other than the federal terrorist trials). But this was a job that, in spite of the threats, I loved. After all, I'd been preparing for it since I was five years old.

"COPS AND ROBBERS"

One of my earliest memories is of telling friends that I wanted to be a criminal lawyer. I was five. The source of my ambition was probably as simple as my parents making the observation that since I liked to argue, I ought to be a lawyer.

In 1950, when I was eight, we moved to Baltimore. In our new home I had my own room and a radio; on Sunday nights I liked to listen to a program about crime, at the end of which the announcer read off the FBI's Ten Most Wanted list. I took notes and fantasized about capturing these criminals and turning them over to law enforcement. On the weekends, my brother and I would make up games about the criminals, playing cops and robbers as we rode our bikes around our safe neighborhood. When we got our first family television set, we were allowed to watch for only fifteen minutes a day during the week and a half hour on the weekends; on Friday nights, the whole family would watch my favorite program, Ralph Bellamy in *Man Against Crime*.

My father, a professor of eighteenth-century French literature and philosophy and a recognized scholar in his field, was teaching at Goucher College. My mother served as his unpaid assistant; between bouts of housework and raising my brother and me, she did background reading for him, typed and edited his manuscripts, and performed a thousand other tasks that aided his writing and his academic career.

My brother and I attended private schools on full scholarships, I at the Bryn Mawr Country Day School for girls, he at the nearby all-boys Gilman School. I felt that I was bright but very young for my class—I was two years ahead of my classmates—and I also knew I wasn't "one of the girls" at Bryn Mawr. My classmates were almost uniformly rich, social, and, of course, white. I was nonrich, a nondebutante, nonsocial; my parents were relatively poor, living only on an academic's salary, at that time around $4,000 a year. They had wanted to send us to a Quaker Friends school, which had students from more diversified backgrounds, but Friends had offered only half scholarships.

I kept on saying that I wanted to be a criminal lawyer and nobody in my family told me that was a ridiculous idea, even at a time when there were very few women lawyers in the country—1 or 2 percent—and almost none in criminal law. Certainly my mother never suggested that such a goal was beyond me. From the time that I was very small she would tell me, incessantly, that I must become an independent person, have my own career, that I could do anything I wanted to, and that I should always aim for the top. Her daily mantra was the question "Leslie, are you doing something constructive?" Most of the time, I was. In my class of thirty-three at Bryn Mawr I was one of the top students, and we were doing some serious intellectual work, studying Greek, Latin, and French. Sometimes the mantra became a bit much; I learned to prop a large history book in front of me, to demonstrate to my mother's watchful eyes that I was indeed doing something constructive, but concealed behind it a mystery story. Enough was enough.

Recently, I was struck by a phrase used by Gloria Steinem, to the effect that we as women are all living out our mothers' unfulfilled lives. I believe that was true for me and for many women in my generation who were driven to accomplish things. My mother was—is—an extremely intelligent and capable person, but her life in the forties and fifties was entirely constrained by her husband, the mores of the time, and the circumstances in which she found herself.

I also share with the women of my generation a certain lack of self-confidence. No one wants to believe this, because I have achieved some success, but I've always had to overcome doubts about my "worthwhileness" and intellectual capabilities. Some of these doubts are due to what I perceived as my father's awesome intellectual abilities and the fact that he directed his intellectual interest toward my brother, and successfully so, since my brother has become a brilliant mathematician whose field is the theory of numbers, and a wonderful, interesting man.

If I hadn't had my mother there, encouraging me, I don't know what would have happened; but she was there, and her daily exhortations left me no choice but to achieve. "You can do more," she'd invariably say, and ask, "Well, what's next?" Today, at ninety, she is still asking me the same question. I know that she is proud of me, so I ask, in return, if anything that I do will ever be enough to satisfy her. She lovingly replies, "Never—you can do more."

Mother's constant encouragement was primary for me, but I also got a lot from my father, even though he was emotionally somewhat distant, absorbed in his own intellectual work. Widely read, able to speak four or five languages, he inspired my respect for intellectual matters and for the rational analysis of ideas. He was decisive and so am I; he was compulsive about being prepared in every situation and so am I; and he was an incredibly hard worker and I think that I am, too. My father also inspired us with a love of reading. He read to us almost every night, until I was about ten, from such diverse material as Edgar Allan Poe (what nightmares I had after "The Pit and the Pendulum"), Plutarch's *Lives*, Aristotle, Dickens's *Great Expecta-*

tions—still one of my favorite books—from Homer, and from Greek mythology, my absolute favorite.

My mother and father's joint concern for family has certainly inspired my goals and values: Family is always first.

Another motivating factor was being atypical in my school. All around me girls were "coming out" as debutantes, being readied for marriage; when they went to college, it was more to look for a mate than to obtain an education that would enable them to have a career. Not in their social set, I could be different in many other respects: When you do not completely fit in and you are not the most popular girl in the class, you find other ways to prove yourself. My classmates respected—and sometimes resented—me because I did well academically, because I didn't conform, and because I was two years younger. I had skipped a grade when I entered the school and another after my family and I spent a year in France (and I attended a French lycée and studied subjects like Greek and Latin in French) while my father was on two prestigious grants, writing a book. But when you're fourteen and your classmates are sixteen, the two-year difference is huge, especially in social terms.

One other story from my Bryn Mawr years. Like most other girls I wanted to be an actress, and during my senior year I appeared in Shaw's *Pygmalion*. I thought I had performed well, but after the play my parents took me aside and said they felt it their duty to inform me that I had no talent as an actress and should, therefore, pursue other directions for a career. I was devastated.

Radcliffe offered me a full scholarship. I believed that it had a greater academic reputation than the other colleges to which I'd been accepted and been offered scholarships; and it was coed. I was sixteen when I arrived in Cambridge and was soon overwhelmed. Radcliffe was always really Harvard, academically, and after the Bryn Mawr School, Harvard was huge and imposing. I loved it.

Among my classmates were Elizabeth Holtzman, who later became a congressional representative and the district attorney for Brooklyn, and Ruth Messinger, who was Manhattan Borough president and ran—unsuccessfully—for mayor of New York City. We were not particularly friends at Radcliffe, though we were aware of one another. (Also among my classmates was Ted Kaczyinski, the Unabomber—Harvard class of 1962. I don't think I knew him, but who knows?)

In the fall of 1958, the Harvard environment was an eye-opener. I had not been permitted to date in high school, but at Radcliffe I began to do so, and in the process of making up for lost time I went a little overboard, occasionally having three or four dates in one day—coffee, lunch, drinks, and dinner. Freedom at last! Of course, we had to return to our dorms by 1:00 A.M., but that curfew seemed incredibly liberal to me back then.

Academically, the university was not inspiring. I'm sure this was due to my immaturity, not to Harvard's inadequacy. However, one of our children recently attended Harvard and despite graduating magna cum laude also found it academically uninspiring, although he, too, loved the experience. I remember one exciting course in constitutional law, but not much else. My grades slipped as I became engaged to a handsome Harvard jock. The plan was that I would go to a Harvard-Radcliffe one-year graduate program in business administration, which would give me a degree that would enable me to support my husband while he went to law school; then, when he was making money, he'd support me while I attended law school. When the personal relationship fell apart in the middle of my grad school year, I wanted out of the whole plan, but my parents had already paid the part of the tuition for the business program that wasn't covered by a half scholarship and insisted that I complete the year. Our undergraduate class of 1962, by the way, was the last ever to receive degrees from Radcliffe; thereafter, female students would collect Harvard diplomas. It was in response to the university's attempt to change the language on our diplomas from Latin to English that I took part in my one and only student protest and received my first and last whiff of tear gas. It was strange to be on the periphery of a riot and the recipient of police action; today, it makes me think that I wouldn't have done well at a university later in the sixties, during the real student protests.

After obtaining my business school certificate in 1963, I ran off to Paris, where I'd found a job as an executive trainee for a forklift company. My French was fluent, and the position served to get me away from the United States so I could think about what to do with my life—God knows I hadn't the slightest interest in forklift trucks. I still wanted to go to law school, but my parents had no intention of subsidizing any further education, because they were not pleased by my apparent lack of direction. Shortly, they flew over to Paris to demand that I return to the United States, and we had a negotiation. I agreed to come back on condition that I attend law school; my father had become dean of the graduate school at Case Western Reserve University, and because of professional courtesy extended to faculty members he could obtain a no-tuition place for me at its law school, if I qualified. I had always wanted to go to Yale, but I had no money and in those days there were no student loans to women aspirants. I realized that Yale was a pipe dream and that I'd better settle for what I could get. The deal was consummated, and I made a date to return—after a few weeks of hanging out in Europe with a boyfriend and, unbeknownst to my parents, of hitchhiking with him from place to place. After all, I had to have some fun, especially before returning to the bosom of my family.

In 1963, Case Western Reserve was a small law school; it is much bigger and better now;* and back then we had only two women in our class. Some of my professors were openly skeptical of women in the law. Their attitude smacked of the provincialism I felt—with youthful arrogance—that Cleveland embodied; and which I hoped would not be replicated once I got into the legal profession in a larger, more cosmopolitan city. During my first weeks at law school, one of my classmates came up to me and said, "You went to Radcliffe, right? So you must believe in free love. . . ." His remark cemented my view of Cleveland and my law school.

Cleveland law circles were still obsessed with the Sam Shepard case; it had recently concluded, but talk of it reinforced my interest in criminal law. There was nothing practical about criminal law in my classes, however, and absolutely no practical courtroom training; this was typical of all law schools at that time. But on the whole, the three years I spent at Case Western Reserve Law were beneficial. I lived at home and got to know my parents as adults; and because I was attending a small school, I was able to become associate editor of its law review and to take part in moot court competitions on the state and national levels—I eventually got to argue in front of Supreme Court Justice Potter Stewart. Moot court fueled my interest in trying cases, although I turned down the opportunity to apply to a special program in Washington, D.C., to become a lawyer for the indigent; there had never been a woman recipient of this award and it intrigued me, but others talked me out of it. And my parents talked me out of joining the Peace Corps.

I had gotten to know a junior partner in a top Cleveland law firm from moot court, and he encouraged me to interview with his firm for a summer job. My gender-neutral first name came into play. The partner who was to interview me did not look at

*I am flattered to have been asked to be their law school graduation speaker this year (2002).

me when I entered the room; he made some comments about my excellent law school record and said, "Have a seat, Mr. Crocker." Once he looked up and saw me, he did a double take and ended the interview with, "I'm sorry. There's been some mistake. We don't hire women in our law firm." I was shocked, in part because of his lack of hesitation about expressing his prejudice and in part because nothing like this had ever happened to me before. And there was no redress; this was 1965, before there was any possibility of filing a federal antidiscrimination law suit for gender bias, and besides, that sort of thought would never have occurred to me then.

After the abruptly terminated interview, I went home and cried; as usual, my mother helped me return to my senses. Her no-nonsense attitude, minimal sympathy, and rousing "Stop feeling sorry for yourself—move on!" forced me to rally.

This was the first blatant discrimination I'd experienced, though there had always been some of the more subtle kind: From men in the law school and from professors, I'd occasionally heard the old chestnut that I was "taking up a place that a real breadwinner should have had."

When I applied for a permanent job, I received offers from several large firms in New York and in Washington and chose Kaye Scholer in Manhattan, because a family friend was a partner there and another partner was a woman. None of the other firms at which I'd interviewed had a woman partner. My mother's voice was influential here, too: "Go to the best firm, take the best job, do the best you can. After that, you'll be able to do anything you want."

When I graduated from law school, as number one in the class—number two if the count included transfer students—and had my offer from Kaye Scholer in hand, my parents celebrated and chose that moment to tell me one reason why: They could now rest assured that I would have a career as a lawyer, not as an actress. Back when I had appeared in *Pygmalion*, they

17

confided, I had actually done a superb job. As they had sat in the audience at the play, they had worried that I might try for a career on the stage, with what they were certain would be attendant heartbreak and a life of personal chaos. To discourage me from such a career path, they had told me I had no talent for acting.

New York was a wonderful place to be a young professional in 1966. I had spent several summers working there and had visited relatives there many times, so I was comfortable in the big city, and my income from Kaye Scholer was adequate to take care of my needs. I had a good social life. The only problem was the job. I had known what the drill would be for a new associate in a "white shoe" firm, and the people there were very nice; but the kind of work I was permitted to do—basic research in the library, dull corporate cases, minimal client contact—was not to my liking. Only occasionally would I get to talk to a senior partner and, of course, I was never involved with the dynamics of the interesting cases—although I did, once, get to attend a business meeting with some of the Rolling Stones, one of whom invited me to London for the weekend. I understood those strictures, but after spending six months at Kaye Scholer, I knew I wanted out and that I must do criminal law or no law at all. The other new woman associate, who hated the work, left the firm after a few months, but I stayed, believing that I needed to put in more time before moving on.

I decided to apply for a position in the United States Attorney's Office for the Southern District in Manhattan. A number of former Kaye Scholer associates had gone there, and the work sounded exciting. But in the fall of 1967, when I walked into that office and asked for an application for the criminal division, they looked at me as though I were crazy and told me that they accepted women only in the civil division. Incredulous and devastated, I didn't bother applying. Time for a new plan! Friends recommended the Manhattan District Attorney's Office, then run by the legendary Frank Hogan. I set up an interview there and also (on the same day) at Legal Aid, which was in the same building. I had no real preference for the defense or the prosecution side, I just wanted to work in criminal law. At the DA's office I ran into a friend from Harvard who encouraged me to work there, and I was told that there was one relatively senior woman in the office and three who were junior.

After several midlevel interviews, I finally met Hogan. He sat behind a huge desk in an impressive office filled with mementos and photographs of himself with various high-ranking politicians. Hogan looked like a gray-haired leprechaun, immaculately dressed and buttoned up and puffing on a pipe. He acted as though he were the patriarch of a clan, the stern grandfather who would not put up with any nonsense. He did not try to put me at ease, and I got the impression that he did not have much use for women lawyers. He tossed me a few softball questions about Kaye Scholer and then asked, "Are you married?"

When I told him I was not, he asked, "Have you ever been married?" I answered no again, and we went on to other matters, but versions of this question kept surfacing and I wondered if he thought something was wrong with me. I don't think he was implying that I might be a lesbian; that idea was far from the forefront of most people's consciousness at the time. But when he asked for the third or fourth time if I had ever been married, my answer was a snippy, "Mr. Hogan, if I'd been married, I'm sure I would remember it." He didn't like that retort at all. This was an era when an interviewer could ask you any question about your background, and you were obligated to answer or risk being rejected.

"You know, if you come to work here, I may want you to go to the appeals bureau," Hogan said.

That would mean more library work. At Kaye Scholer I was making $9,500 a year, and I was more than willing to take a pay cut to $7,000 to work in criminal law—but not to sit in another library. "I have no interest in the appeals bureau," I told Hogan as politely as I could. "I can sit in the library at Kaye Scholer and make more money and be in more pleasant surroundings. I'm interested in becoming a criminal *trial* lawyer."

This response truly miffed Hogan. He seemed to be affronted by my addressing the issue so directly—but I saw no other way to proceed. I knew what I wanted and felt I had no choice but to articulate it then and there. Hogan responded that he'd put his assistants wherever he saw fit and that if an offer was extended, I'd have to go where he directed. He was going to check on a few things, and I should sit in the waiting area. I wondered if he was going to call the marriage bureau in the Municipal Building to find out whether I had ever been married!

After an hour, the offer came anyway. I knew Hogan had not liked my forthrightness, but I had good credentials, his assistants with whom I'd interviewed had apparently spoken well of me, and there was no particular reason to say no to me except that I was a woman who did not know her place and was a bit too aggressive. Perhaps Hogan convinced himself, or let himself be convinced, that it was important for an assistant DA to have a reasonable quotient of aggression. I never found out what he really thought.

I also received an offer from Legal Aid that same day. Legal Aid actually had more women on staff, but friends talked me out of working there, saying that it was easier to go from the DA's office to other work at a higher level than to do so after a stint at Legal Aid. Moreover, a senior attorney at Legal Aid advised me that it was a horrible place to work, a place where women "got no respect." Years later, I would try cases opposite this lawyer, and later still, he argued before me when I became a judge. We never got along that well, but the advice he gave me in 1967 was good, and I took it, accepting Hogan's offer to start at the DA's office in January 1968.

The Manhattan District Attorney's Office sprawled over several floors in 100 Centre Street in lower Manhattan, the massive criminal courts building erected during the Depression. The office had a well-thought-out ladder of apprenticeship. First you worked in the complaint bureau, then graduated to the indictment bureau, and eventually went to the criminal courts bureau, where you began with misdemeanors before working up to trying felony cases in the supreme court bureau. After that, there were a number of possibilities. Each level was an education in itself, and I went through them in the same sequence as did the men who entered the DA's office at the same time. My dreaded fear of having to sit in a library doing research again never came to pass: I was never sent to the appeals bureau.

In the complaint bureau, you dealt with people coming in off the street and evaluated their complaints. The basic task was to determine whether there was anything criminal in what they presented, as most complaints do not involve criminally actionable matters. Some could be referred to the consumer fraud bureau of the state's attorney general's office, rather than written up for action by our office, and other complaints had to be handled by other city and state agencies. This was also the bureau that staffed the complaint room, where police officers came to have actual arrests drawn up as charges in a "complaint." My first day in that room, a cute young cop approached and said, "I've got a half-and-half and a French." I had no idea what he was talking about—surely not the eighteenth century or the French I knew! Seeing my bewilderment, he took pleasure in explaining that these were terms relating to prostitution, specifically sexual intercourse combined with oral sex—his exact words were a bit cruder. Until the time I started work in the DA's office I'd almost never used (or regularly heard) profanity in daily speech, so I blushed. Then he asked me out. I turned him down, but I was sure that back at the precinct they had a good laugh about the incident.

I quickly learned a lot of four-letter words and street expressions from the cops,* but I was also learning much more from them.

At the request of my mother—who else?—I started a diary; overwhelmed with work, I soon put it away. But recently, when I found it again, I noted some entries about the police from my first month in the office, things like "People say you can't really believe the cops" and "You have to be very careful about what they say." Today, those notations appear to me as spillover from my vaguely liberal Radcliffe days. That attitude toward the police changed rapidly once I entered the district attorney's office, and perhaps the rapidity and direction of the change was why I so readily stopped writing the diary. When I began in the complaint bureau, I was not only baby-faced but also wet behind the ears. I had to learn about the real world—fast—and I did; the cops taught me about it. And soon, in the office, the talk was about serious crime, drugs, rape, double and triple murders. I was exposed to a world wholly different from any I'd known, peopled by criminals and cops, in which the division between bad guys and good guys seemed crystal clear. This world was far from that of my parents' salonlike existence, and I was enthralled with it.

I was captivated, first of all, because it was the real world, or certainly an important part of it, and because it highlighted moral divisions that previously had seemed only theoretical and

---

*I also came to appreciate cop humor: One cop used to tell me "Feel safe, sleep with a cop; feel safer, sleep with his partner too."

remote from my life. There is a wonderful simplicity and straightforwardness about the cops and what they do in the world of crime, compared, for instance, to the complexity and nuances of my father's environment of eighteenth-century French literature and the "philosophes." Most cops are men and women of action, not quiet contemplation. They apprehend the bad guys. In my experience, cops are generally good people, most of whom try very hard to *do* good—and out on the streets there are sizable numbers of bad guys, really evil people, committing despicable crimes. I had never known much about these criminals and their deeds, but on learning in detail about some of their crimes, I began to understand that there was, indeed, pure evil in this world and was glad that law enforcement was there to apprehend criminals and bring them to justice. Long before September 11, 2001, I began to see cops as heroes, people to whom loyalty and courage meant more than anything else and who inspired those qualities in me.

I have always been a staunch believer in "truth, justice, and the American way"—in other words, in the American system of justice. Mine is not a blind or unquestioning faith. Certainly our system is not perfect; it has plenty of inadequacies, but it works, and it works better than any other system I have seen or studied. It guarantees accused people a significant number of rights, bends over backward to constrain law enforcement and prosecutorial excesses, and provides for extensive judicial review of courtroom practices and judgments. We hear a lot about the few cases where justice has gone wrong, but in the overwhelming majority of cases, the American justice system works fairly and appropriately.

In that system, the prosecutors have the task, in conjunction with the police, of bringing the bad guys to justice. In all my days in the district attorney's office I encountered very, very few defendants wrongly accused of crimes. In this regard I can't help recalling a defense bar dinner a few years ago at which I was a guest and Alan Dershowitz of Harvard was the keynote speaker. I'm not a fan of his, but that evening he said to this audience of defense lawyers words to the effect of "Let's face it, most of our clients are guilty—almost all—of some criminal conduct related to what they are charged with." This rare moment of candor amazed me.

Of course, I had issues with the system when I was a young assistant DA, as I do today. Early on in my time in "the office," as we called the DA's office then (and now), I had to deal with some of the Columbia University student protesters. They were charged with minor offenses, disorderly conduct or obstructing governmental administration, and I wasn't certain that they should be in the court system. "How can you do this?" some of them asked me; "You're, like, one of us." I was around their age and had some sympathy for them—students who were anti-authoritarian but not criminals. Ambivalent about their protests, I was happy when the prosecutions were dropped or they were given slaps on the wrist and no jail time for their minor offenses. Later on, I had to prosecute people for acts that were considered criminal but which I thought very minor, like masturbation in a public rest room. Those prosecutions gave me pause as well. Roust these people as a public nuisance? Of course. But send them to jail? I never did.

Mel Glass, the head of the complaint bureau, was a terrific boss; two or three times a week he'd gather up us neophytes and we'd have lunch in his office while he instructed us on courtroom procedure—who sat where, who did what, the actual nuts and bolts of what went on. Finally, here was something real and practical; I was hooked! After I'd been in the complaint bureau for a few months, Mel took me aside and said he wanted to talk to me. I worried that I'd done something wrong but couldn't imagine what it might have been. When we were seated alone in my office, he said, "I was extremely skeptical about you; I didn't think you should be hired and I didn't want you in my bureau, because you're a woman and I didn't think you could handle our work. I just want to tell you now that I was wrong about all that. I'm really happy that you're here."

I was deeply affected by his remarks, on two counts: First, I hadn't known about his antipathy, and second, I had changed his mind. I had thought that I was doing my job properly and was fitting into the office well. We, the new people, palled around together, had lunch out together, and all got along. I had thought there were no "female issues" with me. No one had to be overly careful of my feelings; there was no danger that I would run away or cry because the details of some complaint were too vivid or gruesome; no one had to avoid contact with me at the "wrong time of the month"; I wasn't there looking for a husband or on temporary assignment before leaving permanently to become a wife and mother. But I recognized that in the almost all-male world of cops and robbers, women had just not been accepted yet. There was also an office legend working against me: It was said that the one senior woman in the office who had once attempted to try a serious case had become so unnerved that she had been unable to do so and instead had settled for a less stressful permanent position in the indictment bureau. Such tales made me more determined than ever to succeed.

Another encounter in Mel's office was with the leader of the prestigious homicide bureau. John Keenan—tall, thin, thoughtful—was a well-liked and greatly respected legend around Hogan's bailiwick for having argued and won some very important and serious cases. In Mel's office I gushed to Keenan, with absolute sincerity, that my greatest wish in the DA's office was to accumulate enough experience so that someday I could work in his bureau and try homicide cases. Keenan looked horrified at the idea. Though he was polite enough not to say anything discouraging, I quickly realized that I'd put my foot in my mouth and that I would have to prove myself worthy to him before he or anyone else in the district attorney's office would consider allowing me to do what I really wanted. Well, so be it: another challenge.

It was while in the complaint bureau that I met my future husband. The previous fall, I had been in the hospital for very minor surgery and had shared a room with an older woman who had undergone more serious surgery. Her daughter-in-law and I became friends, and she elicited from me a recitation of the men I was dating, all of whom she deemed unsatisfactory. "The right guy for you is my best friend's pediatrician," she opined, and asked if I would agree to having him call me. I did, just to be polite, but promptly forgot about it when he didn't call right away. Six months later, my new friend and I were chatting about another matter and she asked if Fred Snyder had ever phoned. I said he hadn't, but now the name was in the forefront of my mind, so the next night, when Fred did call—a coincidence, we later determined—I recognized the name and he was impressed, though only in the negative sense, because (as he later told me) he wondered if I'd been sitting by the phone for six months, waiting for his call! Long story short: We went out for dinner, got along famously, and spent every possible moment of the next ten days together, having a wonderful time. "What's next?" he asked me, and then answered his own question by proposing, "Let's get married." After contemplating his proposal for at least sixty seconds, I accepted it and then rushed to telephone the news to my mother. She asked me only whether the wedding would be held soon.

"But, Mother, don't you even want to know who the guy is?"

"If he's good enough for you to want to marry, then I assume he's okay. Just hurry up and do it, and elope. We don't want to waste time planning a big wedding."

That's my mother, a real sentimentalist.

We got married three and a half weeks later; eight people were present. That was thirty-four wonderful years ago.

After some months in the complaint bureau, I "graduated" to the indictment bureau. This was a logical next step; the young DA has to prepare and "present" cases to the grand jury, so you get a chance to be on your feet but not in an adversarial situation—there is no judge, no defense attorney (in those days, ever), and most of the witnesses are there because they're your witnesses. Some years later, Judge Sol Wachtler would immortalize the sentiment that "a grand jury will indict a ham sandwich, if the DA wants it to." That's not quite true, but near enough. I didn't like the indictment bureau, in part because it was headed by a nasty guy who played favorites and in part because I still wasn't in a courtroom trying cases. So I was happy to soon move up to the criminal courts bureau.

Criminal court was where young ADAs got to try misdemeanor cases. Felony cases, the more serious cases, were reserved for the supreme court and, in those days, for the corresponding supreme court bureau of the DA's office. In the era before a United States Supreme Court ruling that a defendant facing a year or more in jail had a right to a jury trial (misdemeanors were punishable by up to a year in prison) we tried our cases only before judges. There were a zillion cases to try—or, in court parlance, to "dispose of" by plea or trial—and nobody expressed any overt concern about whether the young DA prosecuting them was female or male.

What a zoo! You'd walk into a courtroom and there would be defendants everywhere, lots of lawyers, people cramming the audience benches, a judge working as fast as he could. The DA's court assistant would hand you a bunch of folders, twenty or more, for a single day. Each was a different case that you were expected to try or otherwise dispose of: prostitution, minor drugs, shoplifting, anything that wasn't a felony. Most defendants were represented by Legal Aid, and its lawyers were attempting to get through as many cases as you were. Your colleague from the DA's office would have just as high a stack of folders and you'd tag-team—you'd be in the hall, talking to your witnesses, while your partner was in front of the judge with a case, and then when he finished with his case it would be your turn in front of the bench.

We were trying these cases "off the papers," and it was done with hardly any preparation. You'd glance through the documents in the folders, trying to absorb what you needed as you walked toward the hall, calling out the name of the cop or witness who'd been involved. You'd meet him out there and for a few minutes discuss what the case was about. Then you'd go back in, the clerk would call the case, and you'd be on, generally with the cop as your witness. The whole trial would last about a half hour. If the case was unusual, like endangering the welfare of a child—I couldn't believe that crime was only a misdemeanor—I'd flag it and ask to have it held over so I could take the folder home and really prepare; but otherwise misdemeanor court was rapid city.

In my very first case, the opposing attorney wasn't from Legal Aid but was a private defense attorney long notorious in the courthouse for representing prostitutes, homosexuals, and cross-dressers and for her continual spoken stream of obscenities. She'd roam the courthouse, looking for business and cursing out the cops wherever she found them. My case was a prostitution case, and I put the cop on as a witness—all very routine. But when the defense's turn came, this lawyer did something unusual: She put the defendant on the stand. I was shocked enough by that turn of events and listened with trepidation as this attorney elicited quite a story from her client. The defendant claimed she wasn't performing sex for money and had merely asked for a handout, hoping just to get the rent to pay for herself and her baby, because she was afraid of her pimp. I was amazed, first, that she testified at all and, second, that she actually had a story, an involved and convoluted one. I was fascinated. When it was my turn to cross-examine, I asked a few bumbling questions and sat down with the full knowledge that I'd been a total idiot.

The prostitute was acquitted and actually came over to thank me. "Don't thank me, I've been incompetent," I told her. The prostitute's lawyer also thanked me and implied that I'd let her client off the hook because I was a nice person—which really made me feel bad, since that wasn't the reason.

The judge called me to the bench. "Was this your first trial?" I nodded. He explained the kinds of questions that I should think about posing next time, questions that would have shown the inconsistencies in the prostitute's story. I realized that I had a lot to learn.

No one was upset about this not-guilty verdict. It was a given that the prostitute would go right back to her profession and would likely be arrested and in court again within a few days. How appropriate it would have been for someone to have prepared me for these kinds of cases and trials, to tutor me in what to ask of a witness, how to treat cops and prostitutes on the stand; but there was nothing except on-the-job training. Today, there is formal training, but back then—nothing. After this trial, I not only felt stupid, but was determined to learn more so that I'd never be embarrassed like that again. I was at best ambivalent about whether or not prostitution should be considered a crime, as opposed to being decriminalized, regulated, and controlled, so I was happy that the case I'd screwed up did not involve some offense that I considered really serious.

Among my least favorite cases in criminal court were the public lewdness ones stemming from men masturbating or performing consensual sex acts on one another in public toilets, often in the subway. As I said earlier, I didn't consider these acts to be more than minor offenses and a public nuisance, and I didn't think people should be sent to jail for committing them. This determination was part of my evolving philosophy, a belief that one must "do the right thing" rather than blindly do one's job. Accordingly, in public lewdness cases I'd always offer a plea bargain down to a "discon," a disorderly conduct charge (which was a violation, not a crime), and I would ask for no jail time; ultimately, this kind of conviction wouldn't even appear on the person's record. That offer almost always disposed of the case— except with a man who was called "the General" because he said he'd been one in the army. Represented by a private lawyer, he refused the plea bargain and I was forced to take him to trial. His lawyer put the General on the stand, where in his own defense he told a complicated story of how he had been urinating in a men's room in the subway and (contrary to what the cop claimed) was only shaking himself off, not masturbating. His story went on in lurid anatomical detail; I think I was sitting at the prosecution table with my mouth hanging open in amazement. I had no idea how to cross-examine the defendant on this issue and, frankly, no inclination to do so; I just asked a few perfunctory questions and sat down. The General was acquitted, and I went home and told Fred he'd better give me a lesson in anatomy; he couldn't stop laughing.

On the whole, though, I did very well, winning almost all of my hundreds of cases, and was soon considered by the judges I respected to be doing a very good job as a prosecutor. But I'd better tell you about the third case that I lost.

I arrived in the courtroom one day early on in my criminal court career, and there was a buzz going around, people whispering that there was a "famous lawyer" about to appear, F. Lee Bailey, the man who had managed to obtain a new trial and an eventual acquittal for Sam Shepard. He was probably the best-known private attorney in the country at that moment in time. "What's he doing here?" I asked.

"He's handling one of your cases," I was told.

Sure enough, he was, and this was strange since the case was a low-level one, a violation having to do with some sort of harassment—not sexual—by a man against a woman in his office. Something larger had to be at stake for Bailey to be involved, and I learned later that the harassment case was related to a shareholder derivative suit that Bailey's firm was handling, a civil case that probably involved massive amounts of money. The judge asked if I was ready for trial, and I went up to him and pleaded, "Judge, look: I've been in criminal court one month, I've had three seconds to look at the papers, and I have to go up against F. Lee Bailey!" He gave me a fat fifteen minutes to prepare.

Frankly, I don't know that I would have fared better if I'd tried it with fifteen hours of preparation. First, Bailey, a handsome and fancily dressed man, very full of himself, aware of his celebrity, came over to me and told me he was startled by having such a beautiful district attorney on the case. This approach completely turned me off: slick and insincere. But in the courtroom, during the trial, he exhibited star power; with a silver tongue he charmed the judge, ran all over me and my witnesses, and won an acquittal. I had to admit that he deserved it.

After nine months doing misdemeanors, it was time for me to be moved on to the supreme court bureau—but nothing happened. The guys who had begun in the DA's office at approximately the same time as I did were promoted, but I was not. Finally, I was told that Hogan did not feel that women were up to the task of prosecuting felonies. This devastated me. I loved "the office," but my whole rationale for coming to work here had been to someday prosecute the most serious crimes. Now, if I was blocked, I might have to leave and start all over again, somewhere else. I went to Judge Irving Lang, who had been particularly kind to me and who thought I was good at my job; Lang had been head of the narcotics bureau of the DA's office for many years. I told him my story, and apparently he convinced Hogan to give me a try in supreme court. The compromise was to send me to the youth Part of that court (each courtroom is called a "Part"), where the defendants were "youthful offenders" between the ages of sixteen and nineteen, charged with committing serious crimes such as robbery and assault, but where the maximum penalty that could be imposed was four years in a reformatory—rather than the twenty-five years that could be given to an adult for those crimes. I wasn't thrilled by this assignment, but it was a foot in the door and for that I was grateful.

I was fortunate to have as bureau chief in supreme court a very sweet man, Peter Andreoli. His wife was a lawyer, and even though they had five children she had always worked, with great success, and he was proud of her. In fact, Peter Andreoli was the first supervisor I met in the DA's office who was fully attuned to the concept that women could do anything men could do—including prosecute criminals. Peter told me not to feel bad about going to youth Part because if I did well there, he would just move me to a regular Part. "But you're just going to have to do this Hogan's way," I recall him saying, "because that's just the way he is."

I had been in the supreme court bureau only a short time when I returned to my office one day in midmorning to retrieve some files that I needed in court—and heard a noise in my closet and looked in. There was a young male rifling through my coat pockets, removing the money I always kept in them. I was taken aback and, without thinking, made my first and last "collar."

"You're under arrest," I shouted, grabbing him by an arm and dragging him down the long hall to Peter Andreoli's office, all the while saying, "You have the right to remain silent, anything you say can be used against you," and so on. Andreoli couldn't believe what I had done and summoned a DA's squad detective to process the intruder's arrest. Once the detective and the "suspect" had left Andreoli's office, he gave me a stern lecture—in his nice, paternalistic manner.

"Are you crazy, Leslie? This kid could have had a knife or anything! Don't do anything that stupid ever again!"

I guess the kid (who turned out to be sixteen) had been as startled as I was and hadn't thought to struggle or run away. When I thought about what could have happened, I felt shaken; but later I realized, ironically, that the episode had probably enhanced my reputation in the office.

The youth Part cases were far better cases than criminal court misdemeanors: They went on for more than a half hour; they were usually about a week long and involved several witnesses, legal maneuvering—and a jury. My love of acting came into play. A good courtroom lawyer has to be something of an actor, for the jury but also for the judge, and to deal adroitly with the witnesses and opposing counsel. The important United States Supreme Court decisions requiring fairness in the makeup of juries, both in regard to gender and to race, were not handed down until after this time*—so when I was first in front of juries, the juries were almost exclusively male. This was a tremendous advantage for me, a young female who had always gotten along well with men, and I had "good chemistry" with

---

*In 1975, *Taylor* v. *Louisiana* cleared the way for more women to serve on juries. The United States Supreme Court began to address these issues in a progressive manner, holding in part that jury pools cannot systematically exclude distinctive groups in the community—there, women—since the pool must be "reasonably representative" of the community. Louisiana's special exemption for women was held to operate to exclude them from petit juries, "contrary to the command of the Sixth and Fourteenth Amendments."

many of the male jurors. They knew I was married—I wore my wedding ring, and the judges would address me as "Mrs. Snyder"—but they were watching and listening to me. As a courtroom lawyer, you immediately clue in on whether or not people find you interesting or attractive, and when they do, you have an advantage. This has always worked for men—why not for women?

Because we interacted so often with the Legal Aid attorneys, after a few months of handling the calendar and trying cases against one another, we young ADAs and our counterparts from Legal Aid got to know one another pretty well. It was a pleasant change for me to become friendly with other women lawyers—even if they worked for the other side. We were adversaries in the courtroom battles, except when we had to fight a common enemy.

The youth Part judge was disliked by everyone in the system—lawyers on both sides, clerks, court officers, and so on. He was consistently unpleasant—no, nasty—to everyone, and every day found him in a foul mood. If anyone said something he didn't like, he would become apoplectic, turn crimson red, and bite your head off. The ADAs and Legal Aid attorneys consistently conspired to thwart him, agreeing to do things we knew he would not like. After a while, it became obvious to me that his dislike of women lawyers was particularly intense. I brought this up to a court clerk one day, and he told me, "Oh, sure—he hates them with a passion. Didn't you know his wife is a lawyer?" Well, that explained everything.

Once I was trying to pick a jury before this judge. The case concerned forcible sodomy, though I don't remember any other details. I was in the process of asking questions of jurors in the voir dire process when one raised his hand and said, "Mrs. Snyder? I really don't remember what sodomy is. Could you please define it for me?"

I was about to respond with the definition as it pertained to this case—forcible anal intercourse—when I happened to glance over at the judge. He was already past crimson and into purple, and he spluttered, "Any idiot should know what sodomy is!" That, of course, made it impossible for me to answer the prospective juror's question. The poor juror was so mortified that I felt terrible for him. But the incident taught me another lesson: Never assume that all the jurors know what you're talking about when you use a legal term. Explain yourself fully, or you do a disservice to your case.

Sometimes you can't even expect the judge to know what certain legal terms mean, let alone know the law. During my time in the supreme court bureau, I was assigned for quite a while to another judge's Part. The judge in this particular Part was an older man who prided himself on being a "man of the streets," which, I soon learned, in his case meant knowing no law and having no interest in learning any. He saw his mission as disposing of virtually every case by plea—I call this being a "plea pusher." If we DAs did not want to offer what the defendant wanted in order to induce him to plead guilty, the judge would berate us. After a month or two in his Part, during a break he asked me casually if I had any kids. I confided to him some information that was very personal: I wanted a family as much as anyone, and we were working on it, but it wasn't happening as quickly as we'd hoped. He expressed sympathy at my plight. But the next day, when I wouldn't do what he wanted—offer a low enough plea so that the defendant could take it and the case could be disposed of—he said loudly, in open court, "Why don't you go home and have babies? That's where you belong." Not very nice.

This judge also prided himself on being able to sink to every defendant's level—and that could be pretty low. Since he'd do anything to obtain a disposition, he'd order "young punks," as he called them, brought up to the bench, and—off the record, of course—he'd speak to them in what he deemed the language of the streets, audibly enough so that the rest of us could hear him.

"Hey, what the fuck you think you're doing? You think you're smart? I grew up in the streets, and look at me. You better take the fuckin' plea or you're going down." In those days I could not believe a judge would conduct himself that way. But this one did.

And one of the very few women judges had been known to use similar language. Rumor had it that during World War II she had parachuted behind enemy lines on a secret mission. I never learned whether this was true, but she was quite the character—smart and likable except when she yelled and screamed like a fishwife, which happened often enough. One day a defendant said to her in open court, "You can take your fucking sentence and shove it up your ass!"

"No," she retorted—purportedly on the record—"*you* can take my fucking sentence and shove it up *your* ass."

As in every field, you had your good judges, your bad judges, your hardworking and dedicated judges—and your utter incompetents and political hacks. Working in the criminal courts and then in the youth Part of the supreme court, I was rapidly disabused of any notion that all judges were learned, erudite individuals, scholars above the fray. I came to understand that there was not a lot to respect about judges in general and that only individual judges could command respect by dint of their character and actions. I knew that if I ever became a judge, I would aspire to be one known favorably by her character and actions.

After I'd been in the youth Part a while, the rap in the office about me was that I did very well in these trials; I don't remember losing any of my cases, although there was one hung jury. My reputation was of showing great promise and of being "good on my feet."

When Peter Andreoli decided that I had spent enough time

and had proved myself prosecuting youthful offenders, he determined to move me on to try adult felony cases. To this day, I don't know whether he discussed this with Hogan or just did it on his own initiative—but it didn't matter, because now, after what seemed like a quarter century's worth of wanting to do it and of preparing myself, I was ready, willing, and able to bring the really bad guys to justice.

HOMICIDE: BREAKING INTO THE BOYS' CLUB

Prosecuting tough felony cases as an assistant district attorney, I gained a reputation of being feisty and a fighter; one older judge even used to laugh at the passion I displayed during arguments in front of his bench. In a friendly (if bantering) way, he'd ask, "How does your husband put up with you?" and suggest, "Maybe you need some medication to calm you down." Obviously, it was still the early seventies.

At first, the idea of my aspiring to work in the homicide bureau was also something of a joke around the DA's office. "I'm going to be the first woman to try a homicide in New York," I'd tell my colleagues, and they'd chortle and slap their thighs. My tone was light, too, but I wasn't really joking; John Keenan's homicide bureau was where I wanted to be because homicide cases were considered the ne plus ultra, the ultimate. They were often the most complex cases in the system, in the sense that they had interesting forensic evidence, expert testimony, and other elements that added to the mystique. They had the best investigators from the police department and the DA's office working on them, the ADAs who handled them were allowed more time (and better budgets) to prepare the cases, and in the courtroom the ADAs got to argue against the better criminal defense lawyers.

The homicide bureau was also a macho club where the best ADAs and some of the chiefs' personal favorites worked—so the idea of working there was a challenge. I've never thought of myself as a frontline feminist, the kind who deliberately breaks down barriers to show they can be broken, but I wanted to work with the best and to be the best, so I determined to break into this particular club.

After I'd tried a number of high-level felony cases and prosecuted them reasonably well, and won virtually all of the cases, in late 1972 I asked to be transferred to the homicide bureau— and ran into a stone wall.

"You have to see Hogan to go to homicide," I was told. "No one wants a woman there. He'll never allow you to go." Many people in the office, especially the old-timers, preferred dealing with a subordinate than approaching the man whom many treated with such deference that he might as well have been a god. I respected Hogan, but I didn't hold him in awe; anyway, if I didn't ask him for the job, I'd never get it. Most of my colleagues considered it pretty forward of me to even request an appointment.

Hogan saw me, heard my appeal, and said no.

Later I learned that a scandal had recently unfolded in the homicide bureau: On Friday afternoons the "boys" had purportedly been watching hard-porn movies and doing other questionable things. It was clearly time for a change: me! So after a few more months, with more good trials under my belt, I went back to Hogan's office, and again he said no. On my third try, the district attorney puffed on his pipe, leaned back in his chair, clasped his hands sanctimoniously, and said, "Leslie, Leslie, Leslie—I always thought of you as the next Betty Furness." Ms. Furness was then the consumer affairs commissioner of the city of New York.

"I don't want to be the next Betty Furness or handle consumer affairs, Mr. Hogan; I want to try homicide cases."

He sighed and told me that if I wanted to go to the homicide bureau, I'd have to bring him a letter of permission from my husband. I waited for him to chuckle at his own joke, but he didn't; apparently he was serious. The reason for this requirement—he didn't state it, but I knew—was that in his patriarchal view I'd have to do such shocking things as look at dead bodies, ride in police cars to crime scenes in the middle of the night, take statements from murder suspects that were apt to be explicit and gory, and deal with violent criminals and cynical homicide detectives. What my husband's permission would have to do with my being able to function in these circumstances escaped me.

I told the bring-a-note-from-your-husband tale to Fred, who also thought at first that Hogan must have been kidding. Although the request for the letter made for a great story, I had absolutely no intention of giving Hogan such a letter; the idea was absurd as well as insulting. Fortunately, my immediate boss thought so, too. Peter Andreoli spoke to John Keenan and told him, in effect, that I was as good as any of the men in the office at trying felonies and an excellent choice for the first female to try a homicide case. By the spring of 1973, Keenan had gotten over the incredulity that my mention of joining his bureau had brought to his face five years earlier. In fact, he had become a friend and ally (and later a mentor and true believer in women professionals). Keenan personally convinced Hogan to do the unthinkable. I received my transfer, and no further mention was ever made of bringing a note from my husband. I think Fred was disappointed!

When a suspect was arrested for murder, the drill was that someone from the DA's office would be called, at whatever hour, and would ride to the precinct in a marked police car (a radio motor patrol car, called an RMP); look at the crime scene, if that was relevant; interrogate the suspect, if he was willing to talk; and handle the case through indictment and through eventual trial or disposition. (For other felonies, in those days, the routine was different: The DA who would try the case in court didn't get his or her hands on it until after the police work and the indictment phase had been completed by another junior assistant DA.) Hogan didn't want my delicate little woman's hands dirtied by this sordid (in his view) routine, but I was willing—no, eager—to do the work. In fact, I could hardly wait to get my hands "dirty." Initially, the homicide bureau was skeptical of me, too—an attitude that intensified when I became pregnant, which happened, ironically, just after I moved to homicide and after years of trying.

As with any new recruit to the bureau, I was given some "dogs"—old cases that had already been prepared by other DAs and which none of them wanted to see through to trial, either because the cases weren't good ones or because they had been around too long. Energized by finally being where I wanted to be—had to be—I prepared, tried, and won several of these cases. And I also got my share of whatever new cases turned up.

One of the old dogs was a drug-related murder—my first real drug case as well as one of my first murders. There had been two victims; one died and the other survived, but he was also a skel and was now in prison on some other charge. He wanted to get some better deal in exchange for his testimony against the shooter, and this, too, was something I hadn't encountered before. But I got through it and won a conviction. The downside was that for years thereafter the survivor skel kept phoning me from prison.

Some people may resent being called in the middle of the

night to go out on a homicide; I did not. As much as the next person, I didn't like being awakened—but getting involved in a new murder case was well worth it. Always, it seemed, in the wee hours of the morning, a patrol car and two uniformed cops would come to pick me up at my apartment building. Once, when I was very pregnant and was being helped into the back of the RMP by one of the two cops, an older woman who lived in the building happened by and shook her head at the sight. I don't know what she thought was happening to me, but for years afterward, every time she'd see Fred and me she'd look at him with great pity. "Imagine, having your pregnant wife arrested! What could she have done? You poor man!" Anyhow, on this night the patrol car took me up to a precinct in Harlem. The cops explained that this was an instance of a Latino guy who had killed his lover. He wouldn't talk to them, and they didn't think he'd talk to me, either, but suggested I give it a try if I wanted to.

This in itself was a concession, because the cops can keep you out of the loop if they feel like it—they can question the suspect themselves, without a DA present, gather all the evidence, visit the crime scene, tell you that the suspect doesn't want to talk to you, and so forth. After the cops got to know me, that didn't happen. In this instance in Harlem, it even helped that I was a woman, and a visibly pregnant one at that. The suspect took one look at me and said, "You're a woman, you'll understand: I was making love to *my* woman, and in the middle she cries out, 'Juan! Juan!' But my name is *José*. Naturally I was enraged; I lost my temper and I killed her—can you blame me?"

Chalk up one confession. It surprised the cops—and surprised me even more.

Perhaps more so than when trying other felonies, in my days dealing with murder cases I learned something about how the justice system operates at street level—principally because I had to deal with the cops as they operated there. Case in point: another murder in Harlem where there was some difficulty in getting the facts straight because no one in the community wanted to talk. The detective assigned to the investigation called me one evening and asked me to go to Harlem with him the next morning to interview a key witness. The woman hadn't wanted to come downtown to testify or even talk at the precinct but had agreed to see him at her apartment. He thought that if I came along, she might be more willing to give a statement. Next morning I was standing in front of my building when the detective appeared. I could think only of "Superfly"—a big, handsome black man in a red Corvette. He held open the door and ushered me into the car. People on Park Avenue turned and stared.

As we drove uptown, he told me he had to make a stop and that it wouldn't take long. We pulled up in front of a liquor store, and he went in and soon emerged with a bottle of cheap liquor. I was shocked and asked him what he thought he was doing. "Leslie, my girl," he said, chortling, "you better get with the program—this is real life, not criminal law class at Harvard. How do you think shit really happens . . . ?" I said nothing, hoping he wasn't going to do something really improper. Patiently he explained to me that he believed he would obtain a statement from the woman—and that he had to give her the bottle, after she talked to us, as a token of good faith.

We arrived at the apartment, which was inhabited by about a dozen people. The woman and I discussed pregnancies for a while over the coffee she offered us, and she and I agreed that I was carrying very neatly; then it was Superfly's turn to shoot the breeze with her for half an hour. Finally, she told us she had witnessed the murder, laid out what she had seen, and said she was now willing to testify in front of the grand jury. After we'd finished, the detective gave her the bottle of liquor and we left. The bottle was never opened while we were there. I had to agree with the detective that the liquor wasn't a quid pro quo and it wasn't a bribe; it was more of a polite thank-you for having let us come to her apartment. Or so I rationalized. If this wasn't the way I had thought police business was normally done, it made sense in terms of the ways of the street. I still had a lot to learn.

Some prosecutors can become blasé or just very hardened by the cases they have to handle. Murder cases affected me strongly and stoked the fire burning in me to see justice done for a victim whose life had been taken. The murders that moved me the most, possibly in part because I was either pregnant or a new mother when I handled them, were those of children. These also enraged the police; many cops are fathers, and whenever a child is involved as a victim in a crime, the cops always go the extra mile to help solve the case and bring the perp to justice.

The first child murder case that I got handed was a "dog" that had been around the system for several years; I think I was the fifth ADA to handle it, and when I got it I could see why: It was a total mess. The medical evidence had not been put together adequately, the defendant was flaky, her lawyer was a wily and aggressive woman, and there had been plenty of prosecutorial sloppiness involved. A woman with four children, the defendant was accused of having beaten one of them to death. She had an explanation for every bruise on the child's body: He had fallen from the crib, fallen down the stairs, fallen off the swing in the playground. The woman was poor and in obviously difficult circumstances, but the more I looked into the case, the more outraged I became. I investigated and found that each of her other children had had injuries, as well as similar patterns of suspicious fractures and malnutrition. I spoke to various doctors, including Fred, who helped me interpret the medical records. It appeared clear to me that this was an abusive mother and I became concerned about her other children, because rather than being in jail or in psychiatric treatment, she was at home and the rest of the children were living with her.

Dr. Vincent Fontana, chief of the New York Foundling Hospital and author of the 1971 book *The Maltreated Child: The Maltreatment Syndrome in Children*, was one of the country's leading experts on child abuse. After reading his book, I decided to use what was then a rare prosecution tactic, the "battered child" syndrome, as part of my case. The syndrome was Fontana's label for a situation in which the parent claimed that the child's injuries had all been accidental but where medical investigation showed them to be the result of a continuous course of parental abuse. I obtained permission to hire Fontana to be the key expert witness in the case.

In real life and real courts, things are not as straightforward as they are in television courtroom dramas, where an expert witness is hired in one second and in the next is giving the crucial testimony on the stand in the case. There are delays, motions, witnesses who don't want to go to the bother of coming to court—and opposing attorneys determined to throw monkey wrenches into the proceedings. That's what happened here. My initial task was to convince the judge of the admissibility of the battered child syndrome, which was not yet accepted as a routine legal tool. And I had to contend with the defendant's attorney, who was very unpleasant, aggressive, smart, and used to the ways of the system. She claimed that her client was too medically and mentally ill to stand trial. When the judge didn't agree with those claims, the lawyer tried another tactic: She made a motion to have me relieved as prosecutor because I was visibly pregnant and this was "unfair" in a child murder case.

So I had to be photographed, front and side view, and have our appeals bureau brief the issue and argue it before our intermediate appellate court—all of which could delay things and thereby make my pregnancy more obvious. Fortunately, and after only a minor delay, the appellate court ruled that I was fit to continue prosecuting the case. Their decision was most flattering: They said I looked only a little fat through the middle, not pregnant! But now I was in my seventh month.

The trial was beginning when I went to my obstetrician for a routine exam. After one feel, he told me, "You're going to lose this baby if you don't go to bed for the next two months." This was totally unexpected, and I was stunned. More than anything, Fred and I wanted a family; I had had a great deal of difficulty becoming pregnant and now wasn't about to let anything happen that would result in my losing this baby. So even though I was in the middle of a murder case that I had finally brought to trial after it had been stalled in the system for years, I went to bed. My priorities were clear.

I hoped that another ADA would be assigned the case and, after two or three weeks to prepare, would step in and continue the prosecution that had been so carefully constructed. The DA's office had asked the judge to declare a mistrial on the grounds that I had become medically unable to prosecute the case, and he did. While the defense can raise all sorts of issues to obtain a mistrial, the DA has to be careful in doing so lest you allow the defense to claim successfully that their client has been put in "double jeopardy"—tried twice for the same offense, a major constitutional prohibition in our American system of justice. And it was a claim that this defendant made, of course. The matter went up to the appellate court, which ruled that this particular dismissal did not subject the defendant to double jeopardy. But by this time another year or two had elapsed, I was no longer in the homicide bureau, and all charges—for a number of reasons—were dismissed. It always galled me that this woman who, in my opinion based on the evidence, had murdered her own child was never even tried for that horrible crime.

Another child murder was at least as bad. There was a couple, both junkies, a young man who was a Charles Manson type and his girlfriend, the mother of two children, one of them an eight-month-old boy. While the mother was absent on some errand, the infant wouldn't stop screaming, so the boyfriend knocked the child's head against the wall repeatedly until he stopped crying. The mother came home to find that the child was not moving. They debated and delayed for a while, then took the child to the hospital, where doctors were unable to save his life. In the initial investigation, the young mother, although grief-stricken for her son, protected the boyfriend—the murderer of her own child. As I would learn to my chagrin, this was not an unusual scenario.

The case was assigned to a very good homicide detective, the sort who can get along with anyone. Good homicide detectives have to be con men because they have to get people to believe them, to trust them. They deal with the scum of the earth, people who've committed horrible crimes, yet the detectives must be able to talk with a suspect as though they understand the extenuating circumstances that would make someone a killer and urge him or her into confessing. "Tell us everything that happened, and maybe I can help you get a better deal. And at least you'll feel better." That sort of line. It's permissible, up to a point, under the law. In this case, the detective obtained a confession, and to prevent the case from going to trial and the difficulties that could be anticipated in countering the defendant's expected insanity defense, we did agree to a plea, twenty-two years to life instead of twenty-five to life. There was not enough evidence to bring charges against the mother on the murder, but her other child was taken away from her because she was clearly "endangering the welfare of a child."

Even when you have a murder case that gets as far as trial, things can and frequently do go awry. I remember one in which the defense lawyer was a friend of mine, a very competent attorney who had been in the DA's office when I arrived there and had since gone into private practice. He was assigned a client under what we call "18B," which refers to a section of law whereby private lawyers who wish to do so—and are qualified—can be assigned to defend people and be paid by the city, although at a ridiculously low hourly rate.

This case involved a good-looking young black man from Massachusetts whom I'll call "Andre." He was apparently sufficiently impressed with his own good looks that he came to New York with a portfolio of photographs of himself and attempted to find work as a model. One day he was in the garment center area and got on an elevator. An older white man was on the elevator; they had some sort of argument, and the would-be model pulled out a knife that (as the medical examiner later testified) must have been similar to an ice pick and stabbed the older man to death. Then he fled, inadvertently leaving the portfolio in the elevator.

The police thought he would try to get out of town and stationed men at the train stations, airports, and the Port Authority Bus Terminal, where they soon apprehended Andre. Shortly, they and my friend who was his lawyer learned that Andre had spent some time in a mental institution in Massachusetts. That fit with my sense of the case, because anyone who would snap during an elevator ride and kill an older and defenseless man he'd never seen before has to be pretty sick. It was a sad, unnecessary crime and a brutal one. My defense lawyer friend's first tactic on Andre's behalf was to attempt to have him declared mentally incompetent and unfit to stand trial. The defense and prosecution psychiatrists disagreed with one another; we had a hearing, and the judge found the defendant competent to stand trial. The trial began. About halfway through it, after I'd presented a number of witnesses, Andre had a fit in the courtroom. He jumped on the table, urinated, and in other equally charming ways acted crazy. To this day, I'm convinced that this was largely an act—but it worked. We had to have the defendant's fitness to stand trial reexamined, and this time the opinion of the psychiatrists and the ruling of the judge was that he was no longer competent. So he was taken to a mental institution for treatment, until such time as drugs and therapy might render him fit for trial. In this case, too, after a year or two had gone by and he seemed ready to be declared competent again, the possibility of a new trial receded to the vanishing point. The key witness had gone back to Hawaii and was refusing to return to New York to testify a second time, and there were other complicating factors. Andre agreed to plead to a reduced charge on an offer from a different ADA and served a relatively light sentence.

It was an instance of system fatigue. I saw a lot of that, and it all worked to the benefit of the defense. Delay and confusion have become two prime defense tactics in our justice system. Defendants and their lawyers wear down the system, knowing that things don't get better for the prosecution with time. Motions go on forever; witnesses disappear, or recant, or turn hostile; defendants drift in and out of mental competence. The next ADA to handle the case becomes more willing to accept a more lenient plea than the previous one.

After our first child was born, in the late spring of 1974, I took a month off. Not surprisingly, there had been no provision for maternity leave in the DA's office when I had become pregnant—but I arranged to take time off and then to work three days a week for the rest of the summer. It was soon decided that a three-month paid maternity leave was appropriate for female employees, but I did not take advantage of the new policy.

District Attorney Hogan had died that spring, and there was an interim DA. An election would be held in November to choose the next DA, and interim DA Dick Kuh was going to be a leading candidate for the position. He had a job in mind for me that he thought ideally suited my talents: chief of a new consumer fraud bureau of the office. I really wanted to do something important, something dealing with serious crimes. My dream was to form a new bureau in the DA's office that would exclusively handle sex crimes. There wasn't another such bureau in any district attorney's office in the country, and I felt that the need for it was clear. Just then, Kuh didn't want to hear about sex crimes. He was more interested in consumer fraud, thought that to be very important, and he wanted only me to take the position. It would be a promotion to managerial status, I would have assistants, he'd assign a top investigator to the bureau, and I could do the job three days a week that summer. I agreed and he scheduled an immediate press conference to announce the formation of the bureau and to introduce me to the public as its head.

I hated the job.

Although I didn't have to go out in the middle of the night anymore, which was a plus now that I had a small child at home to care for, I absolutely loathed consumer fraud work. It was one of those moves that had seemed like a good idea at the time I'd accepted the position, a step up the ladder of managerial responsibility. But I lacked a feeling for the subject; everything else that I'd done in life, and especially in the DA's office, I'd done because I passionately wanted to do it and was interested in the subject—like breaking into the homicide club. Now I was trapped doing something that didn't interest me, and I learned a very important lesson: One should never do anything just to get the promotion or the title, because unless you're interested in the subject, it will bore you to death and you won't do a good job.

If that conclusion seems obvious, please remember that in 1974 not every woman wanted a career, and it was acceptable to quit what you were doing—if you were married and your family could afford the loss of income—and stay home. Furthermore, if you had a career, you were supposed to be grateful for any promotion, graciously accept whatever came along, and never complain. I wanted a career and a family, and I was going to continue to work even now that I had a child, but over the summer I realized that prosecuting consumer frauds was not for me.

What I really wanted to do, had to do, and what really mattered to me was to form that sex crimes unit, because—as I'll discuss in the next chapter—I'd been working since 1970 to change the antiquated laws on rape and other sex crimes. In the fall of 1974, I told Kuh that I didn't like consumer fraud cases and didn't want to continue prosecuting them. I again discussed my interest in sex crimes, and he agreed to let me start a sex crimes bureau, turning over the consumer fraud work to someone else. Robert Morgenthau, who would shortly win election as district attorney over Kuh, would continue, support, and enlarge the sex crimes unit, but it was Kuh who arranged for me to begin it and who obtained a federal grant for that purpose.

I was ecstatic at the opportunity, because for several years the determination had been growing inside of me to do something within the criminal justice system about the rising tide of crimes against women. Now I would have the chance—and the clout—and at least some resources to fight that tide as head of the first sex crimes prosecution unit in the country.

SEX CRIMES,
LAWS, AND
VIDEOTAPE

Two young women dragged off the streets of the Lower East Side of New York City, brutally raped, sodomized, and robbed . . .

A young German nanny working in New York raped, sodomized, and degraded in unimaginable ways . . .

An eighty-year-old woman savagely sexually assaulted by a clean-cut marine with no criminal record . . .

A dentist who delivered a lot more than dental care to his patients . . .

The time was 1970 and the place was the Alphabet City area of the Lower East Side of Manhattan—Avenues A, B, C, and D—then inhabited by a mix of immigrants from a dozen countries and young hippies who couldn't afford to live anywhere else in the city. The streets were littered and crime-ridden, and drugs were rampant. A young man I will call "Trevor Barnes" threatened two young women with a knife, dragged them off the street into a tenement, and in a filthy stairwell raped and sodomized them both. He then took their money and fled.

It was my first rape case as an assistant district attorney in the supreme court bureau, and I discovered that I didn't understand the law.

To the layperson, this double rape would seem to be an open-and-shut case. But at that time the laws about rape were so antiquated that they made it almost impossible to prosecute a rapist successfully. To prove rape or sodomy, you had to have corroboration (additional evidence from something or someone other than the victim) for three "elements" of the crime: the identity of the rapist; that force was used; and that the victim had been penetrated. Because these requirements could so seldom be satisfied, very few rape cases even made it past the grand jury.

Now this one had made it into my hands, and I needed to understand the law in order to properly prosecute the case. What I found in my research made me sick.

The rape laws then in existence in most states had been originally written to protect male interests and property rights. They construed rape as a crime primarily because the rapist's action decreased the value of a man's marital property! The laws incorporated and reflected outdated attitudes toward the roles of men and women in society as well as sexual mores that equated sexual activity by unmarried women with immorality. According to one law review article, "The structure of the laws, enforcement, and prosecution are all based on untested assumptions about the incidence of the crime, the motivation of the criminal, and the psychology of the victim."*

Only between 20 and 50 percent of all rapes were reported to the police. A national survey showed that one-fifth of all the reported rapes never got beyond the police precinct and into the court system, for various reasons including the failure of the police (and of the victims) to preserve the evidence of the crime.

*Legrand, Camille E., "Rape and Rape Laws: Sexism in Society and Law," *California Law Review* 61 (1973).

When rape cases reached the complaint stage, this survey also reported, prosecutors were routinely reluctant to process the charges, fearing the backlash from the occasional filing of what might subsequently be judged false charges that led to harm of "innocent" men.* A widely quoted article in a police magazine suggested that men who raped were not responsible for their actions since they were the victims of "uncontrollable emotions and passions, unexplainable urges, and fierce desires which can be considered impossible to control once they have been aroused."†

Most rape cases resulted in no indictment. Even when taken to trial, rapes had an unusually high acquittal rate, and only 10 percent of convicted rapists did prison time.‡ The reasons for these dismal rates of conviction and incarceration were many. In California, for instance, there was a mandatory instruction that the judge had to give the jury: If a woman had once consented to unmarried sex, she was more likely to consent to it again, and this "evidence" could properly be used to assail the credibility of the rape victim. In other states, if the victim did not submit to a psychological evaluation, or had been the least bit tardy about initially reporting the rape, juries were instructed that these matters tainted her credibility.

An article published in *The New York Times Magazine* in that era had the provocative title "Question: If You Rape a Woman and Steal Her TV, What Can They Get You for in New York? Answer: Stealing Her TV."§ According to Burton Roberts, then president of the New York State District Attorneys Association,‖ New York's rape law was "the strictest in the country," meaning

---

*The statistics in this paragraph, pertaining to the early 1970s, are cited in *Rape and the Criminal Justice System*, Jennifer Temkin, ed. Aldershot; Brookfield, VT: Dartmouth Publishing Company, 1995.
†McLaughlin, F., "The Sex Offender," *Police Chief*, December 1962.
‡Temkin, *op cit*.
§Lear, Martha Weinman, *The New York Times Magazine*, January 30, 1975.
‖ He is also a fine lawyer, superb judge, and good friend.

that it had the most restrictions on the prosecution's ability to convict the defendant. Many legal experts pointed out that corroboration of the victim's word was not required in a robbery or an assault; in such felonies, the report of the victim—male or female—was considered "sufficient evidence" to convict a defendant without any additional evidence or corroboration—but in a rape case it was not.

In the Barnes case, the charges of rape and sodomy had made it through the grand jury because Victim A was able to corroborate Victim B's story and vice versa, including corroboration of the rapist's identity, the force (the knife had been found, too), and penetration (semen had been found inside of the victims' underwear). If there had been only one victim, there would likely have been no case at all.

The case moved me tremendously, especially after I'd heard the two women tell me their stories. My heart went out to them. But I was also enraged about the larger issue, laws that treated women as inferior and made it so difficult to prove that they were victims of this particularly heinous and invasive crime. Where was the justice in that? Or fairness? In 1970, the law still treated rape as though it were a crime exclusively about sex—and it was becoming obvious to me, through listening to these two women and from my research, that the crime of rape was really about power, about humiliation and degradation, almost always of women by men.

All the more reason for being so intense about this case: It appeared solid and winnable because the victims were so credible—two women who hadn't known one another prior to being grabbed off the street and who were articulate and able to give vivid detail about the horror of what had happened to them.

I was looking forward to this dual rape and robbery trial. The case was heard by a judge on the verge of retirement, an old Irish guy who, right off the bat, conveyed his skepticism about having a woman prosecute a serious felony case. Despite his attitude,

the victims' testimony was riveting and gave me reason to believe the case was going well. Their testimony featured such
awful details as one of them menstruating at the time of the rape
and Barnes having yanked out her tampon in order to rape her.
There was a great deal of evidence for the jury to consider. Another reason I thought it was going well was that the attorney for
the defense refrained from doing what many defenders of rapists
did in those days—cross-examine the victims to the point of subjecting them to almost as much abuse on the stand as they had
suffered from the rapist. After I finished presenting the prosecution's case, it was time for the routine defense motions to dismiss. And the defense attorney made those, arguing—as defense
attorneys always do—for dismissal because of a lack of evidence.
In this instance he suggested there was inadequate corroboration
of the elements of each rape and sodomy. It never occurred to
me that this motion would be taken seriously in a case that had
such an overwhelming amount of evidence and corroboration.

But the judge decided to question one aspect of the corrobo-
rative evidence. "How about it, Mrs. Snyder? Where's the corroboration of penetration?" Flabbergasted, I responded that the
answer was obvious: The corroboration existed in the evidence
of semen on the inside of the women's underwear. (At this time,
vaginal examinations of rape victims—for the purposes of going
after the rapists—were not routine.) He refused to accept the obvious nature of the evidence, instead insisting on the hypertechnical reasoning that corroboration of penetration meant nothing
less than semen being found inside the vagina or anus. On this
matter, as in others throughout the trial, he continued to treat me
in a demeaning manner, insinuating that I didn't know the law
and that a woman shouldn't be trying such a serious case.

With the matter still not finally resolved, but as it began to
look as though the judge would throw out the sex crimes
charges, I asked the appeals bureau for assistance. An older, experienced male lawyer in that bureau agreed completely with

my reading of the evidence, and I brought him into court to have him make the argument. The judge greeted his appearance with a snide remark, along the lines of, "Oh, so you think having someone else come and make the arguments is going to make any difference?" Damn right I did, especially if the arguments came from a *male* lawyer. The judge proceeded to dismiss all the rape and sodomy charges against the defendant anyway. I was devastated. But I had to continue on with the trial, and I did, even more determined now to win convictions on the robbery counts, which were the same-level felonies as the rapes and carried the same penalties. The jury convicted Barnes of the robberies. Hooray! But then the judge decided not to give him the maximum sentence, which was 8⅓ to 25 years. Rather, he gave Barnes 5 to 15 years—despite having heard every sordid detail of the brutal attack on the two women. I was truly disgusted, outraged—and without redress.

The women victims were hurt and upset by the verdict. Like me, they were thankful that Barnes had been convicted of something, but they were distraught because their ordeals on the stand seemed meaningless. They had had to go through the humiliating process of recounting in detail the rapes and sodomies, and being cross-examined about them, only to have all of the charges relating to that testimony thrown out by an arbitrary judge.

Thirteen years later, when I had become a judge, a young female ADA stopped me in the hall to speak of Trevor Barnes. She knew I'd be interested because she had the DA's file on the old case I'd done. She told me that she had just successfully prosecuted Barnes for a new rape and that he would be going to prison for quite some time. This gave me some satisfaction, not only because I knew he was a rapist, but also because I knew that I had helped create the conditions whereby such a sick individual could be more easily prosecuted for that awful crime.

My path to helping create those conditions began with this

double rape case. The unfairness of the verdict galvanized me. I said to myself and to other women interested in this aspect of the law, "We have to do something about this. We have to change the law." We all agreed.

In those days I would discuss every case I had with my husband, Fred. Often I'd use him as the ideal intelligent juror and try out my arguments on him or ask him what questions he thought jurors would want answered. He was unfailingly helpful, pointing out things I hadn't thought of or addressed—at least until years later, when he started dozing off during my practice summations, a clear signal that he had listened enough for all those years! When I had earlier brought to Fred my tale of outrage about the rape law, but told him of my resigned belief that one person could not do much to change anything—reinforced by a general lack of self-confidence—he said, "Don't be ridiculous. Of course you can do something about it—and you should. You're smart, you have ideas, and you care. How do you think things get changed in this world? If you feel strongly about the subject, you *have* to do something." And Fred made me feel that I *could* do something to make a difference.

I started small. I wrote up a list of steps that I thought the police ought to take in every sex crimes case so we could better prosecute rape cases, techniques to obtain more evidence and to satisfy the hypertechnical corroboration requirements—things that were not currently being done. These included such matters as instructing the victim not to bathe until she had a medical examination; to have medical exams of the victims performed by nearby hospitals and to retain and properly handle this medical evidence; to retain and voucher all torn or stained clothing from the victim or sheets or anything similar from the crime scene and send these to the lab to be examined for blood and semen evidence; to interview the defendant and elicit statements from him even if they were exculpatory, on the theory that he might say something that could later be shown to be false. I included suggestions for interviewing the victim, asking if the victim noted anything unusual about the defendant, including his underwear, genitals, or other not readily visible area; the language he used; and the defendant's sexual MO (modus operandi). I suggested that police officers not push the victim to be too exact in her descriptions—for instance, how would a rape victim know precisely how tall the attacker was, given the conditions in which the crime was usually committed? It would be better to elicit a description such as "fairly tall" or "medium build" unless the victim was certain; this would avoid problems later in the case.

Not wanting to be presumptuous, I discussed the list with my appeals bureau colleagues, who agreed with it. Then I went to the police department, to the chief of detectives. He and his men—the police department in 1970 was even more of a bastion of male chauvinism than the DA's office—also agreed with it. This was a time before the NYPD had started to set up its own sex crimes unit. They were on the verge of doing so, and my list became incorporated into the basic protocols that were established to help cops learn how to conduct better investigations of rape cases and to gather enough evidence so that these cases could be prosecuted successfully. At that time, most cops did not know—why should they have known?—how ludicrous the corroboration requirements were for sex crimes, how much more evidence these cases required than other crimes did, or what to do to make these cases stick.

The NYPD showed its serious intent to do better in this area by forming a sex crimes unit and placing a good female lieutenant in charge. In addition to adopting my list, the department also asked me to come and lecture to their officers receiving in-house training on the subject. That was a good experience for all of us and led me into a long-term relationship with the department, giving occasional lectures on subjects of mutual interest.

My small success with the list for the police only whetted my appetite for getting at the heart of the matter, changing state law on the requirements for the prosecution of rape and other sex crimes. This was not going to be an easy task. The first law that had to be amended concerned the corroboration requirements. To see what could be done, I met with the newly formed sex crimes unit of the NYPD and with women's groups, including the National Organization for Women, itself less than five years old. This was several years before the landmark case of women's rights, *Roe* v. *Wade*, would be decided by the United States Supreme Court in 1973. It was a time, though, when the "women's movement" was receiving an increasing amount of attention, when Congress was having debates over the Equal Rights Amendment, but when polls showed that more women disagreed than agreed with the goals of the feminists. I was not a joiner and, frankly, didn't want to join any of the women's groups, but I did work with them to try to convince the codes committee of the New York State Assembly and the New York State Senate to alter the corroboration statute. We were joined in our effort by such diverse groups as the state's association of district attorneys and civil liberties organizations; for those groups, as well as for me personally, changing the rape law was not simply a feminist issue, it was an issue of fairness and of improving the state's ability to convict people who committed serious criminal acts.

We had the statistics on our side as well as the moral imperative. Some thirty-three states were in the process of eliminating corroboration requirements. In those states where corroboration was required, the conviction rate for rape was far below what it was in the states that had eliminated the requirement. Also buttressing our position was that crimes as serious as rape, such as assault or robbery, had no corroboration requirement.

Then as now, the assembly in New York was considered a very liberal body—as opposed to the state senate, which is much more conservative. We had a hard time with both and especially with one of the lawyers involved. This lawyer put up a wall that we could not breach. One possible reason behind his position could have been a comment I had heard, although in a joking manner, from several male legislators: "We don't want to make it easier for us to be prosecuted," us meaning males. Maybe these legislators believed that their own extramarital affairs (or whatever) might now be more readily subject to prosecution! We didn't care about their dalliances; our only concern was being able to successfully prosecute rapists like Barnes. Other states were eliminating their rape corroboration statutes; why couldn't New York do so?

The change came in stages; first, the legislature agreed in 1972 to modify the corroboration requirements, eliminating the requirement for proving the rapist's identity but retaining the requirement that we provide corroboration of force or threats of force and corroboration of *an attempt* to commit the particular sex crime even if the consummated crime was charged. This was clearly an improvement over the old law, since it was often impossible to corroborate identity without an independent witness, which was a rare thing to have, and the new "attempt" requirement meant that it would now be sufficient to show semen on the underwear or outside the vagina. But there was still too much extra evidence required to prove the crime, and the victim's credibility was still not accepted. The timidity of the New York State Legislature was excoriated, and rightly so, in a 1972 *Yale Law Review* article entitled "The Rape Corroboration Requirement: Repeal Not Reform."

So we kept up the pressure, and finally, in early 1974, the remaining corroboration requirements for all forcible sex crimes were eliminated. Thinking back on the struggle, I believe that the opposition by the assembly and the reluctance of the male legislators to make it easier for men to be prosecuted delayed the full repeal of the corroboration statute for at least two years— during which perhaps dozens of rapists escaped prosecution for their crimes. And, at this point in time, the rate of increase in reported rape was outstripping the increase in all other categories of crime.*

Repeal of the corroboration statute took care of only half the problem. The other half concerned what was frequently referred to as the second rape, the one that occurred in the courtroom when the defense lawyer confronted the victim/complainant on the stand and grilled her mercilessly about her past sex life and whether or not, by her behavior, she had invited the rape or had consented to it. To put this in context: In rape cases the defendant rarely testifies, but the victim obviously must testify unless there has been an independent witness to all the details, which is rare indeed. Every defense lawyer who understood courtroom dynamics and how to affect juries would "put the victim on trial" through his or her cross-examination, and if the lawyer succeeded in shifting the focus from the defendant to the victim and her prior sex life—which happened all too often—there would frequently be an acquittal, even where the evidence cried out for a conviction. Defense cross-examination of rape victims was often brutal, and most judges would allow every bit of it. In fact, many judges in these cases hid behind the law, saying they had no authority to curtail such questioning, although in my view they could have, on the grounds that it was repetitive, irrelevant, and tantamount to harassment.

Generally, I didn't attend other prosecutors' trials, having quite enough to do to keep up with my own, but I was told about an incredible thing happening down the hall at 100 Centre Street and I went to observe. What I saw was a particularly vicious cross-examination of the victim in a rape case. Now, this victim was a woman who jumped out of cakes at bachelor parties, a stripper, but she said she had been raped, and her complaint had stood up through the grand jury process and was now at trial. The defense lawyer grilled her on the stand for nine

*FBI Crime Reports, 1976.

hours, asking such questions as how many times she had had extramarital sex in the past ten years, whether she had performed oral sex on this or that occasion, whether she had swallowed the semen or spat it out, and so on. I was sickened by this victim's ordeal and by the judge's unwillingness to curtail it. The grotesque detail was irrelevant, and having to recount it in a public forum not only demeaned her, but was also a form of torture that she was forced to endure. She, the victim, was on trial instead of the defendant.

Now, it is clear that in a rape case the defense must be able to introduce any relevant evidence about the victim's prior sex life with the defendant, about how the victim and defendant met, the circumstances of the rape; and a thorough cross-examination is constitutionally mandated. But the lurid detail concerning prior sex acts with people other than the defendant was totally irrelevant and extraordinarily prejudicial.

What was needed to protect victims from this sort of awful questioning was a statute that would shield them. Researching the matter, Judith Grad (of the New York City Corporation Counsel's Office) and I found "rape shield" statutes in several states and wrote our own version for New York. The statute that we drafted forbade most questioning about the victim's prior sexual history unless it involved the defendant. But we included a "savings" clause that permitted the judge some discretion in allowing some prior history into evidence "in the interests of justice," if relevant in a particular case, and only after a hearing, at the conclusion of which the judge would have to provide specific reasons for the inclusion of that evidence in the trial proceedings.

By this time, having been appointed to head the new sex crimes unit of the DA's office, I also had more clout personally than I'd had in 1970; and I was solicited by the New York Women's Bar Association to join them and to chair a criminal law committee. I resisted joining for a while, then decided that

63

women still needed to band together and that their backing and the platform the organization provided would help us lobby for the rape shield law and for other laws that would protect women. The women's bar was important in advancing women's rights, and I was happy I had joined it; eventually I became its president. This time, only a year had to elapse, from 1974 to 1975, before the legislature saw the light and enacted the rape shield law.

On this matter I must include an incident from 1991, when I was privileged to be on a panel for a series of public television programs, produced by Fred Friendly, about the Bill of Rights. On this particular program, the fictional case being presented was that of a "date rape" and the conflicts between the guarantees provided by various amendments in the Bill of Rights. During the program, Supreme Court Justice Antonin Scalia and some defense attorneys were arguing that the female victim's prior sexual history ought to be considered relevant and admissible evidence. My jaw literally dropped open in the camera's view! I explained that the rape shield law served to prevent such information from being admissible, among other reasons because "the victim, as well as the defendant, must have a fair trial," and such evidence was usually irrelevant and prejudicial. Justice Scalia seemed to find this idea offensive and insisted that the victim's prior sexual history might be quite relevant and should not be excluded from consideration. He and I had a bit of a heated exchange, which concluded with my expressing shock that, more than fifteen years after the rape shield law had gone on the books in New York (and had been followed by similar laws in many other states), a justice of the United States Supreme Court would still be making the case for antediluvian attitudes in the courtroom in regard to rape victims.

Beyond the changes in the law, an even more fundamental change was required in the 1970s: Everybody in the criminal justice system needed to understand rape as a crime having to do with power and control and only secondarily with sexual gratification. I had come to this understanding through my reading, through my discussions with other women involved in helping to change the laws, and, perhaps most vividly, through my work as head of the sex crimes unit.

Consider the facts of what we called the "Grand Central" case. A German-born young woman had come to New York City to work as a nanny for the family of the German ambassador to the United States. After working for a while, she took a short vacation and then returned to New York through Grand Central Station, carrying several heavy bags. A large man intercepted her and offered to carry her bags and get her a taxi. Unaware of the danger that such an offer presented, she accepted. The man led her through the station, down several levels into its bowels, and locked her in a dark, internal alleyway. There he proceeded to rape her, sodomize her, and urinate and defecate on her—repeatedly, for hours and hours, and all without saying a word. She screamed, but no one could hear her in the darkness and gloom. Her nightmare seemed to have no end. Eventually, though, her attacker fell asleep and she crawled around the alley, feeling her way until she found a door and managed to force her way through. It was the back door to a restaurant, and the kitchen personnel called the police and obtained help for her. The cops quickly arrested her attacker.

My blood began to boil as I heard the horrifying details of this case. I was again struck by the realization that these events were not understandable as a crime about sex but were crystal clear as a crime that involved the attacker's attempts to humiliate and degrade his victim—in other words, as a crime of domination and control. You didn't have to be Sigmund Freud to conclude that the perpetrator had some twisted need to degrade women. I speculated about the emotional and sexual abuse he must have suffered himself, but I was never able to confirm it in his background; in any event, it was irrelevant now.

My first task was to convince the victim to testify. She had returned to Germany to recuperate and was not keen on coming back to the United States to work with us on the case. I argued with her that unless she testified, the man who attacked her would continue to do the same thing to other women and that she had an obligation to prevent that from happening. Eventually she agreed.

When she returned to the United States, the unit and I did everything possible to support her, give her confidence, and reassure her about testifying. Earlier in my career, I had found it essential to do this when dealing with rape victims, and I made it part of the drill in the sex crimes unit. Even after recovering from the physical part of the rape, these victims continued to suffer. They were totally traumatized and psychologically wounded, at least temporarily. Some had boyfriends and husbands who told them they would never be able to look at them in the same way again, which was further trauma for victims already experiencing psychological problems with trying to have sex again and to live in the world. Not all rape victims have physical injuries, but they all have injuries that are psychic and often long-lasting. Some of the victims we dealt with were children, who could not comprehend what had happened to them and would be scarred for life. They needed our support more than any other victims, and we tried mightily to provide it.

Frankly, it was up to us to protect the victims because nobody else in the system was doing so. Despite having made changes in the laws, we knew that many judges and jurors were still unwilling to accept rape as a crime of control or to comprehend the need to protect its victims from further harm while they were being subjected to the criminal justice process.

Some judges, male prosecutors, defense lawyers, and many

male jury members still retained in their minds the notion that the woman victim might have said no to the man but had really meant yes, and therefore it could not be rape. We still heard defenses on the theme of "She really wanted it" or "She had it coming." In this era, for instance, "legal experts" in the British House of Lords ruled that a man could not be convicted of rape if he honestly believed that the woman had consented to sexual intercourse—no matter how unreasonable his belief might be.*

Things began to improve in the criminal justice system, but it was a slow learning process. I did not think it was my place, as a relatively young assistant DA, to lecture judges on the changes in the law. But when the opportunity arose in regard to a particular case, I did tell them about those changes because I knew the subject and was so involved with it. Many male jurors weren't really swayed by the changes in the law. Why was that woman in a bar? Why did she wear a short dress and high heels? Wasn't that provocation or sending signals that she wanted sex and must have consented? Such questions reinforced the tremendous guilt many victims felt about having been raped, the belief that they had contributed to their own trauma. And these beliefs also reinforced the unwillingness of many victims to testify lest they be subjected to such questions.

In another case I was handling at that time, the victim was a young, good-looking, wealthy white woman who had an apartment on Manhattan's Upper West Side. When I first spoke to her she was making a complaint only about robbery: Five young men had forced their way into her apartment and stolen her money and jewelry. But something about her story didn't feel right; she was not telling all the facts.

I kept questioning her, probing for the real story, to the point of ultimately positing that something more must have happened in that apartment. Eventually she broke down and told me, as I

*The New York Times, May 2, 1975.

had suspected, that each of the five men had raped and sodomized her and then had taken her property—but that she hadn't wanted to file a complaint about the attacks because she didn't want her father to learn about them. I explained to her that she could testify in front of the grand jury and that no one would know about it, including her father; that grand jury testimony is secret and that the indictments that were likely to come out of it could give us the ammunition with which to force tough plea bargains on the defendants. If we obtained those, she would never have to testify in open court. Moreover, I told her, "You're well educated, you can understand this: You're putting any number of other women in danger if you don't tell the truth; rapists are recidivists."

She reluctantly accepted my argument and testified before the grand jury, and we did reach plea bargains with the defendants that put them away for some serious time but also made it unnecessary for the victim to testify in open court—which she might not have been willing to do.

When you care about your cases, you use every opportunity to reinforce them. In the Grand Central case, I placed special emphasis on using the voir dire process for the purpose of educating and even brainwashing the jury. Every good lawyer does this—or tries to. The voir dire is the process in which potential jurors are questioned and then selected. The attorneys for the prosecution and defense are allowed to ask questions of the individual jurors. Today, most judges maintain control, rather than allowing the attorneys to do so, but a quarter century ago, many judges all but slept through voir dire—read a newspaper or a law journal and sometimes actually nodded off—which gave the attorneys their opportunity to tell the jury what they wanted them to think about the case and the evidence. In the Grand Central case voir dire, I told the potential jurors that they must recognize that the evidence in this case would be incomprehensible if they thought of rape as a crime having to do with sexual gratification, but it would be very understandable if they thought of rape as a crime of degradation and control. I'd ask questions designed not only to elicit the prospective jurors' biases, but also to educate them on the law and to display in advance the "weaknesses" of our case and, while doing so, minimize the importance of those weaknesses. Throughout the voir dire and on through the trial itself, I characterized the evidence of urination and defecation as underscoring that the crime dealt with the humiliation of women, not with sexual gratification. The jury, clearly disgusted and repelled by the evidence, convicted the defendant of this horrible crime. But the sentence given by this judge, too, was less than the maximum, something I've never understood.

In one sense, the Grand Central case was atypical: The defendant was a wild-eyed, mangy man on the fringes of society. Many rapists are very ordinary, normal looking, and apparently mainstream. That fact—and it is a statistical fact—was borne out by another rape case that remains vivid in my memory. A white, young, clean-cut U.S. Marine was charged with raping an eighty-year-old woman. This case was handed to me by a fellow prosecutor, because, as he said, "I can't believe they've got the right guy. How could this guy have done this crime?" Now, if the prosecutor couldn't believe it, how could we expect a mostly male jury and a male judge to believe it?

The marine case and the Upper West Side rape case helped underline an obvious point: You can't do the right thing until you have all the facts in front of you.

First I had to be certain myself that this was indeed the likely rapist. I had no formal training in psychiatry, but based on my experience and my readings about sex crimes, I decided that the key to the case was learning about the defendant's personal history. I sent investigators to find out about his family, his school days, and so on. Did he have any sisters? An overbearing mother? Fight with female teachers? Any history of abuse by or of women? We had to continually keep in mind that this fine-appearing young man would probably never take the stand in his own defense but would sit there in his marine uniform, looking good, and that he might well call character witnesses to make him look even better. Ultimately, we learned from our background investigation that this defendant did have a problem with women, many problems, going back to living with a household full of sisters and a domineering mother; he'd had arguments and fights with female schoolteachers; and there had been other warning signs. This background, when coupled with evidence about the crime, made me certain that we had the correct person. But the information about his background could not be brought in the courtroom on its own. If he did not take the stand on his own behalf, we could introduce it only in a roundabout way, through cross-examination of the defendant's character witnesses, if he called any. Then we would be able to ask those witnesses: "Had you heard that the defendant had these specific encounters with women? . . . If you had known this about the defendant, would that have changed your opinion about his reputation for peacefulness/veracity?" And so on.

In fact, this defendant did call character witnesses. Those witnesses who had been close to the defendant said that the information we had learned would not have made them change their minds about his reputation, but other witnesses, those who were pillars of the community but didn't know the defendant very well, admitted that if they had known certain facts, they might not have retained their good opinion of him. Eventually we obtained a conviction. It was satisfying that someone had been found guilty who was especially dangerous to women, because no one would believe he could commit rape. He seemed the perfect candidate to be the recidivist that psychiatrists deem rapists to be, as statistics bear out. And anyone who would rape an eighty-year-old woman had to be considered even sicker than most rapists.

The fight to reform the sex crimes laws was not complete by 1975. A needed change involved the definition of "forcible compulsion," one of the elements of forcible rape and sodomy. The existing standard obligated the victim to have been subjected to "physical force which overcomes earnest resistance" or a threat of physical force that placed a victim in fear of "immediate serious physical injury or death" in order for "forcible compulsion" to be proved. It took three separate amendments before we obtained an acceptable definition in 1983, when it was finally made clear that a rape victim who was threatened or placed in fear of *any* injury absolutely did not have to resist physical force or the threat of it in order for rape to be proved. The new law completely eliminated the onus that had been placed on the victim of having to resist her attacker. Changing this requirement had been another long and painful process, and the changes were resisted by the legislature until the very end.

Even that was not the final word. It was not until the New York State Court of Appeals ruling in *People* v. *Taylor*,* in 1990, that the court officially recognized what victims, prosecutors, and the medical community had long known: Rape is an extraordinarily traumatic event that often triggers the onset of those symptoms in women that we now refer to as "rape trauma syndrome" (RTS). Evidence of RTS is now admissible in appropriate rape cases, not for the purposes of concluding that the victim was or was not raped—that decision is the exclusive province of the jury—but if it is relevant to the case and meets other legal requirements.

Progress on rape was never easy, but at last the extraordinary trauma caused by this dreadful crime was recognized by the law.

*75 NY 2d 277 (1990).

And victims' rights—not just defendants' rights—were finally recognized as well.

In the mid-1970s, the cases kept coming into our sex crimes unit. And many of these cases outraged me, although I couldn't allow my emotions to show. We had to take care of the victims, yet we had to obtain the facts on which to base prosecutions, and to do that we sometimes had to get beyond the victim's need for sympathy. Among the cases that galled me the most were those in which the violence done to the victims was patently gratuitous. A young woman who had escaped the ghetto and was on the fast track until her life was ruined by a rape. Gang rapes, in which the participating males egged one another on to brutalize a woman. A rape in which a young black man said he had been so angered by the presence of a privileged "beautiful young blond boy" that he kidnapped and sodomized the boy in an apartment for days, resulting in trauma that took years even to dissipate partially. As with all professionals, I developed the ability to present a facade of deliberate absence of emotion so I could deal with such situations professionally—but behind it I seethed with anger at defendants who acted like animals, ruined their victims' lives, and showed no remorse. For me in the sex crimes bureau, working on the most vicious cases, the role of prosecutor merged with the role of representing the victim and combined to make me feel that this work was some of the most important I would ever do. In the most egregiously violent of these cases, every corpuscle in me cried out to make certain that justice was done and that appropriate punishment was meted out.

Every time there was an unusual, difficult, or serious sex crime case in the DA's office, it would be referred to us, since our unit was relatively small and had been set up to handle precisely those cases. Eventually we would have four ADAs, one paralegal, one secretary, a detective from the NYPD sex crimes unit permanently assigned to us as liaison to that unit, and ties to two psychiatrists, one specializing in children and one in adults, who agreed to see some of our victims pro bono, at least for consultation. We worked very closely together, shared a relatively private wing in "the office," and handled no other cases. (Now, numerous ADAs are labeled sex crimes DAs but are scattered throughout the various trial bureaus, handling other cases as well as sex crimes.)

One day in 1975, a woman referred to me by the complaint bureau came in with a curious tale. She looked like a hippie and seemed flaky; she was also young and looked even younger than her age. She said that she had had a toothache and had been referred to a dentist in a brownstone in the Chelsea area of Manhattan. The dentist had seen her and said that she needed some oral surgery, and she had made an appointment to have the surgery done soon after. On that date she returned to his office and was taken into a room with a solitary dentist's chair; there the dentist gave her an anesthetic that he said would put her out temporarily while he did the work, so that she would feel no pain. As she woke up in a daze, a state of semi-consciousness, the young woman felt something touching her face and saw a naked penis in front of her, then a pair of pants being zipped up. While she was still groggy and had little control over her body, the person slapped her, grabbed her, lifted her from the dental chair, kissed her, and felt her breasts and thighs.

This was a strange tale. I told the woman I'd look into it. Frankly, although I believed her, I wasn't sure how to proceed. Sometimes, when you have an allegation of wrongdoing by a specific individual, your investigation might cause you to go to him or her and confront that person with the allegation. To do so in this instance would only alert the dentist, who would of course deny the allegation, and it might give him an opening to go on the offensive, file his own complaint or otherwise counterattack. So I hadn't made much headway on the case, although I was trying to gather some information, when—lo and behold—a second woman showed up with exactly the same complaint. She did not know the first woman but gave off the same aura: young, appearing even younger and slightly flaky. And she told us the same story: same sequence of treatment, same chair, same feelings upon waking from the anesthesia, except that this second woman remembered that when she was still semiconscious the dentist placed her hand on his pants and penis, kissed her, and said something about her performing oral sex on him. On arriving home later, she found her underwear wet and her vagina sore, conditions that had not existed prior to the dentist's "surgery."

This victim reinforced the first one's complaint, but now a problem arose because this young woman had initially gone to the local precinct to make her complaint, and the precinct had assigned a detective who had interviewed the dentist and had recommended that nothing be done. It seemed that the dentist had told the precinct detective that the anesthetic he used was diazepam, which was essentially Valium, and that this drug had the known side effect of producing sexual hallucinations. This explanation satisfied the detective, and he was ready to exonerate the dentist or at least to deep-six the case. I confronted the detective and we ended up in a shouting match. I stressed that the dentist's explanation of the side effects of diazepam was not medically sound and was totally inconsistent with the fact that he had asked each of these women out on a date! The detective's airy dismissal of the idea that the dentist could have done anything to the young women provoked me to the point of asking, "What did this guy do—buy you off or what?" I've seldom been so upset with a cop. And one of my reasons for being upset was that I had done some checking on my own, with dentists and doctors, and had learned—as the detective hadn't bothered to do—that sexual hallucinations as a side effect of diazepam were highly unusual, so rare that they were considered to be nonexistent or just a theoretical possibility by other dentists who used diazepam regularly on their patients.

Now I had a serious case. But the evidence came from two women who had been drugged and whose recollections were not entirely clear. There was no scientific or "hard" evidence to corroborate their hazy accounts. I was working with the sex crimes unit of the NYPD, and we decided to try to obtain more evidence via a consensual audio recording. New York State is a "one party" state, in which you can record your conversations with another person if you want to without the consent of the other party. States like Florida and Maryland are two-party states, which require the consent of both parties to the recording before it is legal. (For instance, when Linda Tripp taped Monica Lewinsky, Tripp became vulnerable to prosecution in Maryland for her action because Maryland is a two-party state.) In cooperation with the police, we had the first and second victims return to the dentist's office—separately—while wearing small tape recorders. The dentist made no admissions to either of the victims but did invite them to his hotel room; they refused to go. He offered to inject the second victim with anesthetic again, but she balked. On the tape, he admitted kissing the second victim and enjoying that very much but said no more. He told each victim that he still wanted to see her socially, so at our suggestion the first victim told him to meet her at a noisy, singles-type bar. He agreed.

At the bar, that victim wore a wire, and two undercover cops sat nearby, but the dentist, having been alerted to possible danger to himself by the precinct detective's interview, refused to discuss with the victim what had happened to her—except that she had given him a "fat kiss." He kept the conversation noncommittal and turned on the charm. A clever, cagey guy, this dentist.

Meanwhile, a third victim appeared in our offices. Again, she was very much his type, and the complaint she expressed had become all too familiar. This young woman never resurfaced for grand jury or trial, but we did glean important evidence from her: Her answering machine contained a message from the defendant, asking to come to her apartment with his "bag of goodies" from the office. This evidence reinforced everything we'd learned about the dentist and added more legal justification to our future course of action.

I was all the more convinced that the dentist was a sexual predator, and I wanted badly to see him arrested and prosecuted. It was reasonable to assume that he'd been performing sexual acts on unwilling and unconscious women for years and might have molested dozens of other vulnerable young women while they were under anesthesia in his dentist chair. The more I thought about it the angrier I became, and soon I reached the belief that the best way, and perhaps the only way, to obtain sufficient evidence with which to arrest him was to send a female undercover officer into his office and somehow observe him as he molested her.

Our sex crimes unit had a detective from the NYPD sex crimes unit assigned to it. She was not happy with my idea, since it could put a police officer in potential peril; she also seemed apprehensive about "going after" a dentist. I thought the undercover scenario could be accomplished with a minimum of danger, and I dismissed her other concerns. So I went to the NYPD directly and described the person I needed—young and flaky. The NYPD ultimately said they could not help because they had no officers answering that description; after all, there were still very few women "on the job." The Westchester Police Department had recently formed a sex crimes unit and had a dynamic woman in charge; I went to see her. After I had reviewed the evidence with her, she totally agreed on the use of an undercover as the only remaining way to obtain sufficient evidence to charge the dentist. She told me, "I think I have the perfect person for you. Let's do it—it's the only way you'll ever nail the SOB."

She did indeed have the perfect undercover. This young cop was about twenty-one but looked sixteen and could affect the flaky appearance and vulnerability of the other victims. She was also willing to undertake the task even though she realized that it could be dangerous for her. By this time, we had learned that the dentist had asked each of his victims for details of their personal histories. All were not only young but also lived alone, with no family in the area, and had said they were unemployed at the time they went to his office. This set of circumstances, of course, made them more vulnerable and with fewer resources than if they had lived at home or with a boyfriend or had fellow employees to whom they could have related the tale of what happened to them in the dentist's office. So we naturally chose a history for our undercover that was almost identical.

But having a willing undercover solved only one part of the problem. Now we had to find legal ways to obtain the evidence. An audiotape wouldn't do. You'd hear heavy breathing and maybe other ambiguous sounds, but that would be all. We needed a *videotape* of whatever occurred. All other investigative means had been tried and had failed. Only with a videotape recording could we be certain of anything that took place while the victim was groggy. But there had never been such a thing as a "video surveillance order." I knew that because I had researched it extensively. So I began to draft one, with the help of the appeals bureau.

I had never wanted to work in the appeals bureau—researching and writing were not my main interests—but it was an invaluable resource to me and to every other ADA with a legal problem to solve; moreover, the appeals bureau in our office was always led by brilliant and creative prosecutors. The appeals bureau and I went back and forth on the video surveillance order for a couple of weeks, making sure the language was right. It wasn't a wiretap and it wasn't a search warrant; we made it a hybrid of both. No statute anywhere in the United States covered this situation. But we could be—as we had to be—very specific in our details because we knew the alleged perpetrator's MO: a particular room, a particular chair. We would have to be able to monitor the videocamera from somewhere close by and also to turn on the camera only when the undercover was in the chair, in order not to invade the privacy of other people and to comply with the legal requirements that we anticipated. An important element in wiretaps and search warrants is a section of the application that must detail the probable cause for the intrusion as well. It must also include the information that we had tried other investigative procedures and had exhausted them, with insufficient results—another legal requirement we anticipated. In our order we wanted to satisfy the more rigorous legal requirements for wiretaps, to enhance the likelihood that the order would be upheld in appellate courts later on, should we arrest the dentist, convict him, and the conviction later be appealed.

We also needed to specify how we would accomplish our goal. To learn more about the dental office and to figure out what equipment would be viable in it, we sent in an NYPD officer, one unconnected to our undercover plans and in plain clothes, to see the dentist to inquire about an apocryphal toothache. She had no intention of allowing him to perform any dental work on her since we had told her about the case and his unique techniques, but she looked over the layout as best she could while trying not to appear to be obviously snooping. From her we learned more about the configuration of the offices and enough detail to flesh out portions of our wiretap warrant.

As finally drafted, the surveillance order/wiretap/search warrant included a section allowing the police and investigators, for obvious reasons, the right to break into the brownstone at night and plant the video equipment prior to the undercover operation itself. Fortunately, the dentist lived in the suburbs and not in the brownstone. Even more opportune for us, the old building in which his office was located had been modernized and his office had dropped ceilings. This detail, which might seem trivial, was in fact critical: Without those dropped ceilings there would have been no way to plant the camera to capture him "at work" and therefore no investigation and no case. As they say, for want of a nail . . .

With the head of the appeals bureau, I went to the new district attorney, Robert Morgenthau, to discuss our application. We did this because the application was unusual and we wanted to be certain that he agreed we were doing the right thing; after all, the target was not a drug dealer but a "respected" medical professional. Morgenthau asked us some good questions and then signed the document—as the law requires.

Now we needed the signature of a judge.

I thought that any good judge, confronted with an application for an unusual, groundbreaking wiretap/surveillance order, would want to take it under advisement for a day or two, would read it carefully, and might possibly not want to sign it at all simply because it was unprecedented and many judges don't like to break with precedent, since that can lead to reversal on appeal. Moreover, signing off on this intrusive an order ought not to be done lightly. To bring in an example from a later date, in the present as a judge I review a great many wiretap applications, and I require that such applications be submitted to me at least one day in advance of when they are needed so I can read them carefully to determine whether or not they are legally sufficient. The applications run to dozens of pages and occasionally far more. And the video surveillance order that I had in hand to give to a judge in 1975 was lengthy as well as unusual.

Hearing my doubts, a colleague in the DA's office said, "You want your order signed? Come with me," and took me across the street to 111 Centre Street and into the courtroom of a supreme court judge before whom he had appeared many times but whom I did not know. We received permission to approach the bench; I handed the judge the application and he asked, "What's this about?" I launched into the beginning of what would have been a lengthy explanation of the matter—reflective of my intense interest in the case, of all the work we had put in, and of the unusual nature of the request—but he cut me off by saying, "I don't need to know all that. Tell me *briefly* what it's about." My colleague took over and in less than three minutes provided a wonderful summary, throwing around such phrases as "We need to go into an office, put in certain equipment, do a video recording." The judge nodded, picked up the application, and riffled through the pages, spending perhaps a tenth of a second on each one. After about five minutes, he signed the order and handed it back to us. I was nonplussed.

"But you said you wanted somebody to sign it," my colleague teased. "Does it matter if he knows exactly how much of a bombshell he signed?"

Well, I supposed not.

Now, signed application in hand, we could send in the techs. This was to be a classic black-bag job—a break-in to a private facility by a law enforcement agency—but it was court authorized. That night, police technicians got in and installed the camera in the appropriate dental office and the recording equipment in the basement. The brownstone's basement was a rat-infested, uninhabitable black hole—but it had room for all the monitoring equipment and the cops manning it for the purpose of keeping the dentist and the undercover under constant surveillance.

The day before, the undercover had waltzed into the dentist's office complaining of a bum tooth, and we waited to learn if he would bite. We had previously sent her to another dentist; she did have an impacted wisdom tooth, but this dentist assured her and us that there was no reason to take it out just then and no physical basis for her toothache. The dentist asked her all the questions that we had expected, examined her, and recommended surgery. She said she could not have the surgery that day and made an appointment; that was the pattern followed by the other victims, and we wanted to replicate it here so as not to alert our target. He agreed to do the surgery on her a few days later. A midnight test run of all the equipment showed that everything was in working order. The operation was a go.

Usually, an ADA does not go out on an arrest, and we weren't supposed to—but I wanted very badly to be in on this one, and the police agreed to permit me to sit in the monitoring car. (I never asked for permission from my office, lest it be refused.) In the monitoring car, I would hear the audio from the cops in the basement, who were monitoring the video and audio in the dental office. What I'd hear would not be the dentist or the undercover, but the cops' observations based on their watching and listening from their positions.

The day came. The monitoring cops went into the house during the overnight hours and stationed themselves in the basement in force—they wanted to be able to reach the undercover quickly in case anything went wrong. Early in the morning, more cops wearing the uniforms of Con Edison, the electric utility, took up positions on the street, in work vans, and near manholes, ostensibly doing repair work. We were in the monitoring car outside on the street as the young female undercover walked up the stairs and into the brownstone. She was carrying a tape recorder and transmitting device in her purse so that the audio would be recorded. She had also had her clothes dusted with fluorescent powder that would stick to the dentist's hands should he attempt to remove those clothes.

Everything worked as planned. She was ushered into the dental operation room, the same one described by previous victims and the only one covered by our surveillance order, and was seated by the dentist in the "special" chair. As the undercover would later recall, the dentist promised her "a very erotic experience." The videocamera was turned on by the cops below; they kept up a steady, whispered patter, letting all of us know how things were progressing. I heard lines like "She's going into the office now. . . . He's sitting her in the chair. . . . He's giving her the anesthesia." They could see the video of him putting her under and the undercover beginning to drift into unconsciousness. After about two minutes of complete silence—the proverbial eternity—the cops shouted through our earphones, "He's grabbing for her breasts."

For legal reasons I wanted to let the action go on briefly, so that we would have video of him in the act of reaching under her dress or performing some other relatively minor sexual act, but the cops naturally did not like the idea of their undercover being in possible danger of sexual violation and overruled me. I could understand their position.

"He's going for her. Quick! Let's go! Everybody in! Go, go, go!" the cops were yelling. The "Con Ed" workers ran toward the house, and from inside the brownstone the monitoring cops came up the stairs from the basement, and all burst into the dentist's office, where the undercover was semicomatose. I was some steps behind them. One of the detectives who raced in ahead of me observed him massaging the nipples of the undercover's breasts. Later, he would testify to this at the trial, but those actions were not captured on tape because of the angle of the videocamera.

By the time I arrived in the brownstone's inner office, the cops had made sure that the undercover was safe and had been taken out of the operating room. The dentist was standing there, surrounded by police officers. He was tall, not handsome but imposing, with graying hair, wearing a well-tailored suit with a white smock over it.

"I'm Assistant District Attorney Leslie Snyder. You are under arrest and we have a warrant to search your premises." I handed over the warrant.

He took it in his hand, looked at it a moment, and said, "Well, Leslie, I'm going to eat my lunch." And he proceeded to do so.

I was amazed. Here he was, his whole life coming down around him, his shocking secret exposed, and he sat there calmly eating a peach.

His pose as Mr. Totally Cool held up for a while as the cops searched the office looking for evidence to corroborate the stories told by earlier victims. Later on, the dentist called his lawyer before being taken away in handcuffs. But he never appeared flustered.

I prepared the case for the grand jury. I learned from the videotape and audiotape recordings, as well as from the undercover, that while she was unconscious the dentist extracted her tooth, raised her blouse, and examined her chest with a stethoscope. During the minutes that she had no control over her movements, he lifted her out of the dental chair—they were alone the entire time—pulled her toward him and between his legs, rubbed his hands across her back and around her breasts, and grabbed and massaged her buttocks.

The video, combined with the undercover's testimony and reports from the earlier victims, was enough to produce a solid case. Eventually it was taken to trial, and I must note that the legality and propriety of the video surveillance order was upheld in New York's appellate courts and that the United States Supreme Court denied certiorari—refused to hear the case, in other words—in effect confirming video surveillance as a lawful new form of wiretap. The dentist was ultimately convicted of two counts of sexual abuse, a class D felony, for subjecting one victim and the undercover to sexual contact while they were "incapable of consent by reason of being physically helpless." He received a sentence of only four months in jail. He did, however, lose his license to practice dentistry.

I did not take the case to trial. In the summer of 1976, when it was still in the pretrial phase, John Keenan asked me to leave the district attorney's office and join his new office, that of the New York State Special Prosecutor Against Corruption in the Criminal Justice System. It was an opportunity that I seized; I was to be his chief of trials and to try some very significant cases; the work seemed important and intense, even though it dealt with the dark side of cops' lives. I will tell the story of my work for the anticorruption office in the next chapter, but for now I want to note that one of my jobs there was to be in charge of recruitment for the office, and in that capacity I encountered the name of this dentist once again. A young man recently out of law school applied for a job with the office and ended up interviewing with me. In the course of our conversation, after we'd spoken about his school record and why he wanted to work here, and had spent at least fifteen minutes together, he mentioned that his father was a dentist from Westchester.

Alarm bells finally rang in my head, and I looked closely at the name on his application for the first time—it was the same as the dentist's.

"Is your father the man I prosecuted?"

"Yes," the young man said.

"Don't you think you should have told me this earlier?"

"Why? What difference does it make?"

I immediately terminated the interview.

Well before the dentist's trial, I began to hear that my successor as chief of the DA's sex crimes bureau was saying bad things about me. She claimed that the dentist case had insufficient evidence—because the video stopped too soon—and sent word to me that "if I lose this case, I'll make sure people know it's your fault." Not only did she not lose the case, the conviction made her reputation. In fact, based on the hard work that my staff and I had previously done, the sex crimes unit continued to operate and to expand its purview.

Even though I went on to other positions and eventually to a judgeship, I have maintained my interest in rape and other sex crimes, which have become a worldwide matter of concern. A 1997 conference on rape, held in Tokyo, identified thirty-five countries where wars or armed conflicts have given rise to epidemics of violence against women. In places like Bosnia, Rwanda, Cambodia, and east Timor, mass rapes have become one way that invading armies punish their enemies. In such situations, investigators have found certain common elements: The women involved in the rapes are of relatively low status; there are few or inadequate statutes against rape; the judicial systems are unequipped to handle sex crimes; the victims have no way to assure their safety from recriminations should they file charges against their rapists; and there is, as always, great difficulty in documenting the cases. Learning of such events and conditions, I can only be thankful that in the United States we have reformed our laws, made it possible to prosecute the crime of rape successfully, and educated both men and women in reducing the incidence of this terrible crime.

A WALK ON THE DARK SIDE: INVESTIGATING CORRUPTION IN THE CRIMINAL JUSTICE SYSTEM

Defense lawyers like to say that as a judge I am pro–law enforcement and too tough on the defense in general. I don't believe I'm guilty of either charge—among other reasons, because I'm not oblivious to the problems cops can have or to the obligations of defense lawyers to protect their clients. I've taken my own walk on the dark side, in the form of prosecuting police for corruption and of being a criminal defense attorney.

My journey to the dark side began when I was head of the sex crimes bureau of the DA's office, with one very troubling case. There was an unusual complaint referred to our unit: A junkie and sometime prostitute claimed that a police officer had sodomized her in a back room of a precinct in Harlem. According to this woman, she and her boyfriend had been in a car, driving through Harlem. Since they were both white, the cops had evidently concluded—accurately—that they must be looking for drugs and pulled them in on a pretext, a traffic violation; a minor amount of drugs was found in the car. This was in the middle of the night, with only a skeleton crew manning the precinct. The arresting officer had let the boyfriend go but took her back to the station house and told her that he was going to lock her up unless she gave him a "blow job." After protesting, the woman did as the cop demanded. She was then released, and no charges were filed against her. Soon afterward she made her complaint.

I was skeptical of the woman's story when I first heard it from her, but the more I investigated the more convinced I became that she was credible. For instance, she said she had spat the cop's semen on the floor in a particular place; when our investigator went to the precinct there was a suspicious stain on the floor, precisely where she had said it would be. I decided to present all the evidence to an investigative grand jury, allowing its members to scc and hear everything so that they could make an informed decision as to whether or not to indict the cop. While in short, clear cases most grand juries are rubber stamps for the prosecution, investigative grand juries are different. Together the prosecutors and the grand jury see the evidence unfold, and neither usually knows initially what the grand jury's ultimate decision may be. That was what happened here.

The grand jury thought the woman complainant was credible but wanted to see and hear all relevant evidence. We subpoenaed the memo books and logbooks from the precinct; I called witnesses who had been at the precinct at the same time that the cop and the victim had been there. The grand jury then wanted to hear from most of the cops on the overnight shift. Much of their testimony conflicted with the documentary evidence: The cops were lying! Some of them, I later learned, believed their fellow officer had done what the prostitute alleged, others did not, but they were united in their willingness to do anything to protect one of their own. This was the first time I had ever seen the vaunted "blue wall of silence" in action.

Since cops stick together to protect their own, an individual cop's sense of right or wrong in regard to the facts of this case seemed to be irrelevant.

John Keenan, whose advice I sought (as I often did), helped me keep some perspective by pointing out that while some of the cops might be lying, their behavior did not mean that the cop we were investigating had done what the woman accused him of doing.

The grand jury was incensed. Its members wanted to indict the cops for perjury; things were getting out of hand. I convinced the grand jury that, in effect, Keenan was right: We shouldn't try to indict the police force for its self-protective actions, but rather hold the one offending cop responsible. They agreed.

Several cops who knew me called to say that this stuff—cops having sex in the station house—went on all the time in precinct houses on the midnight shift, but, for me, the fact that it went on regularly did not make coercing sex any less intolerable.

I had a trial preparation assistant (TPA) named Ronnie, and we diligently prepared for trial. In the courtroom, the accused cop waived his right to a jury trial and instead opted to have a judge decide the facts as well as the law. Such trials proceed in the same manner as jury trials but much faster. The judge, another old-timer, was bright and acerbic, and he liked me, so initially I wasn't worried about the case. I put on witnesses, we brought in the circumstantial evidence like the stain—the lab had not been able conclusively to identify it, as this was well before DNA testing began to be used, but the existence of the stain corroborated the woman's story—and I thought the prosecution had gone well.

The defense decided not to put on any witnesses except the defendant. From the stand, under his attorney's questions, the cop smirked at me as though to convey that this whole judicial procedure was a scam and he was going to win. Under my cross-examination, the cop denied the "blow job" but didn't deny the parts of the woman's story that were undeniable, such as that he had stopped her and the boyfriend and brought her to the precinct. But his answers to my questions became completely incredible as he tried to describe why he had let her go without charging her with a crime, having previously determined to release only the boyfriend.

In my closing argument, I stressed that the cop had lied on the stand and throughout the process and identified what he had done to the complainant in terms of abuse of power, charging that he had employed sodomy to degrade his victim in addition to gratifying his own sexual pleasure. He continued to smile broadly at me as I made these statements, but in the gallery the cop's wife started to weep audibly. I wondered if she had experienced the need for control and the desire to degrade that I was convinced motivated him. Throughout my closing, the judge asked me hostile questions and evidently did not listen to me at all—because he already had his verdict written out and delivered it as soon as I'd finished. Defendant acquitted— not guilty! I put on my professional face to hide my disappointment, but Ronnie wept, claiming over and over that "the contract is in." Shortly after this, she left the DA's office and went into another line of work.

It was not long after this case concluded, and after John Keenan had prosecuted the high-profile Phillips case, in which a police officer was accused of murdering a prostitute—there was a hung jury, but Phillips was convicted in a second trial—that Keenan was appointed to head the office of the Special Prosecutor Against Corruption in the Criminal Justice System for New York State, and I joined him as his chief of trials. In September of 1976, after almost nine years in the DA's office, I was ready for a change and a new challenge.

Several years earlier, the Knapp Commission had uncovered and documented evidence of systemic corruption in the NYPD. Its major revelation was of the existence of "the pad," a list of police officers in every precinct who were regularly accepting bribes. Some cops actively solicited money from businesses, criminals, and others for looking the other way at illegal activities being carried on under their noses or engaged in more active criminal behavior. These "meat eaters" were invariably not only the most aggressive at taking money, they ironically were often the most active and gutsy in the street—had the most citations for "collars" (arrests), awards for heroism under fire, and good recommendations from their superiors, and they regularly went after the really bad guys and put their lives in danger. On the other hand, there were also "grass eaters," passive cops who wouldn't shake people down but who contributed to the corruption by accepting shares of the pad money and by not reporting the corrupt activities of fellow officers to higher authorities. The awful thing was that the corruption was systemic, in every precinct, and affected nearly every cop. Because of internal pressures in a precinct, it was very difficult for a cop to stay *off* the pad. This situation, police corruption in general, and the attempt to get rid of it was widely reported and was the subject of the film *Serpico*.

I was shocked to learn about the pervasiveness of the pads; I could imagine a bad apple here or there but couldn't bring myself to believe every apple from every tree or precinct was infected. Since cops had become my heroes, it was difficult for me to believe how deeply and broadly this corruption reached. Like most young ADAs, I had had a period of total enthrallment with the police. It was pleasant, in a complex world, to believe that you and the people you liked—your heroes—were on the right side of things, doing good. Learning about "the pad" undercut my idealization of the police. From that moment on, while cops have remained my heroes, I have understood that, as with the rest of life, the universe of good guys versus bad guys isn't as simple as I'd once believed it to be.

The corruption extended beyond the police to judges and politicians, including some longtime political bosses. In the wake of the first big revelations, Maurice Nadjari had been appointed as the special anticorruption prosecutor and had secured a number of high-profile indictments—before he was, in effect, fired for overreaching and for unscrupulous and unfair behavior,* and John Keenan was appointed to succeed him.

When I first envisioned the cases that were awaiting trial, I thought they'd be not only interesting and tough cases but challenging. That would be a side benefit, of course, since the main benefit would be to try to rid the city of some corrupt public servants. I planned to try many of the cases myself and also to help the other prosecutors in the office do so. Keenan wanted me to retain the most difficult cases and those of the most senior officials. It sounded like an exciting challenge.

One of my auxiliary jobs at the special prosecutor's office was, as I've mentioned earlier, hiring people for the office. Under Nadjari there had been forty people in the trial bureau and at least an equal number in the investigations bureau. We had many applicants whom we knew from the DA's office, and we hired some of these, including the chief assistant, to the severe annoyance of District Attorney Morgenthau; I believe he never forgave us for "raiding" his ranks.

*In April 1977, Justice Leonard Sandler of the New York State Supreme Court dismissed the counts of one Nadjari indictment, against the Bronx Democratic chairman, because of what the judge called the "shockingly improper and prejudicial manner" in which evidence was introduced to the grand jury (*The New York Times*, April 27, 1977, IV, 20:1). Furthermore, as the *Times* reported on March 28, 1977 (p. 57), "In Mr. Nadjari's nearly four years as special prosecutor, not one major political figure, prosecutor or judge was convicted and sent to prison. The few convictions that were obtained against judges, prosecutors and politicians were reversed on appeal."

When I started to delve into the details of the high-profile cases, I found, to my dismay, that they were a mess. Reviewing the grand jury minutes, I ran into numerous examples of over-reaching by Nadjari and his staff, instances of relying on evidence that they must have known would be inadmissible in a court proceeding, of bullying witnesses, of asking overly leading questions—the whole catalogue of no-nos that every good prosecutor learns to avoid lest he or she risk having cases dismissed or reversed.* The errors were rampant.

Corruption cases are famously difficult to prosecute. It is hard to find people willing to cooperate, and you don't have a great deal of leverage with which to encourage lower-ranking defendants to incriminate the higher-ups. Police officers, especially, are reluctant to turn state's evidence against one of their own. Since it is difficult to obtain enough evidence to indict and convict a defendant for a substantive crime like bribery, which has legal requirements that are hard to prove and usually takes place in circumstances that are concealed, you end up indicting people instead for perjury or contempt. The special prosecutor's office (SPO) received little help from most of the district attorneys in the affected jurisdictions, who saw our office as infringing on their turf. Last but not least of the impediments to proper prosecution were some of "Nadjari's people," certain employees of the SPO whom he had hired and who stayed on after he left: Still loyal to him and invested in what he had done, they fought against us newcomers every inch of the way—sometimes to our faces and as often behind our backs.

One day I had the difficult task of telling my boss, John Keenan, that most of the major cases we'd inherited from Nadjari were so compromised that they would never stand up in court. Thereafter, most of the indictments of the bigwigs were

---

*One example of what had galled Justice Sandler was an instance in which a Nadjari assistant took the witness stand himself before the grand jury in order to introduce evidence—a clear and prejudicial violation of proper procedure.

settled either by pleas, by outright dismissals that we signed off on, or by motions to dismiss that were brought successfully by the defendants' attorneys. These outcomes were black eyes for the office and disappointments for me, too: There went the most interesting cases in the office and the most interesting opportunities for a trial lawyer.

I was left with a handful of police corruption cases. John Keenan was a personal friend of one accused cop's family, so he could have nothing to do with that case and asked me to handle it, which of course I did. I wasn't happy with the case, either, because the man being accused was a high-level police inspector—the highest-ranking officer in the department to be prosecuted—and the witnesses against him were corrupt cops themselves, dirtbags who were pointing their fingers in the hope of receiving lighter sentences. But the cop was charged with perjury and the evidence was there. While I was preparing the case for trial, a detective friend of mine called to invite me to lunch. I was delighted to accept, as anticorruption prosecutors were not very popular and I had not seen him for a while, although we had once worked on many homicides together. Quite unexpectedly, in the middle of the meal, he began asking me questions about my witnesses, wanting to know who was going to testify against the officer and if we had any "surprises" to spring. I was stunned at this improper attempt to gain information and upset that my "friend" would sink to trying to do this—and then annoyed that he thought he could sweet-talk me into divulging anything. Oh well: As I've said, every good cop is a good con man, and good con men just keep on conning. He got no information from me, of course; all I had to show for the lunch was a bruised ego.

We went to trial. The inspector's defense attorney was a former law partner of the then police commissioner and a very adept courtroom practitioner as well as a charmer. My witnesses were low-life cops who had been caught and had turned against a superior officer. His character witnesses gave off an aura of respectability: a well-known priest, top brass of the NYPD, and the like.

The culmination of the trial was summation day. I had prepared my remarks over and over, even rehearsed them before Fred the previous evening, but when I walked into the courtroom my heart sank. Along one side of the room, every seat was taken by high-ranking police officers, in uniform and wearing every decoration and medal they had ever earned. I had to walk down the aisle in front of this sea of blue, and the eyes on me were not friendly. On the "bride's" side of the courtroom I had very little company—two people showed up from my office. Nobody else wanted to be seen as supporting me or the case. The phalanx of uniformed officers definitely had an effect on the jury; I could see it as the defense summation unfolded. The sea of blue made me angry because I knew that the cops in those rows really knew nothing about the particulars of this case and were there only to show brotherly support for their comrade—and certainly not support for the pursuit of justice. I delivered my summation entirely while facing the jury and thus had no visual contact with the audience, which helped me forget the sea of blue and concentrate on doing my job.

I lost the case. The inspector was acquitted. But the NYPD had conducted its own administrative review of his alleged violations of trust, which culminated in a departmental trial. Based on the evidence that we had produced in our case, and other matters, the trial commissioner recommended dismissing the inspector from the force. That should have been the end of the story, but it wasn't. The police commissioner was a terrific commissioner and I respected him; but despite his close connection to the inspector's lawyer, he refused to disqualify himself from deciding whether to ratify or reject the administrative trial commissioner's recommendation. Overruling it, the police commissioner allowed the inspector to remain on the force without even a reduction in rank. I later learned that the trial commissioner, who eventually became a New York State Supreme Court judge, had vigorously protested, but to no avail.

Once the major cases in the special prosecutor's office had been dismissed, there were only lower-level cases to deal with and the job became uninteresting. I would rather have been prosecuting murderers and knowing that I was doing some good in doing so. No one appreciated the work of the special prosecutor's office—not the police, not the various district attorney's offices, not the elected officials, and certainly not the public. It was disheartening. I also felt alienated from my office, which was still infested with Nadjari holdovers. I took time to do things with my kids. There was a flurry of interest in John Keenan's possible appointment as police commissioner—he would have been a great one—and of my going along with him, but that didn't happen. When Keenan left the SPO to become head of Off-Track Betting, at his request I stayed on for a few months and then left—to go into private practice as a criminal defense attorney.

ON THE
OTHER SIDE:
FOR THE DEFENSE

It was a moment in my life when my kids were very young and I wanted to spend more time with them. To do so, I had to have some autonomy and be able to control my hours. It was primarily for these reasons that I formed my own firm. Well, I may have been a good mother and trial lawyer, but I wasn't a very good businesswoman; I hated asking clients for money, and I didn't protest enough when an acquaintance said he wouldn't refer cases to me because my husband was a doctor and therefore I didn't need the money as much as his male friends who were breadwinners. In 1979, women still had to put up with that double standard.

There were some referrals for sex discrimination cases and some for criminal cases, but most of my practice came from my signing up with the homicide and felony panels to be available for assignment to defendants too poor to hire their own attorneys. The pay schedule for this work was pretty bad, but I hoped that by doing it, I'd gain experience and earn some referrals. The money was secondary: I wanted experience and flexible hours far more than the pay.

Perhaps the most significant lesson I learned as a defense attorney is that good trial lawyers always try to win their cases, regardless of "doing the right thing." And the desire to win is paramount even when the person you are defending is a horrible human being: You go in there and fight hard and try every ethical tactic to suppress evidence, to win an acquittal or a hung jury, or to get the case placed on hold until the prosecutors tire of it. Instance in point: I had a case in which a man was accused of robbing someone at gunpoint; the cops' behavior in finding the gun was suspicious, and I succeeded in having the gun suppressed as evidence. I felt good about that—but it didn't change the real fact, that the gun had been in my client's possession. I rationalized that if the people I was defending were not innocent, nevertheless I was definitely upholding their rights as individuals and, by inference, the rights that all of us have, which must be protected. I saw, once again, that a trial is not—as I once believed—a search for truth, but a search for the truth under strict rules of evidence, rules that could result in the suppression of actual evidence of guilt.

I sometimes had to visit clients in jail and was not always treated well there, either by the corrections officers or by the other prisoners. I had to endure being "flashed" more than once during such visits. My worst experience with an incarcerated defendant occurred when I was to appear in federal court to represent a bank robber—an alleged bank robber, I suppose I should say, though since his face appeared on the bank videotape and clearly showed him committing the robbery, the use of the term *alleged* seems absurd. He was a young man whose primary concern, as he expressed it to me, appeared to be in obtaining a photo of himself from the videotape of the robbery; he seemed quite unconcerned by the overwhelming evidence against him, which included red dye on his clothes—the result of the bags of stolen money exploding and drenching him with it. The feds had the clothes as evidence, having apprehended my dodo defendant within minutes after the crime. Anyway, in

1979–1980 there were still very few women practicing criminal law, and the courts, especially the federal courts, had no provisions for protecting them from their own clients. Since I had to interview my client at length, the officers locked me in a room with him; I assumed they would stay right outside the door and could be summoned at a moment's notice. This reasonable assumption turned out to be totally wrong. When my client tried to feel me up in the middle of the interview, it took at least ten minutes for help to arrive. I never again put myself in that situation.

Some cases I wouldn't handle, but I tried to be well prepared for those I did and to do a reasonable job in the courtroom. It was odd being in a courtroom on the defense side; the court officers didn't treat me as well as they had when I'd been a prosecutor. I knew their changed attitude wasn't personal.

One of my most memorable cases involved the vicious murder of a woman by a real low-life. This man had gotten in touch with a respectable woman he had once known and somehow renewed their acquaintance, getting her to accompany him to his rooming house. After several weeks of an apparently normal relationship, she disappeared, and her chopped-up body was soon found in a barrel in front of his building. Assigned this case, I counseled my client to jump at the five to fifteen years offered by the DA. He refused.

I explained to the defendant that he was being accused of a particularly vicious crime and that chopping up a woman and stuffing her body parts in a barrel was not likely to earn a jury's sympathy. He pointed to his rap sheet, which said that he had not been convicted of a crime in years, and insisted that this meant he deserved a break. I was leery of this rap sheet; there was a gap in it of some years, and he had been in too much trouble prior to that gap. I told him of my misgivings and also said, "You have to trust me. I'm your lawyer, and you've been around enough to know that I can't tell anyone what you tell me, but you have to tell me truthfully what happened during those years or I can't do my job."

He wouldn't talk and claimed he'd been working throughout the blank years on the rap sheet. This was a frightening and clearly violent man, and after a certain point I gave up my inquiry. It wasn't rational for him to think he deserved a break for this heinous crime, but he wanted to go to trial. The morning of the trial, the ADA—a wonderful woman with whom I later became close friends—waived the defendant's updated rap sheet in front of my face. "In that blank period your defendant committed another murder, Leslie, and he was only out because it was reduced to manslaughter on a technicality. Now there are no offers and I'll be asking for the max."

I wasn't surprised, but I affected dismay to the ADA; and to my client I said, "I told you so." He wasn't surprised, either, and didn't seem to care. On to trial we went. Since the prosecution now considered my client to be a recidivist murderer, they became even more determined to put him away for a long time. They had been able to have the case assigned to a really tough judge known as "Maximum Scott," which, obviously, was not a good omen for the defendant's future. Further difficulties for us centered around the defendant's pants and shirt, which had been found after a search warrant had been executed. Forensic techniques revealed that there were hidden bloodstains on the clothes and on the walls of his room—lots of blood that had been invisible to the naked eye. Some of this blood turned out to match the victim's, whose blood type—unfortunately for my client but fortunately for society—was extraordinarily rare.

I knew very little about blood, but I studied the subject, obtained permission from the judge to hire my own serologist, and used the knowledge gained to conduct a decent cross-examination of the prosecution's expert. When it came time for my summation, I couldn't find very much to hang my hat on—but then, many good defenses begin and end by getting across the notion that in our system of justice the prosecution has to prove its case beyond a reasonable doubt and to avow that in this instance it hadn't done so. I had nothing real to say on behalf of my client, but for three hours I hammered on that point; I told the jury a story along the lines of, "Maybe this happened, maybe that happened, we'll never know exactly what happened, and you can't be sure that the crime went down the way the prosecution alleges that it did." The ludicrous nature of some of these arguments embarrassed me!

The jury was out deliberating for three days. That's usually a sign of a problem, but in this instance they eventually came back with a unanimous verdict: guilty. I felt good that I had kept them out that long. Maximum Scott gave my client the max, twenty-five to life—and I was not unhappy. I was satisfied that I'd done my best in the courtroom, given it my all, but I was also immensely relieved that the defendant had been convicted, because the evidence of his guilt had been overwhelming and it would have been a travesty of justice if he had been freed to walk the streets—and kill—again.

Another accused murderer appeared on the surface to have nothing in common with the man who had chopped up a woman and stuffed the body parts in a barrel. He was young, with cow-silk blond hair, and looked like a hick off the farm, with all the polite and deferential manners that one might expect of a farmboy from the South. But he and his twin brother were accused of thumbing a ride with a young man and woman and then killing the man after beating, raping, and sodomizing the woman and leaving her for dead. She had survived, and now the twins were in New York, facing extradition to a southern state that had a death penalty and was not averse to executing murderers. I was assigned to represent one brother who wanted to fight extradition, while another lawyer represented the other. In my questioning of my client, he would repeatedly say things like "We are so grateful to have you representing us" and would invariably address me as "ma'am." It was difficult to believe that such polite young men had committed this terrible crime, yet the evidence was there.

At the extradition hearing, I was faced with the unpleasant task of interrogating the woman who had survived the attack and who had been severely injured. Though conflicted and ambivalent about doing this, I believe that I nonetheless did a creditable job—for instance, going beyond the obvious to question her about a hunch I'd had: "You were doing drugs, weren't you?" The young woman admitted that aspect of the situation: She and her boyfriend and the twins had exchanged various drugs, and everyone had been quite high at the moment of the crime. This information cast a shred of doubt as to the full culpability of the twins. I must have appeared upset at my own efforts to impeach a rape victim, as the judge in the case spoke to me later and commiserated with me about the difficult defense duty of having to closely question the victim of such a vicious crime. The twins were ultimately extradited anyway.

It bothered me as a defense attorney not to like so many of my clients, so it was a relief when I was asked to represent a group of four clients who were very likable. They were four young black corrections officers accused of an assault on an inmate. They explained to me that because they shared a background with many of the inmates, they frequently felt sorry for the prisoners, but that sometimes, no matter how much sympathy they had, it was still necessary to use force to keep prisoners in line.

The proceedings were scheduled for a Bronx jury trial, and by the time the prosecutor and I had conferenced the case ad nauseam, and the corrections officers union had lobbied for its members, in the middle of jury selection the DA finally allowed the four men to plead guilty to a violation. This meant that the incident would not show up on their records as a conviction for a crime, so they would be able to keep their jobs.

After three years as a defense attorney I came to feel that, while I very much believed in our system of justice and in the adversarial nature of our courts—which are based on the principle that every defendant is entitled to a defense and to competent legal representation—every defendant was not entitled to have *me* to defend him! I began to turn down more and more cases and to listen more carefully to the people who were calling me and asking if I was ready to come back to a full-time job and to public service. After turning down a hefty fee by refusing to represent an alleged child pornographer, I knew it was time to move on. If I didn't want to represent alleged pornographers, rapists, drug dealers, or mobsters—what was left?

When an offer came along to work in the public sector with John Keenan, my mentor, I gratefully—and very quickly—closed my practice. I became deputy criminal justice coordinator for the city of New York and coordinator of the Arson Strike Force, positions involving policy and planning and drafting legislation, among other things. I'd had my time prosecuting corrupt cops and politicians, had my time on the defense side, where I'd learned to appreciate the very difficult job of being a good criminal defense lawyer, and I'd learned also that my heart wasn't in that job. Having looked at life "from both sides now," I thought that becoming a judge might be the next logical step.

ASSUMING
THE BENCH

When I joined the DA's office, I had wanted eventually to be a judge. That ambition faded when as a prosecutor I had to appear in front of more than a few political hacks, incompetents, and just plain lazy judges. Also, colleagues in the DA's office told me that if I wanted to be a judge, I'd have to join a political club and curry favor with the judge makers. I had zero interest in doing that.

There are two methods of becoming a judge: winning election to the bench or being appointed by the mayor or governor. For generations, appointed judges connoted men (and a few women) who were the cronies of politicians or whose appointments were political payoffs; one example was the bevy of "midnight appointments" made by one mayor in the 1970s during his last night in office—many of those he chose were long-time political hacks, or "pols." But once he had appointed them, nobody could get rid of them until their terms ended. Perhaps it was in reaction to those midnight appointments that Mayor Ed Koch began a program of selecting judges for appointment solely on the basis of merit. This was an incredibly unusual thing for a mayor to do—to deliberately create an independent, meritorious judiciary—and it is greatly to Koch's credit that he not only began the system, but also insisted on keeping it clean.

Koch's creation of an independent judiciary was a bold move. His judicial appointments partially balanced out the elected (and sometimes incompetent) judges and reinvigorated the judiciary at a time when competent judges were needed to deal with rising crime rates. Koch also chose younger people as judges, men and women in their late thirties and forties. Most elected judges had won office strictly because a powerful political leader permitted them to, often when they were in their fifties or older. Under Koch's system, lawyers could apply for or be recommended for judgeships; applicants had to complete extensive questionnaires and were then evaluated by the city bar and the Mayor's Committee on the Judiciary.

I felt that I was well qualified to be a judge, having served for many years as a prosecutor, as a bureau chief in the DA's office, as an anticorruption prosecutor for the state, as a criminal defense attorney, and as a criminal justice coordinator. And after several years as a private defense attorney, I had realized that I really wanted to return to public service—that nothing else in the work world gave me equivalent satisfaction. But I had no political connections and no power base, so running for an elected judgeship was out of the question.

It costs money to run a campaign for an elective office. Who, other than friends and family, is most likely to contribute to the election campaign of a would-be judge? The lawyers who practice before their courts, of course. So, often, elected judges end up indebted to the lawyers who appear before them who donate or collect money for their campaigns. In states like Texas, where judges have to run for reelection every four years, there is an additional problem: a screening committee so ideologically fixed in orientation that it will not permit anyone who does not agree with its ideology to make it as far as the ballot. In Ohio, a contest for a seat on that state's highest court in the year 2000 cost between $5 million and $12 million—where twenty years earlier the cost had been under $100,000. Similar stories have been reported in other midwestern and southern states. Also prevalent in new judicial campaigns have been attempts to test the limits of ethics rules that forbid judicial candidates from signaling how they will vote on future cases by making thinly veiled promises to sustain or overturn controversial decisions.* (The United States Supreme Court reviewed the constitutionality of these limits, in *Republican Party of Minnesota* v. *Kelly*, argued March 2002.)

In New York, the Office of Court Administration (OCA) has called upon bar associations to form judicial election campaign committees to monitor candidates' compliance with various professional, ethical, and judicial codes of conduct. Nationally, the American Bar Association is about to begin a major effort to improve judicial selection in all states, emphasizing ethical campaign practices while continuing to advocate merit selection of judges.†

Anyone in favor of merit selection obviously decries the increasing current practices of candidates for judgeships attacking their opponents, indicating in advance what their rulings would be, and refusing to disclose sources of campaign contributions. Catering to people's fears, spending massive amounts of money, and seeking (and paying for) enormous amounts of publicity are unprofessional, unseemly, and possibly unethical. Such tactics limit the number of good, experienced, and talented people who will make themselves available to become elected judges. If we truly want a criminal justice system that is above reproach, we have to find ways to reform the laws on campaign finance, insofar as electing judges is concerned, to enforce the ethical

*Glaberson, William, "Fierce Campaigns Signal New Era for State Courts," *The New York Times*, June 5, 2000.
†*New York Law Journal*, October 16, 2001.

rules on such campaigns and to eliminate ideologically based screening committees.

At the urging of my husband, around 1981 I began the application process for a mayoral appointment to the New York City Criminal Court bench. I put in the required documents, I appeared before the committees—and I waited. Everything went smoothly, if slowly. Nothing happened for long stretches of time. I knew that John Keenan, whom Koch respected, had put in more than a good word for me, but someone was opposing my appointment.

"The knock on you," Koch said when we finally met for the last interview in the process, "is that you're too aggressive and too independent." I wanted to answer back, "How can you of all people accuse me of that, since the main knock on *you* is that you're too aggressive and too independent?" But of course you don't say that to the mayor. So I told him I was assertive rather than aggressive, and that that was a good thing. He peppered me with all sorts of questions, and afterward I felt the interview had gone badly and that I would not get the appointment.

But back at work the phone rang, and it was the head of the Mayor's Committee on the Judiciary, offering me the judgeship.

I did not formally "assume" the bench until March 1983. And the delay of several years between application and appointment turned out to be for the best, because during those years I spent more time with our children. The interval also enabled them to grow up a bit so that when I did take the bench they were able to stay longer each day in school, which meant that not too many hours would elapse between the moment school let out and when I returned home.

Every state's court system is structured differently, and even the names of the courts change. In New York, the highest court is the New York State Court of Appeals. I sit on the New York State Supreme Court, which is New York's highest *trial* court. Lower courts in New York consist of the civil court, to which one must be elected via political club support, and the criminal and family courts, to which one must be appointed by the mayor; there are many miscellaneous other courts. Criminal and civil court judges can be promoted administratively by the Office of Court Administration and designated to be "acting" supreme court judges;* family court judges are also "acting" supremes. Or one can be appointed by the governor, in New York, to one of several other judgeships (as I was several years ago).

There are four intermediate appellate courts ("appellate divisions"), each serving a particular geographical area. Then there is the highest appellate court, the Court of Appeals, led by a smart, dynamic woman, Judge Judith Kaye. All appellate judges are appointed, but those serving on the intermediate appellate courts must first be *elected* supreme court judges. However, any lawyer or judge who qualifies can become a judge of the highest court, the Court of Appeals. This really makes sense—*not*.

The official charts of New York's court system on the following pages make it easier to visualize our complex structure.†

If New York State's court system seems complicated and confusing, it is. However, for the past several years Chief Judge Kaye has been attempting to reform our system by proposing

*The New York State Constitution designates a finite number of elected judgeships for each county. However, owing to the high volume of criminal cases in New York City, the courts have had to designate numerous acting supreme court justices.
†Charts courtesy of Office of Court Administration; reprinted from *State of New York, Report of the Chief Administrative Judge of the New York State Court System* for the calendar year 1/1/96–12/31/96.

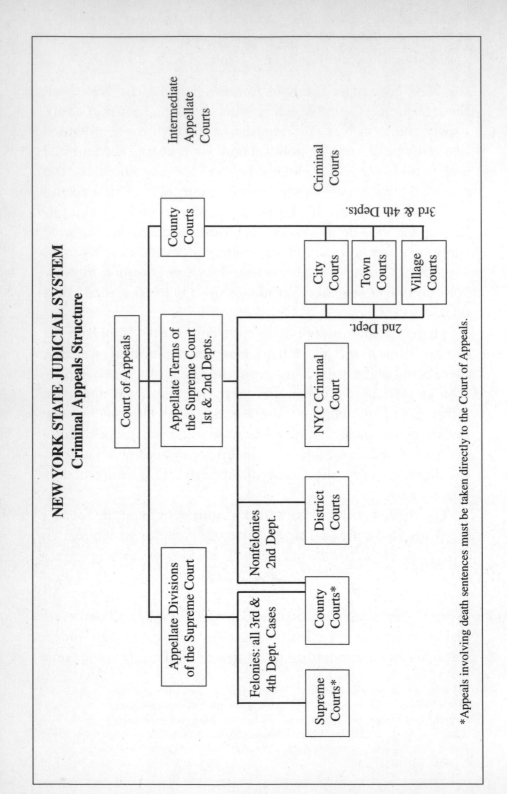

NEW YORK STATE JUDICIAL SYSTEM
Criminal Appeals Structure

Intermediate Appellate Courts

Court of Appeals

Appellate Divisions of the Supreme Court

Appellate Terms of the Supreme Court 1st & 2nd Depts.

County Courts

Felonies: all 3rd & 4th Dept. Cases

Nonfelonies 2nd Dept.

Supreme Courts*

County Courts*

District Courts

NYC Criminal Court

City Courts

Town Courts

Village Courts

Criminal Courts

3rd & 4th Depts.

2nd Dept.

*Appeals involving death sentences must be taken directly to the Court of Appeals.

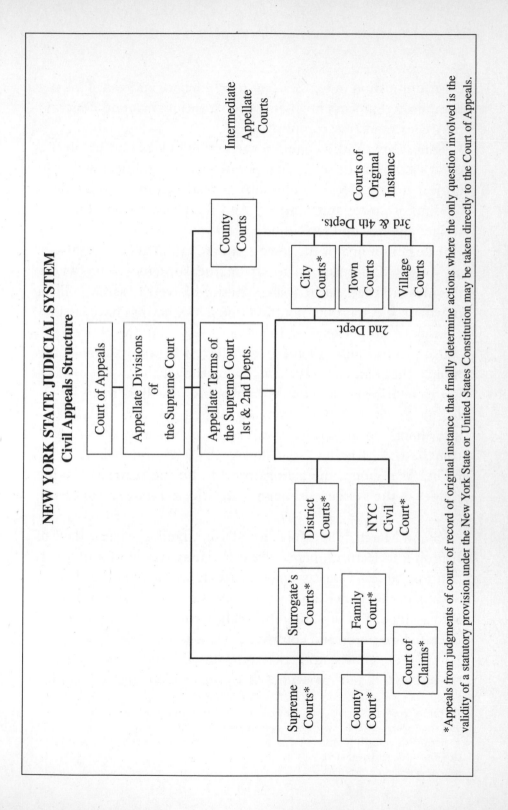

NEW YORK STATE JUDICIAL SYSTEM
Civil Appeals Structure

Court of Appeals

Appellate Divisions of the Supreme Court

Intermediate Appellate Courts

Appellate Terms of the Supreme Court 1st & 2nd Depts.

County Courts

Courts of Original Instance

3rd & 4th Depts.

City Courts*

Town Courts

Village Courts

2nd Dept.

District Courts*

NYC Civil Court*

Surrogate's Courts*

Family Court*

Court of Claims*

Supreme Courts*

County Court*

*Appeals from judgments of courts of record of original instance that finally determine actions where the only question involved is the validity of a statutory provision under the New York State or United States Constitution may be taken directly to the Court of Appeals.

court unification in her State of the Judiciary address. This is a complicated process involving a constitutional amendment and may take years to accomplish.

While New York's system for selecting judges now involves a great deal of merit screening, politicians and political clubs are critical to any elected judgeship and still exert a tremendous amount of power and control.* And the process of becoming a judge depends upon what judgeship you pursue.

I began on one of the lowest courts, criminal court, but—as all judges do—I aspired to sit on the supreme court, where felonies are tried, as an acting.† Actings have the same judicial powers as electeds, but not the same perks; actings have smaller chambers, no personal secretary, and less clout. Moreover, because elected judges have been elected to their seats on the bench, they can do pretty much what they want to—like refusing to take cases they don't want or are unwilling to try or refusing to review applications for search warrants or wiretaps after hours. As an acting, however, if you don't work hard, you run the risk of being "sent down," back to criminal court, by OCA. As a group, the actings tend to be the hardest-working judges in the system, although many elected judges work hard, too.

So, in March 1983, after virtually no training—a few days of listening to lectures, many about the importance of arriving in court on time—I was assigned to AP-1, an "all-purpose Part." I assumed the bench and was—supposedly—magically turned into a judge. You don the robe, walk into a courtroom, sit on an elevated platform, and confront a sea of faces: defendants, their lawyers, the prosecutors, the court officers and clerks, families of defendants and sometimes of victims, onlookers—all looking

*While there have always been allegations of corruption involving political bosses and their clubs, 2002 has seen new ones involving Brooklyn judges.
†"Acting" is actually a misnomer, as one can be an acting supreme court justice indefinitely, once designated.

to you for decisions. You suddenly realize that you are responsible for all their cases—and that there are a great many, at least a hundred cases a day, often more than 150 a day, each requiring at least one decision, which means you have to be very decisive. Some judges are indecisive, others are not quick at deciding—for both these types, the work in criminal court can be disastrous. Every minute or two or three, a new defendant is brought into the courtroom by court officers from the adjacent holding pens, while the defendants whose cases have already been heard are returned there. Still other defendants come from the audience, since many in criminal court are out on bail.

For the criminal court judge, as well as for the lawyers, the process has less to do with the individual defendants than with the paper packages that detail each case. "Blue backs," blue-backed folders an inch or two thick, hold individual misdemeanor cases. You have only a few moments to look over "the papers" as the case is being called, which means you must be a quick study. Most matters in the court to which I was assigned were misdemeanors, but since it was an all-purpose Part there was a bit of everything—motions, bail applications, pleas to be taken.

My very first day in AP-1 was quite an eye-opener. A young but experienced court officer named Eddie was the "bridge man," the officer responsible for the Part getting through its daily calendar, calling each case into the record (the position is now called "bridge officer"). After I'd done a few cases, Eddie advised me, "Judge, we'll be here till midnight if you don't move faster." I tried to move quickly, spending just a few moments on each case. Shoplifting. Possession of pot. Criminal mischief—stealing hubcaps. Turnstile jumping. Appearing before me on each case was an assistant DA and an attorney, usually from Legal Aid. Together with Eddie, they taught me what the markings on the folders meant. Eddie's running monologue provided me with tips on the individual lawyers who were appearing in front of me—which of the Legal Aid people, for instance, thought the courtroom was a soapbox and were inclined to climb on it during a bail application or to attack the police on every occasion. Eddie had a strong opinion about everything.

"C'mon, Judge, we're gonna be here all night! Faster, Judge, you gotta be faster!" Faster became possible after about three or four hours, when I got the hang of it. You had a minute or two to absorb the essentials of each matter and then to make a decision. These weren't trials—there wasn't time for trials in an AP Part. It was just decisions, one after another. And each decision was made or plea taken in a very short time. Discouraged and exhausted, I looked at Eddie at 3:30 in the afternoon and asked, "How many more, do you think?"

"You're done, Judge."

"What? You SOB! I should whap you—you told me we'd be here till midnight!"

In a single grueling day I'd learned the basics of how to handle this kind of courtroom. And he was right about moving fast; judges often stayed much later into the evening to get through as many cases as we did by midafternoon and without accomplishing any more. I became extremely fond of Eddie, who was intelligent, fun, and a very good teacher.

A lot of what I did in criminal court was refereeing deals. The prosecution would offer a defendant a reduced charge in exchange for a guilty plea, and the defense would try to bargain down the penalty. The ADAs had room to maneuver but had to follow certain office policies. I had more latitude, though it was circumscribed by statutes and practice. The DA might want six months, the Legal Aid lawyer two; they'd stick to these positions partly because each had turf to defend and didn't want to appear too eager to back down; so they were happy to have me be the one who split the difference and gave the defendant four months. However, not every case called for a compromise. What could I do with a Legal Aid lawyer who asked for leniency for the defendant because—I swear she said this—"my client only has thirteen prior convictions and one outstanding bench warrant"? Not surprisingly, that sort of absurd reasoning provoked a sarcastic response from the bench. And there was no deal or compromise for that defendant.

Once, a prosecutor and a private defense attorney agreed on a plea and sentence for a defendant in a case, but I rather sharply disagreed with their solution. The defendant, a male teacher in a private boys school, was charged with endangering the welfare of a minor; along 42nd Street he had picked up boys between the ages of nine and fourteen and paid them for sex. Though the teacher had not physically forced the boys to do anything, in the eyes of the law—appropriately—the boys were too young to be able to consent to sex. The defense attorney didn't want his client to lose his teaching license and had convinced the ADA to go along with a plea that would allow him to keep it. They even had a letter from the school saying it would permit him to return to work if he wished to. What was the school thinking? Were they so desperate for teachers that they wanted a pedophile to continue in a position of trust with their children? I was astonished at their complacency. I refused to agree to their bargain and fashioned a tougher one: The teacher would plead guilty to a misdemeanor, and I would give him probation—but he would lose his teaching license.

After that case, I went home and gave my kids an extra hug.

In my time in criminal court, I presided over only half a dozen misdemeanor trials. If you were good at handling and "moving" your calendar, you were rewarded by being stuck in a calendar Part, which was much harder work than presiding over criminal court trials. One trial I particularly remember because of my interchange with an old-time detective in front of the jury. I was still a relatively young female; the detective was testifying and said something I did not hear clearly.

"Detective, I'm sorry—I didn't hear what you just said. Could you please repeat it?"

The detective looked at me for a long moment, clearly annoyed at my interruption, and finally replied, "Yes, *dear*."

The all-female jury looked as though they wanted to strangle him, so I refrained from saying anything in response. Later, in the hall outside the courtroom, however, I approached him. "Detective, you don't have to call me 'Your Worship' or even 'Your Honor,' but it might be a good idea to call a judge 'Judge' in the courtroom."

He looked at me as if he were seriously considering my remark and then said, "Anything you say—*honey*." I gave up.

Aside from the occasional trial, I was assigned to AP-1 most of my time "downstairs" in criminal court.

Because of the overload in our jails and often too lenient plea-bargaining practices, I saw that it was possible for an individual to be arrested and even convicted many times before any jail sentence was imposed. First time on a minor charge would be an ACD—("adjournment in contemplation of dismissal"). Next time it would be a violation, which was not a crime. Then maybe there'd be a second violation, followed by a class B misdemeanor, with no jail penalty. A bit later there'd be a class A misdemeanor with a CD ("conditional discharge"). Next time the charge would be a felony, but the defendant might well be adjudicated a YO ("youthful offender," if between the ages of sixteen and nineteen), which would mean he would have no criminal record, and he'd be placed on probation. The time after that it would be a real felony and he'd get probation, since it was his first felony. Then, finally, a felony conviction *with* jail time, although it might be minimal time. *Whew!*

I had to dispose of many cases by plea even when chagrined because that plea wasn't going to solve the underlying problem. An example: A woman shoplifts to support her drug habit. We might try to find an appropriate drug treatment program for her, but 1) she had to want it; and 2) it must be a program that would accept her. More often than not, one or the other prerequisite was lacking. If her record was bad enough, we had to take her out of circulation for a while by putting her in prison and hope that during her incarceration she'd get some treatment for the drug problem. The operative word was *hope*, and, even then it didn't seem very likely.

What happened in my AP-1 courtroom wasn't pretty, but in a crude way, justice was done. Being a judge in criminal court meant getting through the day's calendar (a printout listing each case to be called that day) and disposing of as many cases as possible—more or less administrative work. Being fair to both sides (which I thought I was doing) was not the main criterion by which a judge's competence was evaluated. Your ability to "handle your calendar"—dispose of cases—was. I did it well enough so that after two and a half years on the criminal court I was reappointed, this time for ten years. Shortly thereafter, I was selected by OCA to become an acting judge on the state's supreme court.

Now I could *really* be a judge.

In 1986, since I was junior to many judges already on the supreme court bench, I was assigned to one of six drug Parts. All six of us assigned were the most junior judges on the New York County Supreme Court. The drug cases were serious cases, but ones that the older, more senior judges didn't like handling, perhaps because the same sorts of defendants, evidence, and circumstances seemed to appear over and over again. Drug cases were not considered prestigious. But I was thrilled to be on the supreme court bench and happy to take the drug cases. At least these were felonies, and in doing them, I would actually get the chance to preside over trials.

I hardly knew anything about the drug world. As an assistant DA, I had tried only one minor drug case. When I became a supreme court judge, the crack epidemic was just beginning, and most cases that I handled were relatively simple buy-and-busts or observation sales. An undercover police officer would walk into a known drug location, buy crack with marked bills, and leave; soon after, cops or detectives would arrest the sellers and recover the marked bills that, along with the crack bought by the undercover, would become the prosecution's evidence. Some interesting legal issues, often about search and seizure, arose because of variations in scenarios. Was the defendant merely a steerer or lookout? What sort of observation post (OP), if any, had the police used? Could the person in the OP really see what he or she claimed to have seen? Did a "ghost" trail the undercover? If so, what did he or she claim to have seen? What should or should not be admissible as evidence?

The cases were also interesting because they allowed me to experiment in mastering the dynamics of a courtroom. The lawyers who faced me were better than those in criminal court; there were juries to contend with and the niceties of trial procedure. How should I keep attorneys in line when they sought to control what went on in the courtroom, without violating their ability to defend their clients? Learning how to preside over a trial properly and fairly was, I discovered, a process of feeling your way along. Obviously, nobody came around to tell us how best to do it. The most important thing was to stay constantly alert—or risk losing control of the proceedings. You had to think about what each side was or wasn't doing and whether some move that they planned might be disastrous, either for the trial record or for the fairness of the trial.

As a judge, I learned you were challenged in court *every day* by lawyers. During one typical morning, I had to contend with nonsense from two seasoned lawyers, both of whom I liked personally. Here, adapted from the court record, are some of the interchanges. First, the ADA had delayed giving an important investigative report to the defense.

> *Judge Snyder:* (to the ADA) You don't seem to understand the fact that by not turning this report over in a timely fashion, defense counsel structured his cross-examination of the last witness so that, in essence, he would end up being sandbagged by your redirect, if I let you ask the questions you now want to ask. Don't you understand that a lawyer as experienced as the defense counsel would never fashion a cross-examination that would make him susceptible to that kind of redirect? He didn't know about the police report. You did not turn it over when you should have!

The ADA fought me on that for three or four minutes. "You can't ask the questions, period, no argument," I repeated. She brought up the issue anyway, three times more before the morning was done, begging me to change my mind, as she wanted to bring out something in redirect that she felt was extremely important to her case. Since I knew her to be literate—and to have a sense of humor—I retorted:

> *Judge Snyder:* Listen, Ms. ——, I'll consider changing my mind when Zeus descends from Mt. Olympus or when Athena is hatched, once again, whole from his headache. Don't expect a deus ex machina ending—this isn't Sophocles or Euripides!

She couldn't stop laughing, but no one else had any idea what we were talking about.

A few minutes later, defense counsel attempted to introduce into the trial other material that I'd ruled inadmissible—a "fight" that had taken place—during routine questioning of a witness:

> *Defense Counsel:* How far away is the parking lot from where this fight took place?
>
> *ADA:* Objection.
>
> *Judge Snyder:* About how far away were you from this woman?
>
> *Witness:* About maybe the same distance where he is standing now.
>
> *Defense Counsel:* And were you on the same side of the street as the fight, or was the fight on a different side of the street?
>
> *ADA:* Objection.
>
> *Judge Snyder:* Sustained. Don't shake your head, Counselor. You are going to have to abide by my rulings whether you like them or not. What's the next question?
>
> *Defense Counsel:* Where does the woman live, if you know?
>
> *ADA:* Objection.
>
> *Judge Snyder:* Sustained.
>
> *Defense Counsel:* He testified on direct that she lived at a certain address, didn't he?
>
> *ADA:* No, he didn't.
>
> *Defense Counsel:* I thought he did.
>
> *Judge Snyder:* It's totally irrelevant. You know what the issues are, so get to the point.

Both sides argued frequently and wasted a lot of time, prompting me eventually to this, at sidebar:

> *Judge Snyder:* That's enough! The reason I seem to be in a very bad mood, and I am, is that I don't understand what either side is doing here. We have taken ninety

minutes to question a doctor, and it should have taken fifteen minutes, frankly. You're asking pointless questions, Counselor—how can you ask if the injury was life-threatening when the victim was stabbed eight times in the chest and received ninety-two stitches? How much do I have to say? The man was only in the hospital a few days, but they initially thought he was going to die. . . . You heard the EMS worker; your questions seemed pointless—pointless, I'm sorry, that was my impression. Just try to get to the point—please!

A few minutes later, in front of the jury, the defense lawyer seemed to be stalling and I had to add, "You can question him as much as you need to without being totally repetitious, Counselor. Incidentally, we are not leaving until we finish with this witness—I don't care if it's midnight!"

In another case, a pregnant female defendant stood before me with her lawyer. She had repeatedly refused to plead guilty, although the sentence offer was probation and her attorney was clearly frustrated with her.

"Your Honor, I've advised my client to plead guilty to this most reasonable offer and discussed it with her on many occasions. She is still refusing the offer."

"Well, Counselor," I responded, "that's unfortunate since it is a good offer given the seriousness of the charges, but it *is* her decision. . . ."

"Well, Your Honor," he replied, "I just don't understand it. It must be the raging female hormones. . . ."

There was dead silence in the courtroom as the female court reporter, some female court officers, and I all looked at each other.

Finally, I said to the attorney, "I can't believe you just said that, and in front of a female judge. . . . Maybe I should send you for a 730 exam [to assess mental competency] and certainly for sensitivity training."

In drug cases there were also frequent challenges, of sorts, from occasional visitors to the courtroom like the defendants' girl-friends, mothers, or grandmothers. They would always talk and make faces, objecting to things that I or the DA said or did and trying to signal "their" defendant or cast intimidating glances at the witnesses against them. When most of the court officers didn't bother doing anything about these visitors' tactics, I'd have to get into it. "If you two can't be quiet back there—de-fendant's friends, I'm talking to you—we will kick you out and you will not return." If that didn't work I'd have to turn to the court officers and say, "If they are going to talk, they are just going to cause problems in my courtroom and are making it very stressful for everyone involved. Put them in different rows, please; put one in the back—I don't know why I have to baby-sit!"

One of my earliest drug cases in supreme court was sent to me by another judge, who telephoned to say that he had offered the defendant, a Mob guy, a good plea, but he had refused to take it. This judge was known as a "plea pusher," someone who ate, drank, and slept pleas, who talked about how many pleas he could get in a day, and boasted constantly about his record in that regard—something I have never been able to relate to at all. He told me he was confident of a plea if the defendant and his lawyer saw that they would indeed be taken to trial—and my courtroom was a trial Part, while his was an "up front" cal-endar Part, where cases were called primarily to see if they could be disposed of early on. This was a class A felony, which meant that a certain amount of drugs was involved. (Class A felonies include murder and possession and sale of larger amounts of narcotics; class B felonies include manslaughter, assault, rape, and possession or sale of smaller amounts of narcotics.)

The change of judge made no difference to the defendant and his lawyer: They wanted a trial, which was fine with me, since I wanted to try cases, and every defendant is entitled to a trial. It became clear, as the trial progressed, that the first judge had not known all the slimy details of the case. The defendant was alleged to have run a cocaine sales operation using his family as cover; the wife, acting as secretary and liaison, was said to have taken phone messages regarding the operation from their home, and the evidence revealed that the defendant used his children as fronts, picking up and delivering drugs when they were with him, as though the family were completing household or school errands. He particularly liked conducting drug business with his nine-month-old baby in tow. (Details like that stick in your mind when you've got kids.)

Short, with slicked-down hair and an expensive suit, this defendant had watched too many "Godfather" movies. His lawyer, equally as well dressed, was known to charge very high fees and appeared to work exclusively for Mob defendants. He, too, was very full of himself, and both he and his client acted as though the courtroom proceedings were beneath them.

An early shock came during the jury selection process. I asked potential jurors, "Do any of you have members of your family, or friends, or colleagues who either have now or have had a drug problem, or have been in rehab, or otherwise have had some close connection to drugs?" At least 50 percent of them answered in the affirmative—50 percent!—and after further exploring the issue with them individually, I had to dismiss them all as potential jurors. This percentage, I later learned, was no aberration, since it would be about the same for pools of potential jurors in nearly every drug-related case that came up for trial in my courtroom.

As the trial of the alleged cocaine seller proceeded, everything seemed to go wrong for the prosecution. The ADA was young and too inexperienced, it appeared, to handle a flamboyant lawyer and a complicated case. He bungled some of the witness presentations. But the major problem was with one detective, one of the key witnesses, who suddenly refused to testify, citing the fact that he and the defendant both had children in the same school.

Livid, I ordered the district attorney to do something about it; I had never heard of a cop "refusing" to testify when he was a potentially important witness. But nothing was ever done, the detective did not testify, and to this day I don't know precisely what happened. All I can say is that in my opinion the evidence clearly showed—circumstantially—that at one point the defendant had been tipped off about a forthcoming search of his house, giving him time to dispose of the drugs that were the object of the search warrant. Only someone inside the police department could have provided such a tip-off. Obviously, this group of cops and this particular defendant were a little too cozy. Also, early on in the trial, I noticed that sitting in the audience every day was a man I recognized as a clerk in the court system; I learned that he was related by marriage to the defendant. His presence seemed inappropriate at best, since he presumably should have been working. When defense counsel gave his summation—with great passion—excoriating the prosecution's lack of evidence and attesting to his client's sterling character as a family man, I had the sinking feeling that the jury was going to acquit.

But the young prosecutor redeemed any earlier missteps by giving a brilliant summation, showing up the defendant for precisely what the evidence had shown him to be: a man conducting a drug operation while hiding behind his children and shamelessly using them for his criminal enterprise. As the prosecutor kept hammering away, I could see the jury physically being won over to his side—heads were nodding, mouths were setting in grim determination. So, very much to the surprise of the defendant and his mouthpiece, the jury voted to convict.

I decided that because of the facts of the case, which I would never have known had I not heard the evidence at trial, and to send this defendant a message of my own, I would have to impose a stiff penalty. The day came for sentencing. Before I took the bench, I retreated to the semiprivate bathroom. The idea that I, a human being, was going to sentence another human being to spend the next twenty-five years of his life behind bars staggered me. That was a lot of power to wield, and I wanted to be certain in my own mind that I should do it, and also that I really had to. I could see no reasonable alternative. Sobered, I returned to the courtroom and sentenced the mobster to the maximum penalty allowed by the statute, twenty-five years to life. Neither he nor his high-priced lawyer was pleased.

This case began my reputation as a tough judge who handed out stiff sentences.

A year or so later, at a retirement dinner, I encountered the sergeant in charge of the group of cops in this case, including the detective who had declined to testify. As I've said, cops are my heroes. Most of them perform dangerous jobs, put in a great deal of extra effort—and never get thanked for it—and a great many risk their lives every day. So when one cop does something wrong and brings dishonor to the vast majority who so diligently hew to the straight and narrow, I get upset. "Don't think I don't know that one of you tipped off the Mob guy about the raid on his house," I told the sergeant. It was pointless to say this, but I just couldn't help myself. He denied it, of course, but we both knew the truth.

In another Mob case, the defendant and his attorney were

determined to appeal the conviction more quickly than the system allowed. Not long after the trial, my law clerk Alex Calabrese and I were sitting in the courtroom when the court reporter who had recorded most of the trial came running in, crying and out of breath. "Judge," she said, "the attorney called me for the trial minutes for his appeal. When I explained that it would be months and months before I can type them up from my steno notes, because I've got many other cases before his, he told me I'd better get these done first, because 'I wouldn't want to see your name on a tombstone.'" She sobbed, and Alex and I were aghast. It was hard to believe that even a Mob mouthpiece would stoop this low. But in my view the reporter was clearly telling the truth and was frightened out of her mind. While trying to calm down, she added that one of the "bosses," a friend of this attorney's, "called me and ordered me to do this transcript next or—and I'm quoting him, Judge—he'd 'jerk my schedule around and screw me.'"

That, too, rang true. Her bosses have a good deal of power in the Office of Court Administration bureaucracy. In fact, the particular boss she named was known for ordering people around all the time, fancying himself a chief judge rather than a boss. He had once come into my courtroom to try it with me. My response was not printable, and our relationship deteriorated further after that encounter.

The court reporter's account of the pressure brought to bear on her was taken seriously enough by the DA's office to lead to an investigation of the boss. But he was an operator, a slick dude who could BS his way through most things; it hardly surprised me when the investigation did not get very far. The ADA in charge was incensed but helpless. No action was taken against the lawyer, and ultimately no action was taken against the boss.

In the special prosecutor's office I had already come to recognize the unfortunate principle that it was highly unlikely that anyone who worked within the criminal justice system would be prosecuted successfully. Now I knew that the protect-your-own-at-the-expense-of-the-system syndrome encompassed bosses in the court system in addition to cops, politicians, and judges. The reasons? Too much inertia, too many friendships, too much nonvenal corruption. I saw these factors operating recently in another instance, with a court officer who bilked dozens of fellow workers out of their retirement savings. I was surprised that none of his colleagues did this man bodily harm, since he had destroyed what they had worked for over the years. He was allowed to plead guilty to a lesser offense and was given minor jail time—basically a slap on the wrist. He had conned so many people in the system; I wondered if he'd sweet-talked the judge on his case or if it was just the system, protecting its own.

In another early case as a judge, I had to deal with a defense lawyer who was consistently an hour late coming to court. The jury was upset at this, as was I—our time was being wasted. On several occasions I'd warned the lawyer not to do it again or I'd take some action. The next time he was late, I imposed a fine. A day or two later, I ran into another acting female supreme court judge in the elevator, a woman I had always liked but did not know well. She'd heard that I'd "sanctioned" this man and told me that she admired my doing so but would never have done it herself, because she wanted to run for election to a supreme court judgeship and the screening process for such positions was controlled by the defense bar. I was taken aback, more by her reasoning than by her candor. I had never thought about my actions on the bench in relation to whether or not they would result in my being unpopular or blocked for election at some later time. If as a judge you can't say and do what you think you should, what's the point of being a judge? This was just one more reason I never wanted to seek election to the bench. I was fortunate to have been appointed by a mayor in-terested in merit—because I soon came to understand that as long as a liberal defense bar was in control of the process for electing judges, I would have no chance of being elected.

You would think that judges, in their "rarefied" atmosphere, would be close comrades-in-arms. In some jurisdictions, such as the Bronx, supreme court judges do lunch together daily and discuss their cases—but not in Manhattan. I like and respect a number of my colleagues, but in general, Manhattan Supreme Court judges tend to be very competitive with one another.

From the moment I became a supreme court judge, I learned that if one Manhattan judge was assigned a high-profile case, ten others would go to an administrator to complain that it hadn't been given to them, while ten more would be thanking their lucky stars that it hadn't been pitched into their lap—be-cause if it had, outsiders might pay attention to what was going on in their courtroom.

After I'd been on the bench for a while, and became dis-gusted at some of the petty jealousy problems, I set up a monthly "ladies' lunch" for female judges—we did allow some male judges to attend, too—and participated in other regular lunch sessions for judges. I even founded the "Dancing Judges," occasional evening forays where some male and female judges went out dancing together. (I have a secret passion for rock and roll and wild dancing.) These comradely exercises all worked well at the beginning, but eventually they petered out.

One of the more "fun" aspects of being a judge has been the weddings I have performed. Frankly, after nineteen years I'd just as soon perform them only for relatives and close friends. But over the years, I've also married a number of defendants be-fore imposing their other life sentences—at their request.

After a year in which all six of us junior judges presided over narcotics cases, half of us were able to escape; the six Parts were reduced to three. I did not seek another assignment because I enjoyed the work and it was challenging. The last thing in the world I wanted was a job in which I might become bored. Serious drug cases were anything but boring: Eventually I came to deal with multiple defendants and lawyers, cooperators, confidential informants, wiretap requests, and other interesting matters. But even early on, the issues were often challenging. And I felt that after a year I was just reaching the point at which I had sufficient expertise in the drug area to do my job as a drug judge well.

At the end of the following year, 1988, the three drug Parts were reduced to one, mine.* My courtroom was charged with handling all A-1 multidefendant drug cases in the system. This turned out to be quite a challenge.

By then I'd learned, because of the death threat from Fitzgerald and the nature of the cases, that being a drug judge involved dealing with some pretty bad people—maybe that was one reason most other judges didn't want these cases. I also enjoyed the extra work. Did a cop and an ADA need a search warrant or a wiretap authorization at a time other than normal business hours? "Sure, I'll do it now or look it over tonight," I'd tell them. I enjoyed going beyond what was required of a judge and being known as a hardworking, tough judge. Did "the People" like to try cases in my courtroom more than the defense? So be it.

*The number of drug Parts varied from year to year, but these Parts generally handled the most serious drug cases and long-term investigations. The growing number of routine drug cases was spread through all the court Parts, as routine drug cases always had been.

After I'd been a "drug judge" for a while, I became something of an expert on drugs and began to be asked to appear on various panels and on television programs such as NBC's *Today* show. ABC's *Nightline* did a documentary on a case in my courtroom. But my most rewarding television experience was as a panelist on several of Fred Friendly's broadcasts about the Bill of Rights, which I've mentioned earlier, in regard to my clash with Justice Scalia. On another episode of that series, about a homicide, Justice Scalia and I agreed on air about the need to allow into the presentencing procedure "victim impact" statements, and he later told me, off camera, "Well, you're not so bad after all." I mention these appearances in part because other judges resented them, even though it was these same judges who had worked so assiduously to avoid handling the cases that were the genesis of all this publicity.

Despite the isolation of being a judge, one could never do it alone. In addition to enjoying my family's support, I've been extraordinarily lucky to have a small but incredibly strong support group at work: my law clerks, Alex and Teresa, and my court clerk, Rocco. Working together, we have made my court run; and they have helped me become the judge that I am today. What strengths I have are certainly due to them; my weaknesses are my own, alone.

I met Alex Calabrese when I was a baby judge in 1983. He was then a Legal Aid attorney and a damned good one. When I had first become a prosecutor, New York City Legal Aid was a tough group full of radical and antiauthoritarian lawyers. In the mid-1990s, a major portion of Legal Aid's funding was eliminated, emasculating the organization, probably because it was a thorn in everyone's side. This sapped Legal Aid of some of its radicalism and caused many of its best lawyers to leave for other positions. But back in the 1980s it had many superb lawyers, and Alex was one of them. Bright, reasonable, and fair, he argued vigorously for his clients but within the bounds of common sense and reason. As a judge before whom he appeared, I liked and respected him. A law clerk serves at the pleasure of the judge and is basically a lawyer who assists the judge with research and with writing decisions. I hired Alex as soon as I became an acting and was entitled to a law clerk, and I was happy to have made this choice, because we got along so well and reinforced each other's strengths. But I had no idea at the time of the significance of the law clerk–judge relationship.

The ways in which individual judges and their law clerks relate are probably as numerous and varied as there are judges and clerks. Some judges and clerks have a close and friendly relationship, some are master-servant, and some have a distant relationship in which the parties are not even pleasant to one another. From the beginning of our time together, Alex and I were a team. He was like my younger brother, someone I could trust implicitly. We discussed almost everything together—the cases, legal issues, our kids. We balanced each other: Whereas I tend at times to be too direct and confrontational, Alex is more conciliatory. As a team, we did good work together. We also became close friends, and our families became friendly, remaining so to this day.

We agreed on a system: When Alex thought I was coming on too strong from the bench, he was supposed to kick me—discreetly, under the bench—and I was supposed to heed his signal and calm down. While I can't recall his ever actually kicking me, he certainly performed the functional equivalent on a number of occasions. However, I didn't always respond in the required manner! More important, we talked law constantly; without Alex I would have been truly isolated.

Together, Alex and I confronted many difficult legal issues and several that were groundbreaking; we'd exchange ideas on such matters until we concurred on the solutions. There were only a few instances when we disagreed. We shared the same, very simple philosophy: Try to do the right thing in every case. Often this meant putting the bad guys away for as long as possible, but that was a function of the kinds of cases and defendants we were handling. And sometimes doing the right thing permitted the opposite: trying every possible way to salvage a young defendant who was enmeshed in the criminal justice system—a person for whom there might still be some hope of rehabilitation.

About nine years ago, because of the extraordinary volume of cases in our courtroom, my added work as chair of the Chief Judge's Advisory Committee on Criminal Law and Procedure, and the wiretaps that I was spending nights and weekends reviewing, I was able to hire a second law clerk. It was to be an entry-level position. Alex and I had worked with Teresa Matushaj while she was in law school and had interned in our court and had found her to be lovely, bright, hardworking, and someone who shared our values. I offered her the job, and she joined us right out of law school. While she was very young, and had little practical courtroom experience, Teresa soon made herself invaluable as the junior member of the team. Nine years later, Teresa and I are still together, and she is my sole law clerk, as Alex is now Judge Alex Calabrese. Teresa and I are very close; I love her like a daughter. With some minor assistance from me, Teresa and my exceptionally able court clerk, Rocco, run the calendar with an iron hand. Teresa is so competent that I am able to delegate to her a lot of the work that to me has become incredibly tedious, which allows me to concentrate my energy on the problem issues.

When I first came to the supreme court, my desire to work hard frightened the court clerk I had inherited, and he almost immediately opted for early retirement. His replacement was Rocco De Santis, who has been my court clerk ever since and is undoubtedly the best court clerk in the criminal justice system. A court clerk is the person who calls the calendar and controls it, under the judge's direction, and handles many administrative court matters. Rocco knows almost everything about the several hundred cases a year that Part 88 handles and can deal with any situation that arises—such as single-handedly preventing an escape during the trial of the Wild Cowboys, which I'll detail later.

Do I sound a bit Pollyannaish in describing my team? Who cares! Unless one is a judge, it is probably impossible to completely understand how important these team members can be to the efficiency and capabilities of a hardworking courtroom.

Today, although Alex has moved on, Teresa, Rocco, and I remain the Part 88 "triumvirate." Some law clerks do eventually become judges, but it is far from automatic, involving—too often—politics. However, Alex's reputation as a fair, ethical, bright, and wonderful human being resulted in his appointment as a criminal court judge in 1997; he has already earned an extraordinary (and well-deserved) reputation on the bench.

Alex, Teresa, Rocco, and I have lunch regularly and do periodic family dinners. We continue to consult one another. We support one another, we care about one another.

URBAN
TERRORISTS

A gang of drug-dealing brothers and cousins, bonded in violence . . .

A gang of young thugs talented only at murder and terrorizing a neighborhood . . .

A young boy shot on his way to school during a confrontation between two rival drug dealers on a street filled with innocent bystanders . . .

Children lured into drug-dealing slavery by an evil "father" figure worse than Dickens ever invented. A man who tortured women and enjoyed it, living by one creed: sex, drugs, and murder . . .

A drug dealer who liked to act the "gentleman" while selling drugs and ordering executions . . . as his four-year-old son played with crack vials and machine guns . . .

Some of the drug gangs in New York City bear similarities to the terrorists who destroyed the World Trade Center and part of the Pentagon on September 11, 2001. While the terrorists killed three thousand people in an instant, drug gangs have caused the deaths of hundreds of thousands of people in America over the years.

The analogy between drug gangs and terrorists was first

brought home to me some years ago when I began to supervise the wiretaps of particularly cunning Colombian drug cells. Back then, these cells were basically run from Colombia by the powerful drug cartels there and by drug lords such as Pablo Escobar. Terrorist cells are known for being highly organized and for each cell being kept in ignorance of the others, so that if a member of one is arrested, he or she can give up other members of that cell only, not those of the other cells. The Colombian cells were organized along the same lines. Members would rent a house in a family residential area of a borough like Queens, a house with an attached garage, so that they would not have to load or unload narcotics or narcotics proceeds from a car on the street. Law enforcement would find it very difficult to conduct surveillance of such a house, since it would be on a quiet family block, and any strange car, even if it contained undercover cops dressed to blend into the neighborhood, would stand out if it was hanging around for any length of time. A male and female pair of cell members would pose as husband and wife, sometimes taking children along to set up house. Newspapers, magazines, and normal deliveries would begin to arrive, and the children would go to school; neighbors would have no idea that inside a home that resembled theirs, major criminal activity was afoot. Huge trucks containing up to thousands of kilos of cocaine hidden in hundreds of cans of tomato paste, or something comparable, would be offloaded elsewhere, and smaller trucks or vans that did not look out of place on residential streets would deliver the drugs to the house; only a handful of people would know what was going on. I was fascinated and amazed for several years as I learned from wiretap applications how the gangs, like the September 11 terrorists, could successfully use an accepted American way of life as a front.

The usual undercover strategies to bring down criminals didn't work with the Colombian cells, either, as they were extraordinarily difficult to penetrate. To be accepted as a member, you had to know someone or be a relative or family member of someone in the cell. It was almost required to have family back in Colombia who could in effect be held hostage—they could be killed if you stole money or drugs or turned state's evidence. And such family members were frequently murdered. Drug kidnappings here in the United States were also rampant, though few of those kidnapped were killed; rather, they were held in order to make sure that debts to the drug bosses were repaid.

New York's neighborhood or street drug gangs are organized on a smaller scale and with less efficiency. While the cartels are clearly international in their reach, the local gangs are not, except that many have roots in places like the Dominican Republic, where they send money and where they flee when pursued by law enforcement. But local drug operations do deal with significant amounts of money, engage in many illegal activities, and terrorize whole neighborhoods, instilling fear as well in the hearts of members, their families, and witnesses to the gang's crimes.

Of course, the analogy with the terrorists ultimately breaks down, because the terrorists are willing to commit suicide and are ostensibly doing what they do for political reasons. Neither the Colombian cartels nor the neighborhood drug gangs are suicidal; they are motivated solely by greed. But still, there are enough similarities so that we must consider the drug gangs to be urban terrorists of the first degree.

Gangs have always been part of New York City, especially in poor neighborhoods, since the earliest days of the city. The notorious "Five Points" area of Manhattan, where gangs controlled every aspect of life in the middle of the nineteenth century, can be seen from the windows of 100 Centre Street; the

Black Hand and other gangs of the late nineteenth century gave way to the Italian and Jewish organized crime gangs of the 1920s and 1930s who ran roughshod over law enforcement while maintaining full control of Prohibition liquor and associated vices. It was only when they grew more violent, becoming known as Murder, Incorporated, that law enforcement and prosecutors really attempted to curb their power.*

Throughout the twentieth century, gangs have sold drugs such as marijuana, cocaine, and heroin in New York. But the level of money that gangs could make from drugs, as well as the level of violence associated with the gangs, escalated seriously around the time "crack" was perfected in the 1980s. As almost everyone knows by now, crack is smokable cocaine, a horribly addictive drug that can be cooked up in a home kitchen. Crack surfaced in New York around 1985 and almost immediately began an epidemic. Within two years, the number of murders in crack-infested areas rose by 50 percent; the number of babies born addicted tripled, as did the number of infants abandoned by their mothers, the cases of child neglect, and the number of children beaten and killed by drug-addicted parents. Experts agreed that the crack epidemic was tearing apart what remained of the already fragile ghetto family. "In New York's poorest neighborhoods, where households are mostly headed by women," *The New York Times* reported,

the switch from heroin to crack as the choice drug of the inner city has had a strikingly destructive impact. For reasons not yet clear, women seem more disposed to become crack addicts. . . . Crack [has] an almost eerie ability to afflict the healthiest survivors in the city's already van-

*See articles in *The Encyclopedia of New York City*, Kenneth T. Jackson, ed. (New Haven: Yale University Press, 1995).

quished neighborhoods, and to steal from their children whatever hopes they once had of eventual escape.*

Crack gave rise to the many drug gangs because its individual units (vials or plastic bags), based on very small amounts of cocaine in rock form, could be packaged and sold for a few dollars each, enabling crack selling to bring far greater profit per ounce to the sellers than regular cocaine or heroin—and enabling neighborhood thugs with only a small amount of capital to start and run enormously profitable operations. Several gangs saw turnovers of more than $100,000 a week in gross sales at one "spot" or location alone. There were so many customers that the gangs would refer to "cheese lines," people queued up outside a spot as though waiting in a supermarket deli line.

In New York City, the task of ferreting out dozens of vicious, violent, and dangerous drug gangs and removing their strangleholds on neighborhoods was tackled by the police in cooperation with prosecutors, most notably by the homicide investigation unit (HIU) of the Manhattan District Attorney's Office. It has been a large, complex, time-consuming, and dangerous task. For me as a judge, presiding over many trials of drug gangs has also been fascinating.

Typical street gang operations, made up primarily of Dominicans or other defined ethnic groups, cook crack in the kitchens of small apartments. It is often put into vials, and the vials are capped and bundled into bunches of one hundred and cached in stash houses that frequently also contain the gang's guns and ammunition. Some stashes are hidden in well-designed *clavos*, or hidden compartments. In one Manhattan Valley stash house, it required the application of a plumber's helper to a floor tile to open the trap; another Harlem gang's

*Kerr, Peter, "Addiction's Hidden Toll: Poor Families in Turmoil," *The New York Times*, June 23, 1988, Section A, page 1.

clavo could be opened only by a complicated electronic buzzer system; a Lower East Side gang had *clavos* built into their cars in such ingenious ways that they eluded many cursory police searches of the vehicles.

"Bundles" are distributed to spots in the neighborhood to be sold, hand to hand, from derelict buildings or concealed locations, often through devices that make sure that the seller and buyer do not see each other's faces. One operation sold crack through doorknobs that could be quickly removed and replaced. The hand-to-hand "pitchers" are frequently crackheads themselves, and such low-level people are referred to by gang leaders as "Dixie Cups" to emphasize their disposable nature. Pitchers usually make $10 or its equivalent in crack for selling a bundle of one hundred vials at from $3 to $10 apiece. Some pitchers work in conjunction with lookouts posted on the streets and on the tops of buildings, equipped with walkie-talkies (or cell phones) to alert the pitchers when the cops are coming. Other gangs have several levels of managers and enforcers; most gangs have at least one enforcer willing to commit murder on command. Cash collected from the sale of vials is usually in single-dollar bills; the Spanish-speaking gangs band the cash in bundles often referred to as *cuentas*, which are taken back to countinghouse apartments for tallying.

The apartments used are seldom the gang members' own but belong to people in the neighborhood; such a ruse kept the police away from one gang's stash apartment for several months. These neighborhood places may at first be offered to the gang in exchange for money or employment, but sooner or later the tenants find themselves tyrannized into becoming all but slaves. Under threat of death if they do not cooperate, they cannot stop becoming more and more involved with the gang's activities—and all too often also addicted to its drugs. Similarly, neighborhood kids as young as eight are used by these gangs, initially to buy otherwise innocuous supplies such as glassine envelopes and rubber bands. Many of these kids are especially vulnerable, as they come from dysfunctional families, have multiple problems in school and at home, and will do almost anything for the "huge" sums of cash—$50 to go to the grocery store—dangled for completing little errands. Gradually they are sucked into the gang's real business, working up the ladder from carrying drugs to being lookouts or pitchers.

Because crack spots are the source of such huge profits, they are jealously guarded not only from police inquiry, but much more from rival gangs who might seek to take over the coveted territory. Guns are routinely carried to guard the stashes and the spots, the runners who take drugs to the spots and return to the managers with cash, and the buys of "weight" (large amounts of drugs), and to intimidate people into either working with the gang or leaving the neighborhood. Enforcers and gang leaders from some gangs would go up to rooftops and take target practice on objects, animals, and people below; nearly every gang's history included incidents where they rolled into a block in their cars and shot it up to send a message either to a rival gang or to the neighborhood about who was really in charge. Many gangs killed rivals or people who got in their way, stole their drug money or drugs or guns, or were presumed to have informed on them or "dissed"—disrespected—them for real or imagined insults. Drug gangs' machine pistols and hand grenades, the leaders' willingness to use violence at the slightest provocation, and their seeming ability to commit murder without being caught and punished terrorized entire neighborhoods for years—until the early 1990s, when a concerted effort was begun by the Giuliani administration, law enforcement, and the Manhattan District Attorney's Office to go after these gangs and take back the neighborhoods they ruled.

Since the mid-1980s, HIU has been devoted to prosecuting violent drug gangs, those generally accused of multiple murders in addition to drug sales. From the very first small pieces of gangs—individual defendants or clusters of two or three—that I saw in the late 1980s, who were dealing drugs and committing murder, cases have been coming my way from HIU. After I did several of their trials, I was assigned most of them, and I've continued to do them for most of my time on the supreme court. In my view, HIU is the outstanding unit in the DA's office, having developed a unique expertise that has allowed it to play a major role in ridding New York City of its most violent street gangs. The unit is headed by Walter Arsenault, an expert in gang prosecutions with a subspecialty in Jamaican gangs—in New York, in Jamaica, and in other places in the world where Jamaicans have immigrated—and a smart, intense, fiercely dedicated prosecutor. The unit also has had many of the best prosecutors and investigators in the DA's office: investigators Terry Quinn and Gary Dugan, and ADAs Dan Brownell, Luke Rettler, Deborah Hickey, Ellen Corcella, and Fernando Camacho, just to name a few. Perhaps what impresses me most—has sometimes bowled me over in the courtroom—is the way these prosecutors put a case together.

HIU's tactics in assembling a case against a violent drug gang known to have committed murders start with amassing materials on each gang member they can identify. This is tough but not impossible to do, since almost all gang members have had multiple brushes with the law and are known to the communities in which they operate. The spots from which the gangs sell crack or other drugs are also well known in the neighborhood and can be observed—though with difficulty, since invariably the gang has lookouts posted at either end of a block and all around the area of the spot. Eyeballing by police officers and investigators from HIU is backed up by photographs and video, from concealed observation posts, of the gang members in operation, sometimes in the process of making drug sales, but at other times just interacting together in ways that show that they know and are intimate with one another and involved together in some business. That's an important point to document, since HIU knows it is going to use the conspiracy statute against the gang and therefore must be able to prove that the individual members are engaged together in criminal activity. The photos, videos, and occasional wiretap recordings are also used as corroboration for the testimony of the cooperating gang members, when the case reaches the trial phase, because in the eyes of the law in New York, the cooperators are viewed as accomplices whose testimony must be supported by other evidence.

From observation, HIU proceeds to small buys, then to larger buys of drugs and sometimes of guns, done by undercover officers with "prerecorded buy money," marked bills that have been previously photocopied. These buys may lead to some immediate arrests, but not yet to wholesale arrests, since the members who are most easily arrested are lower-level pitchers and lookouts, and HIU wants the middle-level and top people as well and prefers to arrest everyone at once at the conclusion of the investigation. Witnesses are identified and found and their statements taken; this, too, is a difficult process because most witnesses are neighbors of the drug gang members and fear for their lives if they provide information to law enforcement about gang activities.

Eventually—usually after many months or more—enough evidence is amassed so that the entire gang can be "taken down," arrested at once. One of the most important reasons for a mass arrest—from several dozen to seventy or eighty people at a time, involving dozens of police officers—is to make sure that no gang members will be left out on the street, able to intimidate witnesses into recanting or refusing to testify. HIU also tries to have some of the defendants separated from the others while they are incarcerated, so that it becomes less possible for the leaders to intimidate the weaker gang members.

After the entire gang has been arrested, steadily, over a period that can extend to many months or even longer than a year, HIU chips away at the gang, trying to induce its members to cooperate, or "flip." This is the point at which I try hard to weed out the low-level defendants and see if I can get these less involved people—many still teenagers—into nonjail, alternative programs that might lead to their rehabilitation. Usually, three-quarters of the gang members will eventually plead guilty or agree to cooperate in exchange for reduced charges and lighter sentences. The cooperators, of course, are the key to making certain that the entire gang will be taken out of circulation; their testimony will show what observation alone cannot—the inner workings of the gang, the role of each member, and such details as which person gave the order to commit a particular crime. An important aspect of cooperation is a phrase from the streets, "Cop to what you do." ADA Deborah Hickey, while prosecuting a gang, explained it to a jury this way: "It's a slang expression, a street expression [that] expresses a basic tenet of ethical behavior: Own up to your own actions. Admit the direction you let your life take. Be honest where once you were not." This is absolutely necessary, because cooperators will be cross-examined mercilessly by defense counsel about their past criminal acts, the deals to which they have agreed, and their supposed incentives for turning against former compatriots—and to answer these tough questions, cooperators have to be brutally honest about everything. If they are not, if they lie on the stand, they face having their cooperation agreements torn up by the DA's office and receiving considerably longer jail sentences than the ones they had hoped to receive in exchange for truthful testimony.

During the pretrial period, defendants and their lawyers know they can take advantage of what is referred to around prosecutors' offices as "Queen for a Day." Defendants can come into the DA's office with an attorney and say anything they want about the crimes with which they are charged and what they know of others' participation. If a plea deal is not worked out, what they say during that "Queen" day can be used against them in court, but only if they choose to testify and if they perjure themselves. Whatever plea is agreed to is written into a cooperation agreement that is made part of a sealed record. When the case goes to trial, the prosecution must turn over these agreements and sealed pleas to the defense. Rumors about who is going to cooperate and what plea agreements they have made often convince more defendants to agree to plead guilty before the case is tried.

Regardless of one's personal opinion of "snitches" or "rats"—as the defense always calls cooperators—their role is critical to law enforcement. However distasteful the idea may be, many cases could not be made without them. The case against John Gotti, using Sammy "the Bull" Gravano as the star witness, is an extreme but well-known example. Many cooperators are violent criminals themselves and cooperate (of course) only out of self-interest: for less time on their own case or for money. Their use, in my view, is absolutely necessary—but a necessary evil.

Listening to cooperators testify can be a sickening and sobering experience. Since most do testify in a brutally honest way, the jury and I hear in gruesome detail about their backgrounds and their many crimes. After a while, it comes as no surprise to learn that most come from dysfunctional families and as a consequence of having almost no parental input have no family values; "right" and "wrong" have no meaning. Most have dropped out of school by the tenth grade and even before that were chronically truant and continually in trouble. The viciousness of their crimes and the totally unemotional manner in which they describe these crimes—as though recounting moves in a chess game—make all who hear these recitations wonder: What sort of a society do we live in that can breed young men and women devoid of all morality and conscience?

By the commencement of the trial, HIU hopes to have as the remaining defendants only the most violent and culpable of the gang members. Trial preparation by HIU is also first-rate and based on the assumption that it will be difficult for jurors to comprehend the entirety of the gang's operation without aids and reminders. One tactic is to display during the prosecution's opening statement a board with photos of all the gang members and lines indicating their positions in the hierarchy and then to point out the members as they sit at the defense table. Then the photos are taken off the board, to be put back on later, one by one, as witnesses on the stand identify members and their role within the gang structure. By the time the board has been refilled with photos, the jury has become able to recognize the individual members, the relative positions of everyone in the gang, and the lines of authority from the leader on down, which aids jurors in assessing individual members' culpability for the crimes with which they are charged.

HIU also uses diagrams and charts to show where the gang's spots are located and the sequence of events during a murder—who shot whom, where particular bullets went or shell casings were found. They also take pains to demonstrate to jurors, who might feel that whether one drug dealer kills another has nothing to do with their lives, that many crimes committed by the gang take place not just in the ghettos but also in the residential neighborhoods of everyday people. Similarly, they try to demonstrate that the proceeds from robberies, muggings, and carjackings in outside neighborhoods are used by addicts and low-level pushers to buy crack and in many other ways end up in the pockets of the drug gang.

Eventually the bulk of the HIU cases were assigned to me, not only because I found them interesting and important, but equally because other judges did not want anything to do with them. When the number of defendants ranges from fifteen to seventy-five, such cases present difficult and messy problems for calendar control. They also take much longer to work their way through the system—for instance, in sorting out the minor players and attempting to rehabilitate those who have not yet become violent. These cases demand supervision and patience in the pretrial phase so that the prosecution can flip the potential cooperators—get them to testify for the government—and obtain more information about the gang; and only the realization, gained from experience, that most gang members will eventually plead out allows a judge to maintain patience with a calendar that for as long as a year seems to be going nowhere.

The judge also has to make sure, during that time, that each defendant is handled as an individual. No plea pushers or disposition nuts need apply for the position of a drug gang judge, lest they go crazy trying to make each individual a statistic. As I've said previously, a handful of judges feel that their job is to get a plea from almost every defendant and that the number of pleas they take, their "stats," are the measure of their value. I haven't looked at my stats in years, and frankly, I don't care what they are, as long as I'm working hard and trying to do the right thing in each case. The statistics are irrelevant to the process of thoroughly working a violent drug gang through the criminal justice system.

Last but not least, many judges shy away from drug gang cases because of the violence of the gang members themselves. Witnesses have been killed or frightened into silence, and threats to the judges, prosecutors, and investigators have become more frequent.

I don't want to sound like a martyr. I don't feel like one. Trying drug gang cases, with all their problems, is what being a judge is all about. In these cases, the issues concern bringing to justice people who have hurt whole neighborhoods, sucked kids into their operations, poisoned thousands with their drugs, and committed many murders. Vicious defendants are a challenge; so are multiple defense lawyers, confrontations in the courtroom, the need to keep jurors awake and involved, and having to fashion new legal tools. On the whole, I have liked handling the drug gang cases because I *always* want to be where the action is and to feel that I am doing, or attempting to do, something truly worthwhile.

In presiding over drug gang cases for many years, I have come to some observations and conclusions. The first is that the issue of bail is the key point in many cases. If a relatively important defendant in a drug gang case gets out on bail, threats and attempts to intimidate witnesses and their families will invariably follow, and there may even be actual assaults or murders. The gang leader who is out on bail will more readily be able to influence his members not to cooperate than if he were still locked up; and his own ability to have gotten out contributes to his and his gang's belief that he will somehow be able to make the case go away, at least the case against himself. On the other hand, when gang leaders or enforcers remain in jail until and through the trial, the leader's power and his gang's belief in his power dissipate rapidly. Leaders who lose control over gang members become unable to prevent co-defendants from cooperating with the DA's office. If they continue to try to intimidate from "inside," from jail, they can be subjected to lockdown, a deliberate isolation technique that further removes them from control over the others in the gang. Therefore, experienced gang prosecutors know that their initial bail applications should contain enough potent material against a defendant to convince the judge either to remand the defendant or to set very high bail.

Lockdown applications and sealed proceedings also become a necessary part of almost every prosecution of a drug gang and involve defendants being locked down both prior to trial and during the trial. In my experience, it is rare to try one of these gangs to a successful conclusion without using these tools, which were developed—too often by me—in the process of trying these violent cases.

Sealed proceedings are a necessity to protect the identities of undercovers or confidential informants, as previously discussed, and whenever such protection must be granted, the judge must take care in the process to make the defense "whole." In other words, the judge must order the prosecution to do the work that the defense would do if it knew the identity of the witness prior to the eve of trial. Thus, the prosecution must search for and assemble not only every conviction in the protected witness's past, but also everything about his or her background, arrests, and drug involvement and prepare to turn that over to the defense at the appropriate moment.

No judge likes resorting to these procedures, but judges who preside over violent drug and drug gang cases must be prepared to use them. While every defendant's rights must be protected, victims have rights, too, and so does society—and it is the judge's role to protect these latter rights as well as those of the defendant. All criminal law involves a balancing of the defendant's rights and society's. Too often, the balance has been tipped too far in favor of the defendant's rights, and in my view, the rights of victims and of society have not received the protections that they deserve.

In the violent drug gang cases, many defendants in effect waived or forfeited certain rights to which they would have been entitled, such as the constitutional right to confront one's accusers, by threatening or even killing witnesses. So society's rights had to be asserted through the ordering of high bail, remand, lockdowns, and sealed protective orders.

All of my drug gang cases have involved long trials, often lasting from three to nine months, and finding and selecting a jury to serve for that long is always difficult. As I mentioned earlier, I have been chagrined to realize that at least half the prospective jurors must be excused from serving on these cases because they or their families have some close, often tragic, connection to drugs. That immediately pares down the jury pool. There are also many people for whom serving on a jury in a long case would be a genuine economic hardship—the self-employed, the proprietors of small businesses, certain employees whose employers cannot afford to pay them or refuse to do so. Most highly paid and highly educated people also cannot give the time and are unwilling to accept the loss of income that being on a long-term jury requires.

Eventually I worked out a system in which I call forty-four prospective jurors into the jury box at once, weeded out of a pool of perhaps two hundred. I hand out questionnaires and question the forty-four orally with the aid of those questionnaires, which allows them to give information about their background quickly. Then each side may ask some questions pertaining to the case or to the prospective jurors' backgrounds. Through this process, in gang cases we generally end up with juries composed of members of just a few distinct groups. First, government employees—post office workers and the like, usually those on a nonsupervisory level, and more blue-collar than white-collar. Other than an occasional teacher, these government employees tend not to be well educated.

A second group is composed of retired people and a sprinkling of the unemployed. These people like to have something to do and to make some money (now $40 a day) for sitting in court for months at a time. (Some of these jurors even like being sequestered and living in a hotel during deliberations. To them it's like a vacation—free meals, a pool, a fitness room, and occasionally a movie!)*

On almost every jury in a long case, in addition to the retired group there are also a few miscellaneous better-educated people,

---

*Our chief judge, Judith Kaye, has recently reformed the jury system. Everyone—lawyers, doctors, and so on—must now serve, and there is no longer any requirement of sequestration.

whom I encourage to participate for balance, even though their participation may be a hardship. When they do serve, they sometimes become the intellectual leaders of the jury, helping fellow jurors go through the evidence and make determinations on the charges against the defendants, which often run to dozens if not hundreds of counts. I tell all jurors in my preliminary remarks that their participation is essential to our democratic process and one of their most important civic duties. I tell them this is *their* criminal justice system, not just the system of those of us who work in it—and that it will cease functioning altogether if they do not participate. The jurors with responsible jobs almost invariably feel compelled to keep up with their work by returning to their offices during evenings and weekends while the trial is in progress. Once in a while, after a trial, a member of this group will tell me that he or she had served because I had convinced them of their obligation to society—which makes me feel good. (In the wake of the September 11 disaster, more people than before have been willing to serve on juries, rather than to seek to get off, because they now recognize jury duty as a way to serve their country and to support our system of justice and our way of life. Unfortunately, there have not been *that* many more "good citizens.")

The Jheri Curls was the first multidefendant drug gang to appear in my court as a gang and to be prosecuted as such by HIU. From the mid-1980s to the early 1990s, they operated in an area between 157th and 159th Streets and between Broadway and Amsterdam Avenues, in the shadow of the George Washington Bridge. They wore their hair in a distinctive way, with the side of the head shaved and permed "Jheri curls" on top, and the leaders drove identical gold-painted cars when commuting into Manhattan from Queens. These Dominicans and Puerto Ricans were also known on the street as the Martinez Brothers gang, after their leaders, five brothers named Martinez, led by the eldest, Rafael or "Rafi," who acted as a father figure. Rafi was a dangerous-looking man and had lived a danger-filled life; he limped and wore a brace on his leg, the result of a head injury sustained when a former drug gang associate shot him during a robbery (he and another defendant later shot the former associate dead). Other gang members were Martinez cousins; it was a family that sold drugs and killed people together, a family bonded in violence. The Jheri Curls had around twenty-five members and grossed $25,000 a day in cocaine sales.

During the two years that the police and HIU tried to amass evidence against them, the Jheri Curls murdered another innocent victim, an older man, for trying to organize the tenants of a building against them—they killed him in broad daylight, on the street, in front of many people, almost none of whom ever came forward to testify. They also killed some people and wounded others for attempting to take drugs from a stash apartment or for crossing them.

The case began when Cesar Martinez was wounded in a shoot-out with men trying to rob him; the Spanish-speaking police sergeant who interviewed him while he was lying on a gurney in the hospital (and who read him his *Miranda* warnings in that language) played on the notion that Cesar might not survive in order to obtain his information. From then on, the cops and HIU carried out intensive surveillance, executed search warrants that turned up guns and drugs, and used undercovers to make buys. The entire gang was arrested on October 22, 1991—together with six guns, nearly a pound of cocaine, an electronic scanner for police radio transmissions, scales, and other drug business equipment.

The nineteen defendants were brought into my court in rows: manacled, glowering men with defiant attitudes who, because there were so many of them, looked very much like a gang, the whole appearing larger and more malevolent than the

149

sum of its parts. This was in a smaller courtroom than the one I now work in, and the distance between the defendants and me was minimal. Their physical presence was overwhelming, and they knew it and played on it.

After hearing arguments from both sides, at the request of the prosecutor, Fernando Camacho, an exceptionally able and likable young lawyer (today an outstanding criminal court judge in Queens), I remanded most of the defendants, because they had long rap sheets and were flight risks with few roots in this country—there was a very real possibility that they might flee to the Dominican Republic if released on bail. Also, the charges against them were the most serious that could be brought: murder, attempted murder, dealing A-1 weight drugs, possession of guns, and conspiracy. This was the first trial in which HIU was attempting to use the conspiracy statute as a way to get at the entire gang as a group, rather than, as they had done in the past, trying to convict individual members of individual crimes.

By the time the case actually went to trial, near Columbus Day of 1992, the initial nineteen defendants had been reduced by pleas to five, including Rafi and two more Martinez brothers. One of the other brothers, the youngest, was to be a major prosecution witness, along with a dozen other "cooperators." This younger brother, Julian, was an appealing person determined not to live a life of crime, but to become a "good American." Despite Rafi's fatherlike position, he had no concern for his siblings and had tried to frighten them into working for him—and later into refusing to cooperate with the prosecutors or to implicate him in any way. Julian had courageously decided to go against Rafi. The specter of one brother "turning" on another is never a pretty one, but in this instance it was justified, although difficult to watch because there was something unnatural about it. For many years afterward, Julian would come back to court to visit the prosecutors and me and to report on his progress. (I haven't seen him lately, though, and hope he is still doing well.)

Among the other cooperators was a low-ranking gang member who, while he was being transported to prison by bus, was told by Rafi and another brother that people who worked with the police would be killed. A third cooperator was a young woman whom Rafi had once shot in the knee and then told not to report it or he would kill her. She had later been forced by him to work as a "mule," transporting drugs and money out of the United States; when arrested at an airport, she had lied to the police about the origin of the drugs, since she expected Rafi to bail her out, but he never did. This young woman would later testify about Rafi's boast to her about a particular murder, in addition to recounting her role of transporting drugs and money.

During multidefendant trials, I tell the various defense counsel in advance that I expect them to divide up their areas of cross-examination so that each lawyer will not ask the same questions of a witness. Obviously, each lawyer must be able to ask questions that concern his or her defendant, and there will always be some overlap, but my procedure is neither unusual nor difficult. In these trials I find that there are frequent clashes with defense lawyers who try to ask improper questions, or badger a witness, or start to lead a witness down a path toward a particular "defense" that would be inadmissible. This irks some defense lawyers, of course; a friend who is a defense lawyer tells me that his colleagues feel that I sense their tactics and put a stop to where they are going too far in advance, thus curtailing their effectiveness. My thinking is different: If a line of questioning is going to be improper, I'm going to stop it as soon as I recognize the potential impropriety. And most of my rulings have been upheld.

One defense lawyer, an old friend, teases me regularly about my bail practices, saying that "remand" is one of my favorite words, and—using a line from a television commercial—comparing my courtroom to a "roach motel," where defendants all check in but never check out!

Despite my toughness on the defense, I generally get along well with defense lawyers on a personal level—probably because they recognize that I am equally as rough on any prosecutor who attempts to go beyond what might be proper. In one trial, for example, the ADA was grilling the father of a defendant and was bullying him, trying to get him to incriminate his son, which of course the father would not do under any circumstances (and the jury knew that). I called a sidebar and, in front of the attorneys for the defense, admonished the ADA for totally inappropriate behavior—having done so less unpleasantly in front of the jury already. I won't allow any lawyer to yell at a witness, or point fingers, or otherwise intimidate a witness—any witness; those tactics simply won't be tolerated. Questioning can be vigorous but must be conducted so that it does not demean the person on the witness stand.

Then there was Richard Giampa, the counsel hired by Rafi to defend him in the Jheri Curls trial. Giampa had a reputation for baiting judges and for being nasty in the courtroom. In a trial in the Bronx, he had called the judge a "wild lunatic," had said that a statement by the judge was "an absolute lie," and had made additional disparaging remarks in front of the jury. His client's conviction was overturned on appeal, and the client was retried before another judge, in large part because Giampa had caused the first judge to act inappropriately. Giampa had obtained outright jury acquittals in two earlier cases, and an appellate court later characterized this conduct as instances of his "engag[ing] in conduct prejudicial to the administration of justice" and stated that his conduct "evinced a flagrant disrespect for the judiciary and a fundamental disregard for the judicial process."* More than one judge had previously cited him for contempt.

Now, a multidefendant trial presents difficult enough prob-

*For all quotes by and concerning Giampa, see the various appellate briefs filed by the prosecution in *People* v. *Rafael Martinez*, et al.

lems for a judge: Each defendant must have separate counsel, and there are also the prosecuting attorneys; the judge must be fair to everyone. Every sidebar at the bench during the Jheri Curls trial involved seven or eight lawyers. All of the defense attorneys other than Giampa consistently behaved well while doing creditable jobs defending their clients. I did clash with a few of them, but it was always done in an atmosphere of mutual respect, and at the end of the trial I complimented them for their able and professional conduct. Today, looking back, I do so even more.

The difficulties with Giampa began during jury selection, when I wanted to seat eight alternate jurors because I thought they might be necessary during what was shaping up to be a long trial. The other defense attorneys were willing to do this, but Giampa refused to permit four more alternate jurors than the law then allowed; so we were forced to seat only four. This perfectly legal tactic is sometimes used by defense attorneys in conjunction with others that prolong the trial, in the expectation that the loss of jurors—which happens—could eventually exhaust the number of alternates and result in a mistrial. But the manner in which Giampa refused to cooperate with his co-counsel set the stage for his manner throughout the case.

During the trial, Giampa consistently asked witnesses the same question four and five times and frequently tried to take a witness over ground covered by the other defense attorneys. His questions were also convoluted and difficult for a witness to understand. Out of the presence of the jury, I warned him about these practices, but he ignored my instructions. In some instances, to cut through the fog, I had to ask the witness a more direct question, elicit the answer, and then tell Giampa to move on. Eventually, after warning him that I'd have to end his cross-examination if he asked the same question one more time, he did just that and I had to order him to sit down. He did so with a grin on his face, as though he had succeeded in inciting me—

153

for the benefit of the jury and so he could have something in the record on which to claim later that I had prejudiced his client and that therefore any conviction should be reversed.

I didn't want to rise to Giampa's bait, but it was almost impossible not to because his tactics were an attempt to take control of the courtroom. During a sidebar he actually grabbed some legal papers out of my hand. Astonished and offended, I grabbed them back, and he later made this the subject of nasty remarks and legal objections. (Of course, I should not have stooped to his level.) In front of the jury, he made snide remarks about my rulings and sent similar message by making faces. He consistently insinuated in his cross-examinations and other remarks—without basis—that witnesses employed by the city or state, such as cops, lab technicians, and the prosecutor, had engaged in illegal behavior; he made vituperative legal arguments that also had no legal basis, frequently objected when there was nothing to object to, and attempted various additional disruptive tactics.

Eventually his actions forced me to hold Giampa in contempt. I didn't want to do this, because to me it was a tacit admission that I was unable to control him; but he left me no alternative. In nineteen years on the bench, Giampa is the only lawyer I've ever had to hold in contempt. This contempt citation was later affirmed on appeal, and he was censured and his license to practice law was suspended for a year, based on a number of similar incidents with other judges as well. This was too lenient a penalty, in my view, for a lawyer whose tactics were consistently to attempt to disrupt every courtroom, prejudice every trial, and by those tactics to obtain a reversal on appeal if there was a conviction. Giampa did not realize that long before the end of our trial the jury saw right through his tactics and held him in contempt as well.

The jury did return guilty verdicts on most of the counts against the Jheri Curls. I sentenced Rafi Martinez to consecutive prison terms totaling 213 years to life; the other defendants received shorter but substantial sentences. The trial verdict, the sentences, and my conduct throughout the judicial proceedings were all upheld on appeal, even though the defendants' briefs were based largely on the supposed errors that I had made in my clashes with Giampa. The appellate division ruling also affirmed the use of many HIU tactics such as the display of the photo board of gang members, which the defense had wanted to have declared inadmissible. The results of this trial, and the affirmance by the appellate court, confirmed that large drug gangs could be prosecuted successfully and encouraged everyone to continue this important work.

Recently I was invited to participate in a seminar in California that featured some Hollywood players as well as law enforcement and other criminal justice professionals. The Hollywood types got their backs up when I spoke about an intimate relationship between drug gangs and their violence and depictions of drugs, gangs, and violence in the movies. The moviemakers, as they usually do, claimed a First Amendment privilege to depict whatever they wanted to in whatever style they chose, and they also claimed there was no evidence that fictional depictions of violence inspired violent acts by real-life people. But they also said that they were aware of concerns like mine and took them into account when deciding what stories to film and how to film them. I am a big supporter of the First Amendment and its right to free expression, but there are definite links between what Hollywood puts on the screen and how drug gangs and other young punks act. In contradiction to Hollywood's self-serving position, a number of gang leaders have told the authorities that they modeled their behavior on Al Pacino's character in the remake of *Scarface;* others used the movies *Nat-*

ural Born Killers or *Menace II Society* as models. Witnesses to real-life shoot-outs report gang enforcers holding and aiming their guns sideways—which makes no sense in terms of accuracy—because the enforcers have seen countless bad guys doing it in movies. Many gangs take their names from violent groups featured in movies or in rap songs, such as Natural Born Killers, Dead Men Walking, and Young Talented Children—just to name three that appeared in my court.

The YTC crew, the Young Talented Children, as they were called, was led by young men nicknamed Yo, Tito, and Chango, so YTC was, they thought, an appropriate name—as well as indicative of the "yellow-top caps," or crack vials, that they sold. At the height of their domination of the neighborhood between 105th and 107th Streets and Amsterdam Avenue, from 1989 to 1994, as Chango later told the court, "We wasn't even valuing money. We were young and spent money on whatever: cars, motorcycles, girls, hotels, guns, anything. We spent money just to spend it so that we wouldn't get caught with it." In the language of the streets, they were "living large," driving big cars, buying fancy clothes, smoking expensive cigars, using expensive drugs, buying ever larger and more deadly guns that they would feel the need to try out on innocent victims just to see how well the guns worked. Chango and his crew were ecstatic after their first murder in the neighborhood because, as Chango later testified, "now we had a body. People weren't going to give us shit anymore." In another incident, two members shot up 112th Street, killing a child and injuring others when they could not find the people who "dissed" them. The real objective of the YTC conspiracy was power, a power that ADA Luke Rettler characterized as "blatant and obscene," the power of life and death over every resident of the neighborhood who was unable to move elsewhere.

For years the local cops were stymied by the Young Talented Children. In court, officers described how difficult it was to approach and get evidence of drug dealing: They would creep up behind the cover of trucks or buses and on one occasion even rode in a concealed position on the back of a garbage truck to jump out to catch the dealers, but they seldom managed to do so because of lookouts on top of tenements and door-lock arrangements that allowed for the dealers' quick escape off the street.

YTC was subtle and street smart, as well as vicious. They sold crack at several locations with varying vial-top colors at each, to make customers think rival operations were competing to offer the best prices and the best-quality product. Once they stole another dealer's money and stash of kilos of cocaine but left enough for the police to find, made fake 10-13 ("officer in distress") calls to bring police to the scene, and made sure that the police found some of the cocaine but not all, which confused the rival drug dealer into thinking that the police, rather than his "competitors," had taken the drugs. After committing murders, they sent people to learn which residents the police were questioning and whom the police suspected. These gang members would also use the chaotic circumstances of the crime scene to spread false information and to find ways to intimidate witnesses into not pointing their fingers at the real killers. They also had a corrupt cop on their payroll who frustrated their prosecution at many points and in many ways; this was well-known in the neighborhood, as the jury and I heard from a mother whose son had been threatened with death but who told her, "You can't go to the precinct—they have a cop." No wonder neighborhood residents didn't trust the police.

In the YTC case, we learned that the defendants were intimidating witnesses from jail by making phone calls to them or contacting gang members who had not been jailed and instructing them to make threats or take action against witnesses. This was when the district attorney's office first asked me to order "lockdowns" of the three main defendants. Now, lockdowns had been used in state and federal prisons to isolate dangerous prisoners, but those were men who had been convicted of a crime and whose rights had been legally curtailed. It was quite another thing to subject a defendant—a person who under our system of justice is presumed to be innocent until proven guilty—to isolation for twenty-three hours a day and permit him only phone calls to and visits with his lawyers. The solution seemed pretty draconian to me at first blush. But the DA's office had plenty of evidence of the defendants' attempts to intimidate witnesses—that in fact they were masters of intimidation—and convinced me that lockdown was the appropriate remedy if society's rights were to be protected. I made an extensive sealed record of the request and the evidence on which it was based, in case the order was appealed, and then issued the lockdowns. It was a first for me, but not the last. Eventually I would become known as the "Queen of Lockdown": I have ordered far more of them than any other judge, because of the number of drug gang murder cases in my courtroom.

Defendants hate this extreme confinement—who can blame them?—but they have always created the situation, necessitating it themselves, thereby forfeiting some fundamental rights. It should be noted that the lockdowns have all been upheld by appellate courts.

An important point was made by ADA Rettler in the YTC trial, a point that HIU has made in each trial: You cannot, absolutely cannot, successfully remove an entire gang from the street without cooperation from some members. This position was perhaps best articulated by Rettler's former colleague, ADA Ellen Corcella—now a major drug and gang prosecutor in Indiana and an excellent lawyer—who argued to some potential jurors in a voir dire, "If you wanted to find out all you could about baseball, who would you ask to tell you? Reporters? Politicians? No, you'd want to hear about it from the insiders, the players. And from just any player? No, you'd want to hear the details from a long-term, experienced player who was savvy and cognizant of all the aspects of the game." The same held true for drug gangs: To learn all about their particular operation, you'd have to hear it from the insiders, scuzzy criminals though they might be. Only the insiders, the gang members, could detail the organization's hierarchy and paint the detailed portrait of daily dealing, assault, murder, and mayhem that the jury had to know. As Rettler put it in the YTC case, "No one is asking you to like these people. You don't have to take these people home when this case is over. We are asking you to listen to them, evaluate their testimony, determine whether they are telling you the truth."

At the trial, ADA Andrea Sacco, an attractive, able young prosecutor, opened by describing the senseless murder of an innocent fourteen-year-old boy, a victim of gratuitous drug-related violence. As she spoke, the boy's mother's hysterical cries pierced the silence of the courtroom, a heart-wrenching sound, and she had to be removed—gently—by relatives and court officers. This was one of eight murders and thirteen attempted murders YTC was purportedly involved in, this one for revenge against rival drug dealers who had kept two of the defendants waiting to buy marijuana. Therefore, they were "going to teach the block a lesson."

Almost always, in these trials, the defense does not call witnesses. But in the YTC case, an overeager defense lawyer decided to call a woman to give one of the defendants an alibi for the time of one of the murders. She got on the stand and said that she and the defendant had been attending a grandfather's birthday party at that particular moment. This was a gift for the prosecution because they were able to show that the time on a clock depicted in the photograph of the party was not the same as the time when the murder had taken place. Proof of a lie—in legal terms, a false exculpatory statement—helped undermine an already shaky defense and greatly aided the prosecution.

In the courtroom I came to know Chango, the leader and clear mastermind of YTC. A killer and a man who ordered others to do his murders, he was nonetheless a real charmer and con man; jurors liked him even though he was seriously violent and had initiated so much violence. He had agreed to cooperate and to plead guilty, so we heard a great deal from him on the witness stand. Many others of the YTC crew pleaded out, and the remainder who went to trial were convicted. I sentenced them each to lengthy terms in prison, long enough to keep them away from society forever.

Chango was represented by an attorney who had made her reputation defending radical minority defendants. She and I had clashed several years before, over her representation arrangement with the head of a smaller drug gang—an arrangement later deemed to be improper and a story I'll tell in another chapter—but this time I had no difficulty with her representation of Chango. She was able to convince HIU to give him a very good plea bargain because he was an invaluable witness, essential to convict everyone else in the gang.

YTC and the other drug gangs made me feel absolute outrage—not because of their courtroom tactics, which were just ways of trying to defend against grave charges, but at what they had done to their communities. And I was glad I felt that outrage. If you stop caring about each case, stop feeling the indignation that is appropriate in these cases, then you should stop being a judge.

Some people argue that drug dealers killing one another is not so terrible. But that notion distorts the reality of their murders. Much of the time their victims are innocent neighborhood people—frequently children. One victim was unforgettable in his absolute innocence: His name was John Paul Valentine, and he was eight years old.

On January 23, 1996, Valentine, a second-grader at P.S. 145 at the corner of 105th Street and Amsterdam Avenue, was walking toward school to begin the day when he heard noise behind him. He turned toward the source, and a hollow-point bullet slammed into his chest, wounding him grievously. It had not been aimed at him but was the result of a shoot-out between rival drug dealers on a street crowded with children. A police car came quickly to the scene, and the responding officer performed an unusually heroic deed: Seeing the gravity of the child's condition—blood pumping out of the little boy's body in great quantities at each heartbeat—he decided not to wait for the ambulance to arrive and almost threw John Paul into the squad car and personally raced him to St. Luke's Hospital, an action that doctors at St. Luke's later credited with saving his life.

The shoot-out had been a complicated affair culminating in two people wielding guns. The day before, there had been an altercation with slugging, kicking, and biting, over whether or not one man had dissed another by refusing to repay $10 he had borrowed sometime earlier. Both men in the fight were crack dealers, and the real beef was whether one had stolen the other's customer. Each planned to settle it the next day and had prepared to do so by carrying the guns that they had left at home during the first fight. Neither of the shooters managed to harm the other with their gunfire, but they did come very close to killing little John Paul Valentine.

One shooter had worn a rubber glove so that he would not have powder residue on his hand, and his gun was ditched by a girlfriend in the river; the other attempted to bury (in a nearby park) the gun that fired the bullet that had smashed Valentine's chest. These efforts to hide their actions went a long way toward proving that the defendants had intended to commit murder when they set out for their street corner firefight.

Before trial, one of the shooters pleaded guilty, leaving one to be tried for various charges, including the attempted murder, gun, and drug counts. This defendant was convicted on most of the charges, including the attempted murder. Among the witnesses at the trial was John Paul Valentine himself, still a little boy, with a wide-eyed, frightened look in his eyes that will undoubtedly take many years for him to lose and will never leave my mind.

HIU's overall strategy was to target discrete areas of the city and attempt to get rid of the gangs that were terrorizing them. Manhattan Valley, just south of 125th Street in Harlem, was one target area. Several gangs operated there, one led by Carl Dushain on 123rd Street, the other by Marvin Shabazz on 124th Street. The level of violence they reached was exemplified by a ceremony held by Shabazz and his underlings on May 24, 1996, when with Moët Champagne and Hennessy Cognac they toasted the murder of Andre Woods, a rival drug dealer who had survived the gang's previous attempts to kill him. Another image of Marvin Shabazz will always remain with me—not of big Marvin, but of his four-year-old son. As the picture was painted—poignantly—by the prosecutor in his final argument, instead of regular toys little Marvin played with bullets of various calibers, crack vials, and drug scales. Instead of finding baseball bats in his closet, he found machine guns. Little Marvin couldn't wake up in the morning in the same way many kids did, smelling fresh coffee being brewed, because his father used the coffeepot to cook up crack.

Chango and his YTC crew were Dominicans and Puerto Ricans, the Jheri Curls and the Wild Cowboys were Dominicans, Fitzgerald and his crew were Jamaicans, Frankie Jaws and his associates were Italian Americans, and Shabazz and Carl Dushain were American blacks—evidence to me that drug gang activity is not specific to any ethnic group; it infects all of them.

Shabazz brought into his orbit an enforcerer, Troy Cochran,

who would shoot or hurt people at his command, and perhaps a dozen boys of thirteen, fourteen, and fifteen, troubled young men from Harlem and Brooklyn, boys who were already using drugs themselves and were beginning to use violence. It has always bothered me that drug gangs are able to attract and enmesh boys that young. What forces are these boys exposed to that cause them to start swirling down a seemingly irreversible drainpipe of drugs, violence, and crime? A typical Shabazz recruit was nicknamed Rook. His mother had been addicted to crack when he was in grade school, so he lived with his grandmother until she died of cancer when he was thirteen; soon, to have a family, he joined the Decepticons, a Brooklyn street gang. Shortly he was "yoking" strangers on the street—grabbing them from behind in a choke hold—with twenty of his pals at a time. "We picked them at random. It was fun. We were young," Rook later testified. He and other young gang members used guns to take occasional shots at rival dealers or those who dissed gang members. Before he was out of his teens, Rook graduated from the Decepticons to take part in Shabazz's operation.

With two dozen recruits like Rook, Shabazz and Cochran tyrannized their block while selling crack and making money. But Shabazz treated his employees well, bought lingerie for his wife (and for various strippers), and cherished Little Marvin—in contrast with Dushain, who regularly beat his employees or had them tortured. The two neighboring drug organizations united against common enemies and did not interfere with one another's operations; however, their leaders did play off each other's images, Shabazz coming across as the gentleman partly because Dushain so assiduously cultivated his "badder" dude reputation. Shabazz was physically attractive, Dushain was unappealing—short, overweight, balding, and bug-eyed, but evidently magnetic to his followers.

When the prosecutor—an excellent advocate—summed up

in the Dushain case, he used the analogy of the Pied Piper of Hamelin to describe what Dushain had done in the neighborhood, luring the children away from their homes and families. To me the more appropriate literary reference was to Fagin, the evil manipulator of children in Dickens's *Oliver Twist*. Like Fagin, Dushain had a nose for kids who were particularly vulnerable, and he knew what to offer them. One needed help in penmanship, another the comfort of a father figure after running away from an orphanage, a third money for the rent. In exchange for his help, he forced girls as young as thirteen to transport crack in their sanitary napkins held inside their vaginas on airplane trips to a southern state; pushed one with a pretty face to lure a man out of a club so he could be ambushed and assassinated; involved them all in "bagging up" his crack and selling it. He would tell the young girls not to use crack but to bag and sell the drug, and invariably they would become hooked themselves anyway; he would force them to perform sex acts on him before he would give them steady jobs in the organization. One girl he liked so much that he nicknamed her "Shitty."

After a few months of hanging around Dushain, the thirteen-year-old boy who had run away from the foster home considered himself Dushain's son and, according to his testimony, "was with him everywhere he went. I would follow him [and] if I woke up and he wasn't there, I would follow him down to 123rd Street." This boy was made to carry guns to Virginia and to sell crack; when he came up short in the money count or when Dushain's videotapes were missing from his Bronx apartment, Dushain ordered him beaten with a piece of wood. Another boy recruit had seen his mother die when he was five and his father when he was eight, and he had been kicked out of his stepmother's apartment when he was thirteen; he took a street name from a comic book—MAGE, "Monster Anger Gone Evil"; under Dushain's guidance he worked toward becoming the person that this name described. A friend of Mage's, fatherless and looking for direction after a stint in the army, was sucked in by the promise of easy money. He would later tell the jury that he would not accept a minimum-wage job at McDonald's, the only other job for which his education would have qualified him. "I will *not* flip a burger," he insisted.

Dushain had been convicted in 1988 of killing a girlfriend but had served only three years. He hit women who crossed him with whatever was near: bricks, pipes, bats, pieces of wood, fists. He ordered one woman who had inadvertently witnessed a murder to be handcuffed and hung from a pipe in a sub-basement dungeon for days, her only companions rats and other vermin. When a gang member brought her food—she was diabetic—an enforcer knocked it from her hands and stomped it into the floor; at last Dushain went down and "rescued" her, pretending to be astonished at her treatment so she would not report the incident to the police. He bathed her wounds, let her have a few days to recuperate, and then put her back to work bagging and selling crack.

To Dushain, the rules of the game were "sex, drugs, and murder." He took care to insulate himself from outright murder by assigning that task to his chief enforcer, "Cash," or by hiring others to do his killings, one of them the young man from Brooklyn who had dropped by to see his friend Mage. Dushain supplied them with guns and the money to buy "blunts," cigars filled with mixtures of marijuana, cocaine, and sometimes PCP, (phencyclidine).

One intended murder victim was a rap disc jockey nicknamed "006," who survived many Dushain attempts on his life. He became a repeat target in part because he was determined to testify before the grand jury investigating the first attempt to kill him. An actual murder victim was the super in the building from which Dushain sold crack. Dushain was convinced that this man had snitched on him to the police; he had Cash shoot him to death even as the super begged for his life. Moments later there was an unrelated gun battle on the street, and Dushain ordered the super's body dragged out to the stoop so that it would look as if he had been killed by a stray bullet during the gunfight.

Later, when the arrests of his gang began, Dushain terrorized his minor associates—a former lover, for instance—by displaying a photograph of a dismembered woman whom he said he had killed and another photograph of his male associates digging an unmarked grave for her body. He told the former lover, "This is what happens to people who cross me." By such means he prevented her from testifying before the grand jury—but not forever, as the police and HIU eventually found her, protected her, and made it possible for her to testify without being further harmed by Dushain.

After Dushain had been arrested and incarcerated pending trial, he continued to try to frighten or entice potential cooperators into turning their backs on plea bargains. He plied his women with instructions—by letter. Some of the letters were turned over to the DA's office and introduced as evidence. He would start out friendly: "Maxine, if we are co-defendants we have to move together, think alike, and by one of us taking a plea bargain, a cop-out, will indirectly jam the other person up.... When you get a chance, ask your lawyer who are the witnesses against you.... Please let me know what kind of questions the detectives are asking about me." Soon he escalated to promises and threats: "I'm working on something to get that conspiracy charge off of us.... If they can't prove it, they lose it, unless you tell on yourself and the only thing they is going to do for you is give you less time and you going to jail anyway.... Call [name omitted] and ask her what was the police asking her each and every time they pick her up from her house." And finally, to Maxine: "Listen up? The DA got to prove that you had full knowledge of exact you suppose to act out.... So to beat this allegation you is going to have to find a alibi for the whole month of February. . . . Why is [the DA] concerned that Maxine needs an alibi for February? Because I know that I never sent you anywhere, to kill anyone? The only thing that's going to protect us from going to jail is that we don't open our mouths."

Similarly, he wrote to Shitty, "No matter what they might tell or ask you, you don't know nothing about Mr. Dushain, or how he make his money. . . ." When this letter did not bring the desired response, Dushain tried harder: "Call your lawyer, let him or her know that you want to speak to your co-defendant attorney [name and phone number omitted], so on the day you go to court he could come down to the bullpen and speak with you . . . let him know to inform me who you feel are standing strong and who should be worried about. . . . Love always, to death do us part, the rise and fall." Still later, the threats are more blatant. "Melvenia . . . told me how Coco is lying on her. Shitty, if I have knew sure that Mel is serious about she's saying about pulling back, I'll have Tai Stick get in contact with Coco and have Shabazz wife Stacy talk to Little and get them to disappear when it time to go to court." He followed with ten specific questions for which he wanted her to obtain answers from other co-defendants.

To Mel herself he wrote twenty letters. "Now I'm facing life in prison. How is we going to have a child now? . . . Hopefully I'll hear from you because I'll have a chance [before court] to speak with the crew about Coco and Little and I need to know the decision you came up with. So I could help you. Mel, if you want to help me, I need this information now. . . . What did you tell [the grand jury] about me sending Maxine and Mel to the Karate Club to kill 006? . . . To answer your question about if or not the DA will be piss off [if you recant]? Yes, he will. But what the fuck can he do? But offer you that fifteen to life cop-out bullshit and take you back to trial. That's when I'm going to keep my promise. . . . Mr. Dushain loves you. Stay strong and together, we'll both make it home." When Mel did not answer the way he wanted: "I may never come home due to you informing these fucking police about a lot of shit that you should have had—shouldn't had open your mouth to. When you kill Hobo, nobody ran to the grand jury telling on you. . . . I don't understand. Why did you do this? Everybody is mostly in jail cause of you. I understand you might be mad at Tai and them, but what did me, Kanika, Shitty, Shabazz and Disco do to you?"

One reason Dushain was concerned about the testimony of these cooperators was that a central charge against him was conspiracy—a charge that would break through the barriers of insulation he thought he had erected to prevent himself from ever being charged directly with murder.

The conspiracy charge, though central to the legal strategy of taking down whole gangs, is a somewhat complicated legal concept, difficult for laypeople to grasp. So when I instruct a jury in one of these gang cases, I pay special attention to it. I begin by defining the charge: Conspiracy is an agreement between two or more people to commit a crime in the future. Then I illustrate the notion of conspiracy with a silly, apocryphal example having nothing to do with the case:

My law clerk Teresa and I have been feeling underpaid lately, so I decide that we should rob a bank. We meet and agree and intend to rob a bank. The law says that after we reach this agreement, if one of us does something to carry the agreement into effect, called an overt act, then we both have committed the crime of conspiracy. So, if I went out and rented a car, intending it to be used as a getaway car after the robbery, we would both be guilty of conspiracy, even though renting a car is not unlawful. Now let's say that Rocco, our clerk, was in the bank at the time we robbed it. Even if he knew about our intended robbery beforehand, he wouldn't be guilty of the conspiracy if he did not *intend* to participate in it or share in the profits. However, if the DA could show that Rocco not only knew us but knew our plans and was one of the members of the group that agreed to rob the bank, and intended to rob the bank, then he'd also be guilty of conspiracy.

Now suppose I made up the plans, but rather than do the robbery myself I decided to go to the Cayman Islands and sit by the pool while the robbery was going down, and to have Teresa rob the bank and then wire me the proceeds. Even though I wasn't present when the bank was robbed, I'd be guilty of conspiracy to rob the bank because I agreed to the robbery and intended to share in the proceeds. . . .

The "story" goes on for a while and discusses various legal scenarios illustrating various conspiracy issues and elements.

The conspiracy charge worried not only leaders like Dushain but also minor players like Shitty. This charge was the stick wielded by the DA's office to convince such minor players to become cooperators.

Eventually, in the Dushain and Shabazz cases, the major players as well as the minor ones were all convicted. While incarcerated, Dushain continued to be a problem, causing repeated disturbances, destroying property, and threatening other inmates and corrections officers.

On sentencing day, Dushain and Cash continued to deny the murders and other crimes and accused the police and prosecutors of putting words into their mouths—words that conveyed their intent to commit murder and their other criminal actions—by means of the cooperating witnesses. In particular they denied the ADA's characterization of them as "monsters."

After their lengthy statements of innocence and accusations of police prosecution conspiracy, which were totally belied by the evidence, it was my turn to speak. "Listening to you both makes me sick," I began. "It makes me sick to have presided over this trial and to have listened to two people who are, obviously, pathological liars, who are murderers, who are truly evil individuals. . . . You *are* monsters, both of you, and you have to be removed from society for as long as possible." I sentenced Dushain to various terms for individual crimes that amounted to a cumulative sentence of 150 years to life, Cash to 91⅔ to life, and (after a separate trial) Shabazz and his enforcer, Cochran, to prison for what would also amount to the rest of their lives. I will never forget how the "gentleman" Shabazz, at the time of his arrest, was more concerned with saving his guns and drugs from the police than with shielding his four-year-old son, Little Marvin.

In the Manhattan Valley cases, there were not many minor players for whom alternative sentences were appropriate, among other reasons because these defendants did not have families or supportive environments in which they could live while receiving treatment and counseling or to which they could return after residential programs. However, in a series of drug gang cases having to do with the Lower East Side— equally violent cases, with equivalent areas terrorized by crack, cocaine, and heroin dealers—the possibility of alternative treatment for the minor players was greater because these gangs were composed mainly of Puerto Ricans. Their families tended to be more intact and present in this country and therefore could provide a more supportive environment for the young people sucked into criminal activity by the gangs and their "easy" money, the young people who, as ADA Deborah Hickey eloquently stated in a summation, sold (and consumed) "tiny glassines filled with false hopes and desperation." The leaders of the Lower East Side gangs, who had committed such crimes as executing a rival while he sat in a barber chair, received the lengthy sentences they deserved, but we could at least provide a chance for a new life to a few of their associates. Sometimes, I must repeat, trying to "do the right thing" means putting defendants in jail for a very long time; sometimes it means finding alternative treatment. In these terribly violent cases, only by feeling that you have done the right thing by everyone can you be internally at peace with yourself.

By the middle 1990s, HIU had locked up and eventually sent to prison more than five hundred gang members from various drug-infested areas of the city. It was an era when New York's crime rate was plummeting, but in the areas where the gangs were being taken down, crime fell even faster than in the city as a whole.* Some precincts saw their rate of drug-related murders go from two dozen a year down to single digits after the gangs that controlled their neighborhoods were taken off the streets.

Over the course of the years, and as a result of presiding over the trials of so many drug gangs and handing down these very stiff sentences, I began to accumulate nicknames on the street. I suppose it's nice to be well known, but not by these particular people, who would harm me if they could. To the skels involved in the drug trade I was the "Ice Princess," because I kept my cool and the defendants couldn't intimidate me, and maybe also because in court I insisted on decorum and on using proper language, of course. When one defendant asked me, "Hey, what language you speakin'?" I smiled and facetiously informed him that my parents had spent a lot of money to make me speak this way. But I don't think any defendant would understand me any better if I used their street language. To them I was also "the Princess of Darkness" for giving lengthy sentences, and "Judge

*See article by Murray Weiss, criminal justice editor, in the *New York Post*, March 18, 2002, in which he refers to New York County District Attorney Robert Morgenthau as saying that in lowering crime, the single most important assault by his office was on drug gangs such as the Wild Cowboys, the Purple Top Crew, and the Jheri Curls, among others. These were all HIU prosecutions and my cases.

232," supposedly the number of years in prison that I meted out to one defendant. Actually, the sentence given to Rafi Martinez was 213 years, but some defendants apparently felt, "What's a few years here and there?" Corrections officers told me that some of my longer sentences had been posted by defendants inside the holding pens for my court, probably to warn others of what might be coming their way.

For a long time, I have also been told that cops sometimes threaten potential defendants with having to appear before me (taking my name in vain?) in order to get them to confess or cooperate. I hope it's an apocryphal tale! I believe they similarly use the numbers associated with our courtroom—we are Part 88 now and in room 1313 on the thirteenth floor of the 100 Centre Street building—to convince potential defendants that their destiny will be decided in that numerically mysterious and significant place. (Fortunately, I am not a triskaidekaphobe!) Law clerks and others in the appellate division, who regularly have to review the transcripts of my trials, have, I am also told, dubbed me "Xena, Warrior Princess" because I so frequently argue with the lawyers and never shy away from such fights. United States Attorney Mary Jo White, a wonderfully able prosecutor and person, couldn't stop laughing one day when she telephoned to alert me that her investigators had taken down a gang selling glassines of heroin with a new brand name and image on it: "25 to Life" and a portrait of a blond-haired female judge who looked just like me. She sent over one of the glassines, and my colleagues in the courtroom framed it for me to hang on my robing room wall. People in the police department told friends in the media about the new heroin brand, and it became a story in the national and even the international press; a friend sent me a clip about it from Australia.

Evidently, on the street there was a lot of wondering as to why I would hand out such tough sentences. The obvious explanation—that the crimes merited such punishment—did not satisfy some criminals, so they made up a story. In this street myth, I had a daughter who became a drug addict and who overdosed and died; so distraught was I over this loss that I vowed to take my vengeance out on the drug-dealing defendants who were convicted in my court, by sentencing them to a collective million years in prison. The point of this tale was supposedly that a million years was such a large number that I needed to sentence individual defendants to longer and longer terms to reach it.

Of course, this story has no basis in fact; but perhaps it makes some defendants feel better as they serve their long sentences.

TAMING THE
WILD COWBOYS

Forty-one defendants. Forty murders. Hundreds of families torn apart. Thousands of men, women, and children addicted. A neighborhood held hostage . . . The Wild Cowboys

By far the worst drug gang and the most complex, chilling, and challenging drug gang case over which I presided was that of the Wild Cowboys.

Taming the Wild Cowboys was a massive job because the gang's criminal activities extended over Manhattan, the Bronx, and Brooklyn. For the first time in memory, the district attorney's offices in all three jurisdictions were cooperatively involved in a prosecution. It was also massive because so many crimes were involved. The Wild Cowboys were believed responsible for as many as forty murders, although the prosecutors were able to obtain sufficient evidence to charge the defendants with only ten of these murders and with myriad other counts of drug dealing, weapons possession, assaults, and attempted murders. The Wild Cowboys' reign of terror lasted from 1986 to September 1993, when the first mass arrests brought the majority of what would eventually amount to forty-one glowering defendants into my courtroom.*

*See Stone, Michael, *Gangbusters* (Doubleday, 2000); and Jackall, Robert, *The Wild Cowboys, Urban Marauders and the Forces of Order* (Harvard University Press, 1997), for two interesting books about the Cowboys.

How does such a gang start? How does it recruit members? How does it become so violent? How does it continue in operation once its crimes become known to law enforcement? The long investigation and trial of the Wild Cowboys gives us a glimpse into some answers to these questions.

Nelson Sepulveda, born in the United States to immigrants from the Dominican Republic, and a dropout from a New York City high school, began in the drug trade by buying prepackaged crack from a neighborhood supplier and then selling the vials out of a ground-floor apartment in the Mott Haven section of the Bronx. It was early 1986, the beginning of the crack epidemic, and there were plenty of customers. Nelson hired a few friends, a fifteen-year-old from across the hall and a thirteen-year-old from an upstairs apartment, and other underage kids, as lookouts and runners. After a few months, when the sales were not going well enough, Nelson brought in his younger brother Lenin, named for the Russian revolutionary.

Lenny was street smart and violent. He proved to be an excellent sales motivator and manager, organizing the operation. There were shift managers to work eight hours at a time supervising pitchers and lookouts, spot managers to oversee individual sales locations, enforcers (all armed with semiautomatic weapons) to guard the movements of money and drugs and to keep the pitchers, lookouts, and managers in line, and kids to fetch both innocuous supplies like rubber bands and to transport drugs, sometimes in their backpacks or lunch boxes. Soon the first spot was pulling in much more money, and Lenny became the gang's leader, as Nelson deferred to his brother's obvious abilities. Old school friends started coming to them for jobs—Dominicans who, like the Sepulveda brothers, had been in trouble since their early teens, had stolen cars, had dropped out of school or been expelled—Nelson had punched out a dean—and had all hung around on street corners smoking blunts. They went into the drug trade because their families were nonexistent or dysfunctional, they had no guidance from schools, churches, or any organized group of adults, and without education they had no prospects of legitimate jobs. Those who moved effortlessly into the crack sales business included José "Paqualito" Llaca, a violent man who loved to fool with guns; Daniel "Fat Danny" Rincon, who intimidated others by his bulk; and Wilfredo "Platano" De Los Angeles, known as "the Dark Man" for his brooding appearance, intensity, and tendency to erupt into violence. The gang was initially called Lenny's Boys but would become known and feared as the Wild Cowboys.

Initial police raids resulted in the arrest of one man with a shotgun, bulletproof vests, and ninety-one vials of crack, but this did not stop the crack-selling operation, which the brothers simply moved out of the apartment and into an inner courtyard. When that location was shut down by the New York City Housing Authority, they transferred to another building, to a concealed, second-floor balcony at 348 Beekman Avenue, which they called "the Hole." Lookouts and escape and disposal routes allowed the gang to evade police attempts to shut them down. The Hole remained open for business 24/7, but traffic was best on weekends and on the days when welfare checks were distributed. A bundle of a hundred crack vials would be sold, on average, every five to ten minutes. By 1987, profit from the Hole was $30,000 a week. The next year, the brothers began to buy unprocessed cocaine and cook it into crack themselves, and the profit soared. The Sepulvedas hired a black limousine to take them around, while Platano drove a white Mercedes-Benz. The gang opened more spots; managers moved up to supervisors and angled to open their own spots.

As the profit increased, so did competition and the level of violence. Enforcers and managers would climb on rooftops to take target practice with their guns, seeing how close they could come to pedestrians without actually hitting them with bullets, shooting out light bulbs and windshields. Neighborhood kids got used to hearing gunfire on the streets, to seeing "cheese lines" waiting to buy crack, to watching drug transactions in every hallway and in many apartments in the surrounding buildings. The gang overran the neighborhood, using other people's apartments as stash houses, cooking galleys, crash pads, and hideouts while intimidating tenants into subservience. Pitchers who didn't work hard enough had their fingers smashed with bricks. "Bottlers," the girls who bottled the crack, were beaten if suspected of "tapping," taking some of the crack for themselves. When two sister pitchers objected to storing crack bundles in their apartment and wanted to stop pitching, Platano ordered an associate to shoot one in the head; she survived, did not tell the police who had shot her—"Snitches get stitches" was a gang motto—and on her return from the hospital went back to selling crack for the gang. Another female pitcher who wanted to stop had a shot fired at her through the peephole of her apartment. Pitchers who did not start out as crackheads soon became addicts and sometimes became prostitutes or muggers to support their crack habits.*

When lower-level gang members were picked up by the police, Lenny and Nelson hired experienced lawyers who got them out on bail. If middle-level people were arrested and scheduled for trial, the gang harassed and intimidated witnesses until they retracted their stories so that the cases against the gang members could not be prosecuted. After a while, when gang members were arrested they would laugh in the face of the

*Most crackheads do not commit crimes that require concentration or take time or planning, as their need for a fix gets in the way.

police and brag that they'd be out again very soon—and they were.

In the spring of 1989, a former spot manager for the gang, a close friend of Lenny and Paqualito's who had gone out on his own but continued to deliver *cuentas* and cocaine for the Cowboys, was murdered, and the gang decided to take revenge on the rival crack dealers they believed were responsible. On September 3, 1989, in a wild street chase and shoot-out, Lenny, Paqualito, and Victor Mercedes, Fat Danny's half-brother, killed two men from the rival organization and wounded two others. The killings became known as "the Double." One victim was executed in a car on the street in front of an apartment building where a young Cowboy associate, Michael Cruz, was visiting his girlfriend; drawn by the sight of people he knew firing guns, the teenager went downstairs to view the dead body in the car up close before the police arrived.

Michael was a member of the Morales-Cruz family, an entire family lured into criminality by the Cowboys, a family that became some of the gang's most poignant victims.* Elizabeth Morales, a single mother, was working nights as a housekeeper in a nursing home when the gang started seducing her children: Tito, the oldest at eighteen, Michael at fifteen, Iris at twelve, and Joey, the youngest at age ten. Tito began as a pitcher, Michael as a lookout (for unmarked police cars) who would take Iris up on the rooftops with him for company, and Joey by doing errands, going to the store to fetch rubber bands for *cuentas* and snacks for the managers. The gang paid Tito for every bundle he sold and plied the other kids with toys, ice cream, fancy clothes, music cassettes, $50 bills, and rides on the back of motorcycles. Platano liked Elizabeth Morales's lasagna and hired her to cook meals for the gang. At first, the gang's attention was

*See two excellent articles about the family, by Robin Pogrebin, in *The New York Times*: "A Family on the Run," September 24, 1995, and "Guns, Terror and Testimony," October 1, 1995.

pleasant and brought in some money. Soon, however, Elizabeth Morales objected and lectured her children about associating with the Cowboys, but there was nothing she could do to prevent Platano and the other Cowboy managers from putting her kids to work at illegal activities and from taking over the Morales apartment and using it as a clubhouse. When Elizabeth Morales told Lenny that she did not want her kids dealing drugs, he retorted, "If they want to live in a man's world, they have to do a man's job." She didn't like Lenny's assertion, but, as she later said, "I couldn't just pick up and move, I had to stay and fight it. Yet I couldn't fight it, because [the gang] had the money. They went over lots of mothers' heads."* She herself also became a worker in the organization, as a bottler.

Detective Mark Tebbens, a tall, imposing, and determined man assigned to a Bronx precinct, began an investigation into the gang in the wake of the Double, and eventually Paqualito and another of the shooters were arrested and sent to jail. Because of what was later shown to be false testimony and intimidation of witnesses, their convictions brought sentences of less than two years apiece. Lenny was not apprehended and the gang's activities continued, including murders and attempted murders that the police seemed unable to curtail. But Tebbens persisted.

When the shooters returned to the streets they went right back to work, joining Fat Danny in managing new locations or "spots." Members of the Cowboys would often be arrested for selling crack or carrying guns, but higher-ranking members would pay their bail or arrange for lawyers to handle their cases and get them out and back on the street quickly.

While Lenny was in prison on another charge, Nelson plotted the gang's worst multiple murder, that of a rival gang selling "treys"—vials of crack for $3 apiece—undercutting the Wild

---

*Quoted in Pogrebin, *op. cit.*

Cowboys' $5-a-vial operation. Nelson obtained the services of the hit man known as Francisco "Freddy Krueger" Medina and bought enough machine guns to do the job from supplier José "El Feo" Reyes. On the night of December 15, 1991, Nelson, Platano, Fat Danny, and other Cowboys, among them Stanley "Trigger" Tukes, accompanied by Freddy Krueger, went to the alleyway where the rival gang conducted its sales. Nelson handed out machine guns from his knapsack and then, at Freddy Krueger's request, left the rest up to him. Lookouts were on rooftops, communicating to the shooters by walkie-talkie. Other Cowboys positioned cars so they could arrive quickly at the location before the intended victims could scatter and leave just as quickly.

While Nelson waited out the event on a rooftop, his men entered the alleyway and started firing, killing four and injuring others. The injured included a crack customer, Janice Bruington, who later testified at trial that she was heartsick to see Stanley Tukes, whom she had known since he was a child, killing another young man whom she'd always known, Amp Green, the seventeen-year-old who was in charge of the spot for the rival gang. After Bruington was shot, she survived by rolling under a car and pretending to be dead. The Cowboys pursued the other injured people, firing at them as they lay on the ground. Before Green died he told Iris Cruz and others who tried to aid him that Stanley had shot him. These brutal murders had about them the air of a massacre and would be referred to forever, both in the gang's lore and by law enforcement, as "the Quad."

The Cowboys were impressed with themselves when the Quad made the front pages of the newspapers. But after the Quad, police investigation of the gang intensified. Stanley Tukes and Platano were arrested. Nelson fled to the Dominican Republic. A Bronx grand jury heard testimony from several witnesses and Cowboy associates, some of whom, like Janice Bruington, lied about what they had seen because they feared reprisals. The gang's activities continued and even expanded to Brooklyn, where they soon resulted in another murder.

Feeling invincible and seemingly able to withstand even intense police pressure, the Cowboys became more brazen and brutal.

On a late spring night in 1992, Paqualito caught Tito Cruz, who had stolen a bag containing cash and crack from the gang, and pistol-whipped him. Then he went to the Morales-Cruz apartment to get the drugs back and told Elizabeth Morales that they had better return all his drugs and money by midnight—or else. He waved his gun at her as she tried to protect her three-year-old granddaughter, who asked if they were all going to die. As the witching hour approached, Elizabeth Morales tried to find the drugs, but her sons had sold most of them and the money was already spent; she gathered what drugs and money she could and gave them to Paqualito.

She knew her family was running out of time. They had no idea when Paqualito would strike, but they knew he would. She had received warnings from other gang members about the danger they faced from him, but no one was willing to help her or her family. They were on their own. Friendships did not last long in the Cowboys' world; you did what you could not to cross any one of them and hoped to stay alive.

So that very night, Elizabeth Morales gathered up the family and they ran, taking almost nothing so that no one would know that they were leaving. Thirteen people crowded into one car; the family made it to a shelter, and shortly thereafter Detective Tebbens took on the Morales-Cruz family almost as his own.

Yet somehow the Cowboys seemed to find them wherever they went. First it was the drive-by shooting of Elizabeth Morales's son Michael in Brooklyn. Then the family was moved to another location and that apartment was broken into while they were out. At that point, Tebbens moved them out of the city, but even in the suburbs they weren't safe. Two Dominican men grabbed Elizabeth Morales one day as she walked home from the store, put a knife to her throat, and told her not to "talk" anymore and that they knew where she lived. Nevertheless, the Morales-Cruz family continued to cooperate. At this point they really had no choice; they realized that even if they stopped cooperating with law enforcement, the Cowboys would find them and kill them.

The role of the Morales-Cruz family in the investigation of the Cowboys was critical. Iris, Joey, and Michael each provided testimony and gave details about the quadruple murders as well as other homicides and the day-to-day operations of the Hole. Joey and Iris's involvement in the gang as children under the age of sixteen also established the critical element of the conspiracy in the first-degree charge against most of the defendants on trial.

It was February 26, 1993. Not half a mile away from the courthouse and not an hour earlier, the World Trade Center had been damaged by a truck bomb, with attendant chaos. In my courtroom we were just finishing up with the Jheri Curls, and while the jury was deliberating in the adjacent jury room, the courtroom was a strange sight—lined with exhibits from the trial, photographs of gang members in their distinctive Jheri Curl hairdos, charts of their organizational structure, plus some guns that had become exhibits in the case. Also, in the midst of these exhibits I had just married a couple—they said they didn't mind, maybe because it was a second marriage for her, a third for him—and some guests from the wedding were still hanging about in their finery . . . when the court officers brought in one of the leaders of the Wild Cowboys, Lenny Sepulveda, in handcuffs and leg irons, along with his lawyer and various family members.

Lenny stared at me. He looked nasty and violent, exuding menace, cursing me under his breath. I've seen plenty of defendants like that: Their stares, their restlessness, their whole beings, convey a sense of evil. You would never choose to be in their presence.

Lenny had been brought in on a charge of jumping bail in a gun case, but I knew that he and his brother Nelson were accused of masterminding as many as forty murders throughout New York City in addition to operating a major drug organization. But my main concern at that moment was to make certain that no disruptions would affect the deliberations of the Jheri Curls jury in the adjoining room. Lenny probably expected to walk out the front door of the courtroom after the bail argument. Why shouldn't he have believed that? It had happened so many times before to him and to the other Cowboys. If Fat Danny was out on bail on the Quad and Nelson had managed to escape to the Dominican Republic without the authorities doing anything about it, why shouldn't he, Lenny, be able to walk out on a mere bail-jumping charge?

So when I announced that for obvious reasons I was remanding Lenny, he had a little tantrum. "Fuck this!" he shouted as he was being taken out of the courtroom and back into the pens.

I've heard worse, but the issue was control, so I couldn't let it go unchallenged.

"What did you say? Bring him back in here." The court officers brought him back. He was still staring insolently at me when I addressed him directly. "You're in my courtroom, now; you may be used to being king on the streets, but you're here now and you're going to obey my rules. So if you curse in my courtroom ever again, you won't be back; you'll just hear the trial as it's piped into your jail cell."

I had to exert control, because I knew that prior to this moment the Wild Cowboys had been able to circumvent the system on every occasion. As I've pointed out, over the years, they had been indicted in other jurisdictions for serious crimes but managed to get out on bail each time and to terrorize witnesses into not testifying. I was determined that they would not get around the system this time. Lenny muttered an apology, and the judicial process went on.

Ironically, Lenny was confined that day in the same holding pen behind the courtroom as Rafi Martinez, the lead Jheri Curl. I have always believed that Rafi filled Lenny in on me, because the next time Lenny appeared in court he was significantly more subdued.

Nelson remained in hiding in the Dominican Republic. Fat Danny and Paqualito still ran the gang and its drug-dealing operations, and they continued to commit violent acts—murders and beatings. It would be another six months until, in September of 1993, the NYPD and the coalition of DA's offices would be ready to arrest several dozen members of the gang in a huge one-day sweep.

I still remember vividly the rows and rows of street-tough, angry defendants, in handcuffs and leg irons, staring at me in defiance as they were arraigned. In early 1994, the extradition of Nelson and Paqualito from the Dominican Republic—itself no easy task—brought to forty-one the total number of Wild Cowboys taken off the streets. Now the prosecution could begin in earnest.

The first shock for me was the request from HIU to have me accept the cooperation agreements of Lenny and Nelson. I had no idea of the discussions that had been going on between the prosecutors and the Sepulveda brothers and their attorneys, but HIU was worried that I might object to proposed sentences that would not result in Lenny and Nelson being put away forever. They were right about that. I was initially very, very skeptical about deals that would keep Lenny and Nelson in jail for only, respectively, twenty-five years to life and twenty-two years to life. Those sentences for the masterminds of an alleged forty murders? No way!

It was at the request of the defense lawyers that HIU came to me with their sales pitch. They asked rhetorically, Why flip the leaders of such a violent gang, charged with ten murders? Because, they answered, it was the only way to obtain their testimony, which was considered critical to taking off the streets forever the most violent members of the gang—Paqualito, Platano, Fat Danny, Stanley Tukes, and Victor Mercedes, thugs who in many ways were more hair-trigger violent than the brothers—and to learn all the facts about all of the gang's crimes. The Sepulvedas' information, HIU insisted, would also help federal and state law enforcement to successfully prosecute drug supplier Jose "El Feo" Reyes, hit man Francisco "Freddy Krueger" Medina, and the Cowboys' gun supplier, Raymond Polanco. In the end, I decided that my faith in HIU, which they had earned over the years, warranted my agreeing to the deals for Lenny and Nelson.

The prosecutors also told me that Lenny was willing to admit and plead guilty to the David Cargill murder. HIU's investigation into the Cowboys had been intertwined with their investigation into the murder of Cargill, a nineteen-year-old college student, in a drive-by shooting on the West Side Highway in May 1991. Law enforcement had been unable to solve that murder; rumors had the Cowboys involved in it, but since there was no drug-related tie to Cargill, investigators had been stumped as to why this shooting had occurred and why the Cowboys would have done it. Lenny's plea to the Cargill murder was one of the most chilling allocutions that I have ever heard. A plea allocution is the verbal interchange between the court and the defendant when a guilty plea is entered. The defendant must admit his guilt and may be asked to recount his crime in detail. Basically, David Cargill was murdered because he was in the wrong place at the wrong time. Lenny and some other Cowboys, as well as Polanco, were in cars on the West Side Highway, returning from a nightclub, when Cargill's truck cut off one of the Cowboys' cars. Lenny had gotten a new gun from Polanco that night and decided to test it out—on the truck that had cut them off. On the first attempt to shoot at the truck, the gun jammed, but on the second attempt a bullet from that gun killed Cargill. The saddest part of the allocution was watching the Cargill family listening to Lenny. Normally, the courtroom is sealed for cooperation agreement pleas, but upon a request from the prosecution and on the consent of defense counsel, I made an exception so that the Cargill family could be present. They needed to know who had killed their son and why, in order to achieve closure and end the speculation that had surrounded his death.

Rumors about Lenny and Nelson's possible cooperation spread among the other Cowboys, but no other defendant knew for sure, since the brothers' cooperation agreements were sealed. These rumors pushed some middle managers into pleas and cooperation agreements themselves. Prior to trial I was also able to extract a few of the minor players charged in the Cowboys' offenses, those who seemed more to be victims than real criminals, and to find alternative sentencing and drug treatment for them.

By the time the trial began, just nine of the original forty-one defendants remained. They were Paqualito, Platano, Fat Danny, Stanley Tukes, Victor Mercedes, and four others, all charged with murder . . . and much more. Over half of the original defendants had pleaded guilty, with the remaining defendants to be tried after the conclusion of this trial.

Jury selection was difficult and lengthy, as in all of my drug gang and other long cases; one potential juror was John F. Kennedy Jr., then the editor of *George* magazine, who was excused because he was unable to serve for an expected six months trial and, in any event, didn't want to. The difficulty of the jury selection process was heightened because the defendants, as was their right, chose to be present as prospective jurors were questioned—instead of remaining at the defense table and allowing their attorneys to ask the most personal questions of the prospective jurors off the record, at the bench, as the law also permits—and to stare in evil fashion at everyone. Their intimidation tactics, I'm sure, did frighten away some who might otherwise have served. But eventually a jury was picked that included, among others, a schoolteacher, a postal employee, and an engineer. In what was somewhat unusual for a long trial, all the jurors were employed. Two-thirds were black and Latino; this statistic was considered a somewhat important factor, since the trial was taking place when the O. J. Simpson case was in the news. Nicole Brown Simpson had been murdered in June of 1994, and the Simpson case was in the pretrial phase in October of 1994 as the trial of the Cowboys commenced. At the beginning, no one in the media was paying attention to our case, in which nine defendants were accused of ten murders and suspected of forty, because none of our defendants were celebrities.

It was mid-October. Opening statements were being given in the Wild Cowboys trial. During a short recess, I was informed of a new threat.

"Judge, I'm sorry to tell you this," a detective reported, "but the Cowboys have made a death threat against you and your family."

"Are you serious?" (Why do I always seem to be asking this?)

"I'm afraid so, Judge. Dan Brownell [the lead HIU prosecutor] has been threatened, too. And Mark Tebbens. Members of

Intell have been briefed, and they're taking these threats very seriously. I think by now you know how bad these guys are."

My heart sank: I absolutely and in great detail did know how very bad "these guys" were. The idea that my family was now included in the threat made me almost apoplectic. No one would give me any more information, lest it compromise my trying of the case. But the threat was considered so immediate and so grim that we had to call my son's school to have him taken right out of class, brought to the principal's office, and instructed to wait there until two detectives showed up to guard him.

That night there was more brass in our apartment than I'd ever seen in a private room. Gathered to talk to Fred and me were a dozen high-ranking people from the NYPD and other organizations. John Miller, then the spokesperson for the NYPD (and now a leading reporter for ABC News), had already told me that the department was going to create a special squad to protect the entire family. Now the brass gave us the nuts and bolts of how the protection would work and a few—very few—details as to why they were taking these extraordinary measures. One, as I later learned, was that the contract on us had gone to the hit man known on the streets as Freddy Krueger. That really worried them.

I hadn't paid attention to this nickname before, but I came to learn that in the horror movie *Nightmare on Elm Street* the villain, named Freddy Krueger, invades people's dreams and kills them in the worst ways they can imagine. (I don't go to horror movies—there's horror every day in my courtroom.) Law enforcement's information was that Fat Danny and some of the Cowboys had given the contract on me to this Freddy Krueger, who was known to have murdered a dozen people. None of these details were shared with me until after the trial.

To shield us from this killer, the NYPD had prepared round-the-clock, full-force protection for our entire family. Detectives would be with us continuously, we would have "security devices" with which to summon aid at a moment's notice, there would be cops in front of our apartment building and an "advance team" if we wanted to go somewhere. I was overwhelmed by the completeness of the security. All I could think of was that it reinforced the notion that the threat was very, very serious. And I was truly appreciative that law enforcement would go to such lengths to protect my family as well as me personally.

We lived in a Park Avenue co-op; and very soon the co-op's board objected to uniformed police standing in front of the building, another security measure that had been implemented. The NYPD agreed to have the cops sit in patrol cars rather than have them stand around and be more visible. But some members of the co-op board were also annoyed by what they claimed had taken place on that first night: A police SWAT team had climbed to the roof, then rappelled down after assessing our building's security—in the process, supposedly freaking out people in other apartments in our building and in adjacent buildings. I had heard and seen nothing of such activity, and the police denied that it had occurred. But a year or so later, after I had become friendly with the lieutenant in charge of our protection "detail," I asked him whether the tale of the SWAT team on the roof was true. He just laughed, which I took as a clear admission that it was.

When the brass cleared out of our apartment after several hours that first night, Fred and I needed to talk.

"Look, I want to keep doing what I've been doing on the bench. But now our family is involved. Threats like these are how violent criminals like the Cowboys take over the justice system and are so seldom brought to trial. They are entitled to a fair trial, and I can give them that—we can't let them beat the system. But if you tell me you don't want me to go on working these cases, that you're worried about our safety, or you think that the kids might be in real danger—then I won't do it."

"Don't be absurd," Fred said without missing a beat. "You can *never* give in to people like these. You have to go on doing your job." He pointed out that the police department's massive protection for all of us should enable us to proceed with our lives—safely. It was late at night, but we called in our kids and told them in outline form about the threat and the protective measures. Our younger son was in high school and would be the most affected.

"Mom," he said, "I'm proud of you and the work you do, and you have to keep on doing it. Sure, it'll be a pain in the ass to have cops with me all the time, but I'll deal with it if it's necessary for you to keep doing your job. It's really important: we can't let the bad guys win."

I've never been prouder of my family or more grateful for their incredible support.

Emerging from the building the next morning, I was amazed to see not only two detectives and a black unmarked car, but also another car for backup and a gigantic armored truck, which trailed behind us on the trip downtown. "Are you expecting an ambush? An army?" I asked the lieutenant in charge of the detail, a very nice guy but ultraserious. He didn't answer but had a few requests.

"We're going to need your blood type, your husband's, your children's, the names of all of your doctors, the closest hospitals, people to notify in emergencies."

I was stunned. Obviously the cops thought they might have to use this sort of information, which meant that the situation was even graver than I'd thought. No wonder they had us being followed by the equivalent of a tank!

When we reached the court building, there was new security inside and outside my courtroom: bomb-sniffing dogs and the detectives who handle them. From that day on, the dogs were brought to the courtroom each morning before the start of business. Alex, Teresa, and I all loved dogs, and after the dogs had done their work in the courtroom, we'd get down on the floor and play with them. Other antibomb measures were put into the courtroom; they're still in use today, so I can't discuss the details.

The trial of the Cowboys proceeded. During it, one defendant asked a court officer if my law clerk Teresa was my daughter; he might have thought so because it was clear to any onlooker that we were very close. The manner of his question was threatening, so police protection was extended to Teresa for a while as well.

Being surrounded by security is a strange and suffocating feeling. People accompany you everywhere. You usually travel by car because walking outside is considered dangerous. Advance teams go into restaurants, sometimes with bomb-sniffing dogs, before you make your entrance. No taking a stroll for coffee with your husband without prior notice—cops walk behind you, and a car with more cops in it trails you slowly. The situation forces you to become more aware of things you usually take for granted—privacy, spontaneity, the degree to which each of us in a civilized society respects the right of others to live as they choose. To retain some privacy, when you ride in the car you and your family have only curtailed conversations and avoid mentioning anything personal. The first weekend, we wanted to go alone to our house on Long Island, but there was information that someone had tried to get the make and license plate of our car, so the police had to accompany us; they parked their car prominently in our driveway and slept in shifts in a spare bedroom. Our weekends had been our time to relax, but that became less possible.

One evening we had tickets for the Broadway play *Angels in America*, and the police "detail" had to accompany us inside the theater. They were looking forward to a Broadway show; but, to their dismay and ours, the play included very realistic acts of simulated anal sodomy on stage as well as anti-American sentiments. The detectives were appalled: What sort of weird, ultra-liberal perverts were they protecting?

One day, an alert was sent to us about a threat from a different drug-related source, a Colombian drug cartel, against certain people in New York connected to narcotics prosecutions, such as the city's narcotics prosecutor, myself, and a few others in law enforcement. The police department told me that over the coming weekend they would have an extra car watching our apartment. During that weekend we happened to be at home and peeked out the window. I couldn't find the unmarked car and remarked to Fred, "Gee, these guys are good," impressed with their ability to blend in without being noticed—until Monday, that is, when the police called and apologized: The unmarked car had been watching the wrong address all weekend.

Get a gun, the cops urged me. Judges are allowed by law to carry guns, and to satisfy the brass, I obtained a secondhand .38 and took some training—enough to convince my instructors that I could pull the trigger and not close my eyes at the same time. But was it really necessary to have a gun when I was accompanied at all times by trained detectives packing nine-millimeter Glocks?

Nine defendants and thirteen lawyers. Seven years' worth of crimes. The logistics to handle all this was complex—extra court officers, extra tables, seventy-five witnesses, hundreds of documents to be placed into evidence, everything taking a long time because moving that number of defendants around itself takes time, as does each bench conference with a dozen lawyers. Each defendant was a frightening individual, and the whole gang together presented the spectacle of a group of seasoned killers who would not have hesitated to murder everyone in the courtroom if the opportunity arose. It was clear from the get-go that this case was going to take all of my concentration and focus just to keep it under control and on track.

The lead prosecutor, Dan Brownell, was one of the mainstays of the homicide investigation unit. A bright, articulate man, he was laid-back on the surface but intense underneath—a "sleeping tiger." He was so laconic that there were times during the trial when I kept waiting for the prosecution to object to certain things that the defense was doing. When Brownell did not, I had to call him up to the bench and ask if he still had a pulse— a query to which he had, justifiably, a number of sarcastic responses. I wanted him to be more active in protesting various defense maneuvers so I wouldn't have to be. Lori Grifa, from the Brooklyn District Attorney's Office, was as intense and high-strung as Brownell was taciturn. Don Hill, from the Bronx, was somewhere in between in temperament, and the three prosecutors' skills were complementary and allowed them to divide up the monumental task of prosecuting all the defendants successfully. Hill, for example, had lived with trying to solve the Quad murders for more than two years, so it was logical for him to begin the prosecution's opening statement with a recitation of the most horrific of the gang's many crimes.

On the defense side there were ten lawyers, among them some who had appeared before me frequently and some I'd never met before. Two from the Bronx were rather unkempt. One experienced defense lawyer made certain that his client came into court washed and shaved, his hair neat, and wearing clean-cut clothes; and that he kept his distance from his co-defendants so he would appear more likable than they did. This ploy did serve to set him apart. Another lawyer was fighting hard for his client until his wife died in midtrial; he could not continue, so the "extra" attorney took over for him for a period of time (the extra attorney had been provided because we had unfortunately known that the wife's death was likely to occur at any time). The only female defense attorney developed a close relationship with her client, one of the most vicious of the Cowboy enforcers. Its potential for repercussions was made manifest when this lawyer received a threat from the family of one of the murder victims and her client told her he'd take care of it. Another familiar presence on the defense side was a bulldog of a former Legal Aid lawyer, whom I knew to always fight hard for his clients. But even he, and the lawyers for the defense in general, came to feel over the course of the trial that the evidence against their clients was so overwhelming and the magnitude of their evil so great that success was unimaginable. The gang's evil wore them down emotionally, as it did Alex, Teresa, and me. Because the tension level in the courtroom seemed multiplied by the large number of defendants, every evening, even if things had gone well during the day in court, we would all be emotionally drained.

One of the charges against eight of the nine defendants was conspiracy in the first degree. This charge carries a maximum sentence of twenty-five years to life. What differentiates it from conspiracy in the second degree, the more frequent charge, is the participation of "children" under sixteen.

In fact, the gang's use of children, which emerged from the testimony of the witnesses, was one of the aspects of their total lack of morality that I found most disturbing. These defendants had seduced and scared the neighborhood children into becoming part of their operation and, all too frequently, turned them into addicts as well.* The Wild Cowboys had ruined many young lives, held whole families hostage, taken over entire housing projects. It was also stunning to learn that every defendant, and nearly every witness connected to the gang, had a long criminal history but had spent very little time in jail. The

*Federal officials in Illinois recently charged thirty-five people with running an international heroin and cocaine smuggling ring, using as couriers women charged with renting babies from poor families so they could transport the drugs in cans of baby formula. This may be a new low. *The New York Times*, December 15, 2001.

defense, of course, by their cross-examinations, wrung from the witnesses all such negative information. They made certain that the jury understood that the cooperators, and even witnesses like Iris Cruz, not only had criminal records but had participated in the gang's crimes. The Morales-Cruz family, not incidentally, continued to be threatened by the gang during the trial; eventually, as discussed earlier, they had to move a dozen times before finding relative safety.

The prosecution called seventy-five witnesses in all. One of the first was Freddie Sendra. He provided the jury with crucial background testimony about the Cowboys from his days with them at George Washington High School and set the stage for all the later witnesses. However, he had a lengthy criminal history, and some of his prior statements were riddled with inconsistencies. His cross-examination by nine defense attorneys was grueling for everyone. I allowed the defense attorneys great latitude since Sendra was one of the first cooperating witnesses to testify.

As expected, tarnishing the credibility of the prosecution's cooperating witnesses was the main theme of the defense strategy, as it is in all drug gang trials. So much of the evidence against the Cowboys was coming from the cooperators that it was imperative for the defense to impeach those witnesses. The other main strategy was more unique to this case—to concede that the individual defendants had dealt drugs, but to argue that they had done so independently of one another and did not "act in concert" or participate in a conspiracy. The defense implied that there had actually been another conspiracy—that the police, prosecutors, and everyone else in law enforcement had illegally conspired to "get" these defendants.

If the implied conspiracy had been true, the prosecution would certainly have presented the jury with a more "perfect" case. This was not a perfect case—no gang case is. Given the nature of the crimes and the nature of the witnesses, no gang case ever will be.

On direct examination, the prosecution asked each cooperating witness to detail the terms of his or her cooperation agreement as well as any prior criminal history and "bad acts." A good prosecutor will always do this, as you don't want the jury to have the perception that you have kept something from them and allowed defense counsel to raise the issue for the first time on cross-examination. And of course, the prosecution had prepared the jury, by their questions in voir dire, to expect what they heard.

The cooperation agreement and the prior criminal history of a witness are two major defense impeachment tools. It can be powerful to show that the witness is getting a "sweetheart" deal. Defense counsel goes into detail as to what jail sentence the cooperator could have received had he or she not cooperated—in most cases significantly longer than what the sentence will be if he or she testifies truthfully pursuant to the cooperation agreement. The cross-examination on this point also allows defense counsel to let the jurors know what sentence the defendant on trial is facing—that is implied, not stated openly, since sentence is not to be considered by the jurors in reaching their verdict. The prosecution, on redirect, must make clear to the jury that the witness will get this deal only if he or she tells the truth.

Sendra remained on the stand for a week. He was followed by Janice Bruington, the fortyish crackhead and longtime resident of the neighborhood who had survived the Quad, after being shot, by rolling herself under a car and playing dead. Defense counsel hammered at her very hard because she, like many of the witnesses, had initially lied in her statements to the authorities—and they wanted the jury to believe that she was lying now. But Ms. Bruington insisted that wasn't so and recalled that her son had told her not to be scared because the

Cowboys could no longer get to her and that she should tell what she knew. "'Mommy, listen, you know, tell the truth,'" she quoted her son as saying and added, "Nobody forced me to tell the truth. I'm telling the truth on my own, because I'm tired. I want to get on with my life. I'm scared to go to this place, that place . . . for so many years. I need a life now." She started crying silently. Her emotionality and unexpected tears showed the jury that, contrary to what defense counsel had implied, what this beaten-down, terrified woman was saying about the Cowboys was the absolute truth.

Later on, I had to caution a second defense attorney to prevent badgering of another female witness; actually, in these instances and others, overly aggressive defense questioning rebounded against the defense, provoking sympathy from the jury for the witnesses rather than impeaching the witnesses' credibility.

Perhaps the most emotionally charged of the prosecution's witnesses against the Cowboys were the members of the Morales-Cruz family, especially Iris, because she seemed the one true innocent in the case, even though she too had a criminal record. By the time Iris took the stand she was a young woman; but as she testified, it was easy to imagine Iris five to eight years earlier, when, she related, Platano would flatten her against a stairwell wall and tell her he was going to make sure that she lost her virginity to the gang. It was easy to picture this beautiful young girl as an unwitting witness to several phases of the Quad shootings, eventually descending the stairs from her apartment into the alleyway to cradle in her arms the head of her dying classmate Amp Green. "He was saying, 'Don't let me die.' He kept on repeating it. I was there, and then I looked to see if the girl was alive. And she wasn't. She was just there, and she had this . . . yellow thing in her a hand, a top, like, Yellow Top. And I was looking to see if she was alive or saying something. She wasn't."

Iris's testimony and that of the other members of her family really got to me. The Morales-Cruz witnesses conveyed, as no outsider could, the sense of how completely the Wild Cowboys had ruined the lives of everyone in their family—a family that typified many others in the project and in the neighborhood whom the gang had totally destroyed.

The continuing danger from the Cowboys was underlined when, in jail, some of them beat up a fellow detainee once they learned he was going to have to appear before a certain judge— me—because they feared he might "snitch" on them. The assaulted defendant was actually coming to court to be sentenced and, prior to being beaten up, had never intended to testify; because of the Cowboys' own conduct, the People gained another witness.

My protection continued during the trial. I was bothered by the fact that virtually no other judge called me to commiserate or to support me for staying on a tough case in the face of death threats. Some judges, I was told, were jealous of the publicity I received because of the threats. When the *New York Post* did a story with photos about the protection, Fred and I were more than incredulous, we were enraged, because in addition to the text being snide—along the lines of "This is what your tax money is paying for"—the *Post* printed a photograph of our building with the number prominently displayed, along with my photo. The newspaper might as well have said to any would-be assassin: "This is where she lives, and this is what she looks like; come and kill her." The *Post* didn't bother to mention that the gang threatening me had committed multiple murders or that I was risking my life to preside over their trial. I later learned that this sordid spread did galvanize our intermediate appellate court to call in the city editor for the *Post* and tell him precisely how irresponsible his newspaper was to run this story.

As I presided over the trial, Alex and Teresa watched the Cowboys watching me to see if I exhibited any fear. Actually, I was too busy controlling the situation in the courtroom to have time to feel fear—or much else. It took all of my attention every day just to make sure that things moved along. So mostly I didn't think about Freddy Krueger—still on the loose someplace—except for those moments at 3:00 A.M. when I'd wake up in a cold sweat from another nightmare.

The danger posed to all of us by the defendants was also evident when a mistake was made in the holding pens underneath my courtroom and Fat Danny almost escaped.

Rocco was in the courtroom alone, during the lunch recess, and heard a knock from inside the door that leads to the holding pen area. Normally, only a court or corrections officer would be seeking access to the courtroom from there, so Rocco opened the door and saw Fat Danny Rincon standing there all by himself, uncuffed, unguarded, and ready to . . . ? Rincon was a huge, menacing man and could easily have physically overpowered Rocco and made his escape through the courtroom and out of the building. Thinking quickly, Rocco stepped into the holding pen area with Fat Danny and closed the door behind him rather than allow Rincon to come into the courtroom. Only then did Rocco ask casually, as though nothing were amiss, what the defendant wanted. As it turned out, Fat Danny had a request having to do with lunch. Rocco told him he would take care of it and that Rincon should return downstairs to the pen and wait for Rocco to solve the problem.

As the defendant disappeared back down the stairs, Rocco summoned officers to meet Rincon there and lock him back into his cell. Only then did he breathe a sigh of relief. Where had the corrections officers been? How had Rincon slipped out of the cell area by himself? Fortunately, Fat Danny never realized that there was not a soul in the courtroom or in the vicinity and that he could easily have escaped.

Rocco did not tell me about this near disaster. Long afterward, Teresa told me. They waited because they were afraid that had I heard about it at the time it happened, I would have been so incensed that I might have tried to hold the entire corrections department in contempt. And Teresa and Rocco may well have been right.

The trial had rolled on for nearly six months; 1994 had come and gone, and we were into 1995, and the jury as well as everyone else appeared to be getting tired of the proceedings—when the prosecution brought on one of its most highly anticipated witnesses, Nelson Sepulveda.

The police had gotten word and informed me that some "friends" of the Cowboys were planning to storm the courtroom during Nelson's testimony, have a shoot-out, kill me—and probably kill Nelson, too, who because of his cooperation with the authorities was not exactly Mr. Popularity with the other Cowboys. In reaction, the courtroom had—once again—been made into what seemed like an armed camp. There were thirty or more court officers, police officers, and other law enforcement personnel all over the courtroom, all with guns. A uniformed court officer stood in front of the bench, plainclothes detectives were seated throughout the courtroom, and next to me, in Teresa's usual place, sat a female court officer in civilian clothes, gun close at hand. My courtroom was probably the safest place in New York City that day.

But before I was ready to face this scene, I went into my bathroom to apply some lipstick. My face stared back at me from the mirror: pale, too pale. I felt my heart pounding. I entered the courtroom, and what I saw—the armed camp—was a frightening sight even if the guns were there to protect me.

"The People call Nelson Sepulveda," the assistant district attorney announced loudly, and as Nelson entered and was led toward the stand, a couple of obvious drug dealers sauntered into the back of the courtroom. Conspicuously dressed with pounds of gold around their necks and doing what we call the "felony walk," they ostentatiously made their way to seats in the gallery. They had clearly come looking for trouble, but when they saw the array of cops and court officers lined up just waiting for them to start something, they must have thought better of it, because they just sat quietly through the testimony.

Beyond the tension created by the armed guards and the possibility of violence erupting right then and there, Nelson's testimony was also electric because of what he said and how he said it. Calmly but in gruesome detail, he laid out the whole string of murders, attempted murders, and other violent acts committed by the gang as though he were glad to have these off his chest. Other cooperators had told us about bits and pieces of the Quad, but Nelson put that massacre in perspective for the jury. "I put a hit on them," Nelson said, identifying "them" as the rival dealers who were selling treys of crack for $3, $2 less per vial than the Cowboys' price. He took the jury through his reasons for the action, the procuring of guns from El Feo and hiring Freddy Krueger, the loan from another drug dealer of a distinctive white Cadillac (which several witnesses had recalled seeing during the murders), the placement of cars and lookouts, the murders themselves—he'd heard the sounds from his hideout a block away—and the subsequent disposal of the guns from the pedestrian walkway of the George Washington Bridge over the Hudson River.

Other witnesses would testify to the gory details of other murders, but none would be as effective as Nelson Sepulveda coolly reciting the details of how the Cowboys had planned and executed the Quad.

It had not been until the day before Nelson was to testify that the prosecution had had to reveal to the defense the precise nature of Nelson's deal. The facts about his deal squelched the rumors of excessive leniency to Nelson by the prosecution—and so took a lot of steam out of the defense's cross-examination of him. They couldn't very well charge that Nelson was "getting off easy" when he had pleaded guilty to serious crimes and was going to receive at least twenty-two years in jail as long as he testified truthfully and completely. The defense had anticipated that Lenny and Nelson had gotten Sammy "the Bull" Gravano kinds of deals, the feds having given Sammy just five years for nineteen murders to flip against John Gotti. Not so here—I would never have agreed to so little jail time for Lenny or Nelson.

Later in the day, after Nelson's stint on the witness stand was finished and he and almost everyone else had been cleared out of the courtroom, the lieutenant in charge of the protective squad and I were standing alone. "I'm glad this day's behind us," I told him, "because I found it incredibly nerve-racking."

"Aw, it didn't faze you at all."

"Yes, it did—really! I was nervous, my heart was pounding."

"I don't believe it. Nobody would ever have known. You didn't show 'em a thing."

Another example of putting one's acting abilities to good use!

When it came time for summations, although the defense took a lot of time and many of the lawyers were quite passionate and articulate, they did not have much to work with. The evidence against their clients was overwhelming. Defense counsel could argue, for instance, that each defendant had acted independently and that there had been no conspiracy, but the sheer volume of consistent cooperating witness testimony showed otherwise. Unlike his co-counsel, one lawyer was fairly effective in his insistence that his particular client—the well-dressed one who had deliberately set himself apart from the other members of the gang during the trial—was not guilty of the one murder with which he was individually charged.

In the middle of the prosecution's summation, one of the defense lawyers called in sick, which brought the trial proceedings to an immediate halt—and, of course, put a dent in the prosecution's momentum. Everyone knew this was a delaying ploy, but I was furious and decided to do something about it. From chambers I telephoned the lawyer's house. He wasn't home, so I spoke to his wife and without too much arm-twisting obtained from her the phone number of his doctor. Then I called the physician.

"This is Judge Snyder from the supreme court in Manhattan. We're in the middle of a trial, and I know that you're treating Mr. 'Jones,' who is the lawyer for one of the defendants here, and I'd like to know how long he'll have to be out of court because of his illness."

His "patient" had not yet arrived for his appointment, the doctor said, and he could not be certain how long any illness would keep the patient away from court until he examined him.

"Of course, Doctor, but when you see Mr. Jones and find out what's wrong with him, please treat him and tell him to come back to court quickly—consistent with his illness, naturally—but I'll have to have *you* come to court and testify about your patient's prognosis."

The doctor took in my message and called back no more than half an hour later to say, "There's nothing wrong with Mr. Jones, and I'm sending him back to court—immediately." When Jones did appear, it was obvious to everyone that there was nothing wrong with him.

Finally, Dan Brownell's summation for the prosecution continued. It took almost two days in April, and by the end Brownell was hoarse and speaking almost in a whisper. But he painted for the jury a clear and detailed picture of the reign of terror perpetrated by the Wild Cowboys. And he did a superb job, as he had throughout the trial.

Finally, in May of 1995, after a trial that had lasted almost nine months, the jury retired to deliberate. This milestone in the trial brought me no feeling of inner peace. Normally, when a jury is out I return to my work in other matters. Since most of my cases are extraordinarily serious, I always care about the outcome and hope that it will be the rational one dictated by the evidence. But I have never felt the kind of tension during deliberations that I did with the Cowboys. Every day I had a knot in my stomach, which seemed to grow each time the jury buzzed: Would they send out another note or a verdict? If a note, would it indicate what they were thinking or doing? After the first five or six days, I was driving myself crazy contemplating the possibility of a hung jury and a retrial. And I'm sure I was driving many around me crazy as well: One day when my wonderful Teresa dared to suggest that "everything will be fine," I snapped at her. "How do you know? Don't be such a Pollyanna!"

Don't ever think that the judge doesn't care about what the outcome will be, especially in a case like the Cowboys: such a long trial, so many horrible crimes, so many victims, such evil defendants. . . .

Jury deliberations seemed endless and were occasionally the source of difficulties, two of them significant. There was one count that involved only the "well-dressed" defendant, and it appeared—from the notes sent out of the jury room—that the jury was deadlocked on it. Eventually they asked if they could render verdicts on the other counts only, and I told them they could. We certainly weren't going to hold up the proceedings for one count—not after all this time (two weeks) and not when the jury seemed ready to reach unanimous verdicts on the many other charges.

The other incident was more troubling. The jury sent out the following note: "If the children under sixteen, little Iris, Joey Morales, etc., were used in any capacity in the drug organization, and their parents knew what they were doing and did not object, call the police, protest, etc., can the defendants be held accountable under the law for their behavior?" The question seemed to imply that the Cowboys might not have been responsible for pushing these kids into working for the gang because it was their parents' fault. This was a potentially very serious point, because it went to the heart of the A-1 conspiracy charge; it was also bizarre.

There was only one possible response to that question. I called the jurors back into the courtroom, reread them my conspiracy charge, and answered the question in the note with a great big "Yes, the defendants could be held responsible, assuming all other legal requirements were satisfied, of course."

That seemed to settle the issue. But the deliberations continued a full fifteen days—quite a long time, but not so long in a case that had itself taken nine months to try and had many counts against many defendants to be considered.

Near the end of the workday on May 15, 1995, the jury buzzed—another note, I thought. But the signal was to inform us that they had finally reached their verdict. No one could quite believe it. I had insisted that the attorneys remain in court during deliberations, to respond to questions from the jury and to be ready in case there was a verdict; but it still took more than an hour to arrange for extra security, to notify all appropriate personnel, and to bring all the defendants into the courtroom. The courtroom was packed when the jury was finally brought in.

The jury found the defendants guilty on all but two counts. On one of those counts, involving the well-dressed defendant—who happened to be a young black male—represented by an able lawyer, the vote had been eleven to one for conviction. We were told long after the trial that there was some belief that the holdout vote had been racially motivated—the defendant, his attorney, and the holdout juror were all black. This was, after all, the time of the O. J. Simpson trial, and racial issues permeated the air. That defendant, incidentally, was later retried in another court, before another judge (and with another jury), and was convicted of the murder charge.

Overall, the jury had done an excellent job. They had listened to the evidence and had deliberated carefully before convicting the Wild Cowboys of nearly all of the terrible crimes with which they had been charged, the only rational verdict consistent with that evidence.

Seeing this case brought to a successful conclusion, which took a long time and a lot of work, gave me great satisfaction—as it did the detectives, the homicide investigation unit, and the Manhattan, Bronx, and Brooklyn prosecutors involved. Some are quoted in two recent books about the Wild Cowboys as saying that they consider getting this gang permanently off the streets to have been the high point of their careers.*

Five weeks later came the sentence. The security in the courtroom was like nothing I had ever experienced before. It made the security when Nelson had testified seem minimal in com-

*See works cited on page 174.

parison. The defendants had nothing to lose at this point, but the courtroom was ready and so was I.

Sentencing can be difficult for a judge, but in the case of the Wild Cowboys sentencing was easy: The defendants had to be taken off the streets forever.

"You have no values," I told them, straining to hold back my anger.

You have no morality. You have no respect for the law. . . . This gang represents the worst fear and dread to society today. Guns, drugs, incredible violence . . . I have never presided over a trial or been involved in a case where I saw whole families destroyed in the way we all saw here. When the Morales-Cruz children took the witness stand, I really almost wanted to cry to see their lives virtually destroyed. . . . These children have a chance at a second life because they have been relocated . . . but as to many other families about whom we heard throughout this case who were sucked into this gang's drug operation in every capacity, children eight years old and younger, they have had no chance. It is one of the most tragic things I have seen in any case: an entire neighborhood almost destroyed by this group.

Some of these defendants sit here smirking and laughing. It's a joke. Nothing affects them. They accept no responsibility. . . . They blame the witnesses because after they tried to shoot and kill them they still came forward. . . . What these defendants cannot accept is that the criminal justice system applies to them and it will work in spite of their best efforts to threaten everybody in it. . . . You thought you were above the law. You think you're above the law. No wonder: You were let out on bail all the time in the past and you committed more crimes and you were still let out on bail. You scared the witnesses off. You laughed in the faces of the police and the criminal justice system. No one could touch you. You could get away with virtually everything. But now, we know this: You are not above the law. . . . Your lives were simple, you had only one law: If someone got in your way, kill them.

After praising the witnesses who "came forward and spoke truthfully despite threats, intimidation, and shootings," I lauded the police, who "did their job, especially Detective Mark Tebbens, bravely and courageously and with absolute perseverance, because it took years. The District Attorney's Offices of New York County, the Bronx, and Brooklyn came together to do their job. And the men and women on the jury did their job. Now I have to do my job."

I sentenced Platano to a total of 133⅓ years to life, Stanley Tukes to the same, Paqualito to 116⅔ years, and Fat Danny to 158⅓ years, and I meted out commensurate lengthy sentences to the other five defendants—a total of 868⅓ years in all. These tough sentences were also meant, I said, as a message "to every other vicious and violent drug gang terrorizing our streets: You *will* be brought to justice, and you *will* be removed from society forever."

The message got across in other ways, too. After the trial, the remainder of the Wild Cowboys, those who had not yet been tried but who had been members of the conspiracy and were charged with its offenses, all quickly pleaded guilty. In the years that followed the Cowboys' trial, at least four entire gangs taken down by HIU also decided to plead out rather than risk trial and the sorts of long sentences that the Cowboys had received.

Federal and state law enforcement pursued El Feo, Freddy Krueger, and Raymond Polanco and eventually brought them to justice—trials and pleas at which Lenny and Nelson Sepulveda were or would have been star witnesses. The brothers' final sentencing had been held off until all such proceedings had been completed.

Much later, we would hear that several defendants serving long jail sentences—possibly including the Cowboys—were getting up a pot of $1 million to take out a contract on me; one of these defendants was purportedly selling his garage in New York City to be able to contribute his share.

On March 2, 1999, almost six years from the date of Lenny's first memorable appearance in my courtroom, Lenny and Nelson were sentenced. The Lenny that I saw on the date of sentence was the polar opposite of the Lenny I had seen six years earlier. Gone was the bravado; instead I saw a man who appeared to be filled with regret, who tearfully apologized to everyone for what he had done, including to the Cargill family, who came to see their son's murderer sentenced. Mrs. Cargill gave a poignant speech about the impact of her son's death on her, on her husband, and on their other children. Although victims may speak at sentencing, it does not usually happen in these gang cases because many of the victims don't have families, and when a statement is made it is usually filled with anger. I was deeply moved by Mrs. Cargill's remarks: Anyone, a mother or not, could not help but feel her grief.

The initial questions that I had asked about this gang had long been answered, except one: Why and how had the Cowboys been able to wreak their destructiveness on our great city for so long? Law enforcement had tried to end their reign of terror with buy-and-busts, surveillances, and arrests. But as the violence had continued unabated, despite the arrests, the police became discouraged and an entire area in the Bronx became lost to civilization. The Cowboys had learned to work the criminal justice system to their advantage, by a simple plan: Hire good lawyers, pay them well, get out of jail each time, and then threaten, intimidate, and/or bribe the witnesses against them, even kill them . . . until there was no case or at best a minimal charge. Their cycle of violence continued until Mark Tebbens and HIU persevered and began to destroy it. Ultimately, after much effort and great determination, the criminal justice system had worked.

Shortly after the trial, a *New York Daily News* editorial said, in part:

> For seven years, the murderous, crack-peddling Wild Cowboys gang bent terrified northern Manhattan and South Bronx residents to its evil will. But death threats against her and her family didn't intimidate Snyder. She coolly dispatched nine gang thugs to life in prison on 88 counts, including murder. . . . Like the Minutemen, Snyder . . . stared tyranny in the face and it blinked . . . and [she] restored life, liberty, and the pursuit of happiness to the formerly fearful. That's what independence—and all-American spirit—are all about.*

This tribute touched me, but the real reward was internal: a feeling that some measure of justice had finally been achieved.

But still there was no sense of triumph. Nothing could bring back the forty murdered people, the thousands of lives destroyed by the gang, or the families infected by their evil. There was only a sense of relief.

---

*"Real Life Heroes," *New York Daily News*, July 4, 1995.

BEING CREATIVE: MAKING LAW

Most of my time on the bench is spent dealing with the routine legal issues of each case. I decide motions, resolve pretrial issues, hold hearings, and preside over trials. Only rarely do judges on trial courts have the opportunity to make law; moreover, there is no way to predict when such an opportunity may arise. Sometimes you will have to determine an important issue and there is simply no precedent in the law to guide you in what to do.

I have had a few opportunities to make law. One arose in connection with what seemed at first blush to be an ordinary drug case involving a defendant named John Seychel. It had to do with a CI ("confidential informant"). In December 1986, a search warrant was authorized for Seychel's apartment, based on the police having received information from the CI who had witnessed preparation, packaging, and sales of drugs from the apartment. Upon execution of that warrant, cocaine and meth (methaqualone) were found, along with several firearms, and Seychel was subsequently arrested.

The case was assigned to me, and in the pretrial phase the defendant submitted a motion to suppress the drugs and other items found in his apartment, claiming that the search warrant was defective, and also demanded to know the identity of the

CI. The prosecution contended that it could not disclose that identity.

This happens, especially in drug-related cases. There are two such reasons for nondisclosure that have been frequently cited (and upheld by appellate courts) in the past. First, the disclosure of the CI's identity could place the CI in danger, presumably from the target of the search warrant; and second, to reveal the facts behind the search warrant before trial would compromise an ongoing investigation. The risk of danger is real, as the cases I've presided over highlight, since the drug world is a very violent one in which witnesses and families of potential cooperators have to live with fear and are frequently the targets of these violent drug dealers. So in the pretrial phases of drug cases, the prosecution often seeks to keep the CI's identity secret, for good reason.

However, at trial, the ground rules on secrecy and concealing identities change radically. Then the defendant has a constitutional right to confront his or her accusers, which means that the CI's identity *must* be revealed, except in very unusual circumstances, if the prosecution intends to proceed with the case, because the defendant's guilt or innocence is at stake. In contrast, the pretrial phase is not considered to be a "truth-finding" phase—motions are brought primarily to suppress evidence, not to determine guilt or innocence, so the prosecution is not always required to disclose the CI's identity.

You might ask why anyone would become a CI, since his or her identity could ultimately be disclosed. The answer is simple: CIs are usually defendants who cooperate either for money or to obtain a better deal for themselves on their own case(s). They know they are assuming a potential risk, but self-interest prevails. Sometimes, particularly in the federal system—but not always—the prosecution agrees to relocate a CI and his or her family as part of the deal, especially in Mob cases. (Who has not heard of the Federal Witness Protection Program, immortalized by Hollywood in vivid, often inaccurate detail? Most states can afford only case-by-case solutions.)

In the Seychel case, when Seychel's counsel brought his motion to suppress the drugs, which would in effect force the prosecution to reveal the CI's identity, the prosecution countered by asking the court for a protective order that would permit it to withhold that information from the defense.

The issue was a fascinating one: Should a prosecutor have the right to conceal the identity of a CI in the *search warrant* situation presented by *Seychel*? While there was a substantial body of law concerning informants, there was no law directly on this point. Any decision we made could set a precedent for future cases. Alex and I worked to construct a way of permitting the prosecution to conceal the CI's identity, which was appropriate in this case, while answering the requirements of the defense for discovery about the factual basis of the warrant.

Basically, we constructed a four-step procedure by which the judge—in this instance, me—would determine whether the search warrant had been based on probable cause, as the law required; whether the confidential informant in fact existed and was reliable; whether the CI would be in danger if his or her identity was revealed or an ongoing investigation might be jeopardized; whether the search warrant could be "redacted" (that is, partially blacked out) and disclosed in part to the defense; and whether it would be necessary to hold a hearing on any of these issues.

I applied this procedure to the *Seychel* case, upheld the search warrant, and granted the People's request for a protective order so they would not have to reveal the CI's identity.

The defendant pleaded guilty, and the four-step procedure did, in fact, become precedent—something prosecutors and courts relied upon in future cases.

None of this ultimately mattered to John Seychel: He was murdered, purportedly by the Mafia, for whom he worked as a low-level mope.* The police were unable to determine whether or not the killing had anything to do with the case.

A few years later, I had to extend the *Seychel* precedent significantly. Once again, the case began as a relatively routine drug matter, against a man named Juan Castillo. In April 1988, one of my colleagues on the supreme court, after examining an undercover police officer and taking sworn testimony from a confidential informant, authorized a search warrant for Castillo's premises. In his apartment, the police found and seized eight pounds of cocaine, a machine gun, two other guns, a large quantity of ammunition, and $28,000 in cash, most of it in $20 bills. After finding this contraband, the police arrested Castillo, and he was subsequently charged with criminal possession of the drugs and weapons.

The case was assigned to me, and in pretrial conferences, the prosecution attempted to resolve the case by means of a plea—but the defendant did not want to plead guilty. He and his lawyer believed they had good reason to have the fruits of the search suppressed. According to the defendant's wife, on the day before the search, two detectives had come to their apartment and had entered the apartment without receiving permission to do so. They had shown her a photo of someone they said had previously lived there and asked if she knew where he was, which she did not. Mrs. Castillo also said the police officers had then searched the apartment without a warrant.

Castillo's attorney asked for details of the search warrant, and the prosecutors asked for a protective order to conceal the identity of the CI. I applied the four-step procedure set forth in *Seychel*. But at the end of it, there was a quandary. Yes, the CI was

*Low-life or bum.

real and existed; yes, there was a real danger to his life; and yes, the search warrant was supported by probable cause. But there were other legal contentions by the defense that required a full-blown hearing. The prosecution convinced me in a sealed record that the identity of the CI was so sensitive that it could not be revealed under any circumstances or the CI would certainly be killed. All attempts to work out a negotiated plea failed; I was going to have to hold the full-blown suppression hearing. But if I did that, and both sides were present, the CI's identity would be disclosed.

So in spite of a lack of precedent and with plenty of concern about conducting a fair proceeding, I decided to hold the suppression hearing with only one side present, the prosecution—in camera and ex parte. Everything would be recorded in a sealed record available for appellate purposes, but neither the defendant nor his attorney would be present, nor could they obtain a copy of the record. This goes against the very idea of achieving fairness in an adversarial judicial system by having both sides represented, and I was not happy at having no alternative.

I decided to proceed, though, because the choice was either to dismiss the case and let the defendant go, despite his having had the drugs and guns in his possession, or to do something without precedent. I was uncertain as to whether the notion of an unbalanced suppression hearing would hold up on appeal; I thought it probably would not. But I called the hearing, without the knowledge of the defendant or his lawyer, and brought in the CI, the cops, and all other relevant witnesses. To maintain balance in the hearing, I tried to ask hard questions, the ones that a good defense lawyer would have asked had he or she been present. If this had been a buy-and-bust of two vials of crack, perhaps I would not have followed this procedure and would not have taken the chance that it might be thrown out on appeal—but eight pounds of cocaine is a lot of weight, indicating a substantial dealer, and the machine gun and other weapons also suggested that this defendant was dangerous. I was convinced that my unconventional solution here was the right thing to do, given the circumstances of the case; it also appeared to be the only solution.

In the sealed hearing, I determined that the first search had been done by the DEA and the second by the NYPD. I found that the two searches were unrelated and that the search at issue here involved no police impropriety. Since I found the search warrant to be based on probable cause, I issued a ruling that denied the defendant's motion to suppress and told the defense that I had conducted this hearing in camera. As we all expected, they objected; any competent defense lawyer would.

To provide the defendant with an incentive to forgo a trial, at which time the identity of the CI would have to be revealed, the prosecution now offered Castillo a very low plea, four years to life. Castillo accepted the offer, a good one, and appealed the denial of his motion to suppress, something that was anticipated and that he had a right to do.

To emphasize what the defense saw as my dramatic departure from precedent and from the two-sides-at-every-proceeding basis of our adversarial system, Legal Aid drew up an appellate brief with a lot of blank spaces. They contended that they had not been able to make intelligent arguments in their briefs because my ruling had denied them the information on which to base those arguments—hence the blank spaces.

To my surprise and gratification, the intermediate court, the appellate division, affirmed my decision without any written opinion. While a decision from a unanimous intermediate appellate court is not automatically appealable, in this case Legal Aid sought and received leave to appeal to the Court of Appeals, the state's highest appellate court. I could readily understand Castillo's and Legal Aid's willingness to "go all the way" on such a controversial issue, an issue that ultimately divided the Court of Appeals.

The majority of judges agreed with my ruling. They wrote in their opinion that the sealed record of the in camera hearing, which included the original search warrant and affidavits, "establishes convincingly that there was support for the determination . . . that the warrant was issued upon probable cause, that the documents supporting the warrant were not perjurious and that the affidavit and oral testimony could not be effectively redacted for delivery to defendant without destroying the informant's anonymity," relying on and quoting from my decision in *Seychel.* They agreed that there had to be a "sensitive balancing" between the defendant's Fourth Amendment rights—in this pretrial hearing—and "society's need to encourage citizens to participate in law enforcement by granting them anonymity when necessary for their protection." They noted that Castillo had not objected to protecting the confidentiality of the CI, claiming only that his rights had been violated by the ex parte hearing. This group of judges conceded that when a judge holds such a hearing "without the defendant's participation it must be particularly diligent and consider all possible challenges that might be raised on the defendant's behalf" but argued that the court had already allowed that procedure in *Seychel* and other cases. The trial court judge, they concluded, could "do a competent job of performing such a straightforward, purely legal task" such as the hearing, and in this case the trial judge had done so capably. They upheld my procedure and decision.

The dissenting judges disagreed. In their opinion, "Depriving a defendant of any participation in or knowledge of a suppression hearing where the issues involve *both probable cause and invalidity because of police misconduct** is without precedent and . . . conflicts with fundamental tenets of fairness and due

*Emphasis in original.

process of law inherent in our Federal and State Constitutions." They claimed that my hearing procedure had denied the defendant his right to confront and cross-examine the witnesses against him and that the possibility of police misconduct and the need for the defense to be able to explore and exploit that possible misconduct outweighed everything else. "The issue here is whether . . . the defendant must be content with what amounts to no more than a paternalistic assurance by the court that it has reviewed the facts in chambers and has decided that, although the defendant may believe otherwise, the police 'didn't violate his rights, after all.'"

There are seven judges on the Court of Appeals. Four—the majority—upheld my ruling, two dissented, and one abstained. I read the appellate decision and, although not happy with the dissent, felt good that the procedure I had followed had been affirmed by both appellate courts. What I had done in this case had been absolutely necessary, given the circumstances, and I was glad that in doing it properly (as the appeals courts agreed), I had established a tool to deal with such extraordinary circumstances in future cases.

I could have avoided the entire controversy and simply dismissed the case when the prosecution refused to disclose the identity of the confidential informant at the hearing I had ordered. But then justice would not have been done. And I would have been dissatisfied with that result. If I'd been reversed on *Castillo*, I still would have believed in my heart that I had done the right thing, but obviously I would never have used that procedure again.

Later, *Castillo* was taken up to the United States Supreme Court, which denied certiorari—that is, refused to hear the case—in effect letting stand the ruling of the state Court of Appeals. The *Seychel* and *Castillo* precedents are now used in other states, including California. Defense lawyers intensely dislike these precedents, at least in part because the in camera procedures these rulings permit prevent them from making the prosecution choose between compromising an informant and throwing out an indictment.

While we all want to be liked as well as respected, sometimes as a judge you have to do things that make you unpopular; it's part of the job.

A third case presented another quandary. The result was not so much a legal precedent as a procedural one. The facts of the underlying case were horrible. Two young, uniformed police officers in a marked radio car on Manhattan's Upper West Side were ambushed by two leaders of a drug gang wielding machine guns as they rode in a rented livery car; almost miraculously, since the cops were badly outgunned, they were not hurt. The livery cabdriver was located and was able to identify the perpetrators, which led to their arrest. The cabdriver testified before the grand jury, but before he could testify at the trial, he was lured to a dark park in the Bronx and shot in the head at point-blank range—in other words, he was executed. This fact came out in pretrial proceedings, and I held a hearing to determine whether the defendants or their agents had been responsible for the murder of the witness. There was only circumstantial proof of this, but I considered it to be strong enough to support a ruling that at the defendants' trial, the livery cabdriver's grand jury testimony could be introduced as evidence. Precedent already existed to support my ruling, although certain legal issues had not yet been clarified. As I discussed earlier, at trial every defendant has a constitutional right to confront his or her accusers. But by ordering the killing of the witness against them, the defendants had in effect waived their right to confront that witness—which was why the grand jury testimony could be permitted into evidence at the trial despite the lack of cross-examination or "confrontation" by the defense of that witness.

The defendants were convicted of attempted murder, and each was sentenced to forty years to life; their convictions were affirmed on appeal. In more recent cases, the ruling at issue has been extended even further.

These cases became the basis of increased protection of the identity of witnesses and confidential informants in New York State and also reflect my view of the kind of work one must do as a judge: balance the rights of defendants against the rights of society. Now that we as a country have been subjected to the tragic, overwhelming destructiveness of terrorism on our own soil, many more people may be concerned, like me, with bolstering the rights of society and of victims in that balance.

Upholding the rights of defendants is also fraught with difficulties and opportunities. Consider my attempt to use the concept of "shadow counsel" in New York State.

In the late 1980s, a well-known lawyer who had handled the defense of many radicals had been hired by the head of a drug gang to represent him and his gang after their arrests. Initially, she had arranged for other lawyers whom she knew (and who perhaps felt obligated to her, although she denied this) to represent the various other gang member defendants—an arrangement that the prosecution claimed enabled the head of that gang to keep track of everyone in it and their legal maneuvers. If true, this was patently unfair to the other defendants, and in other cases has been found to be an illegal arrangement. But during the time it was in force, one of the defendants realized that his lawyer was not helping him and found a way to telephone the prosecutor and say that he wanted to cooperate but was afraid to tell his lawyer, because the information would then get back to the leader, who might very well try to have the defendant and his family killed.

The DA's office brought this defendant before me in chambers to tell me his story—in a sealed, ex parte record, of course.

After hearing it, I suggested that he fire his lawyer; he said he couldn't do that because it would send the same signal to the leader—that he was thinking of cooperating. At first I refused to do anything about the situation because he was represented by competent counsel, but the second time around, when his level of fear for his life had mounted seriously, at the DA's urgent request I did something novel in the state system. I assigned "shadow counsel," in this instance a government-paid assigned lawyer, who would represent this defendant without notifying his current lawyer. The shadow lawyer would conduct all legal proceedings, including any plea of guilty by the defendant, unbeknownst to the original lawyer, who would think she still represented him. The DA had been asking me to do this since the first time he brought the defendant before me.

It did not work out well. For reasons that remain unclear to me, the defendant did not take the negotiated plea, rejected the opportunity for cooperation that he had sought, and went to trial. He was convicted and sentenced to one hundred years to life.

The lawyer was subpoenaed to testify in the grand jury about her fee arrangement with the other defendants' lawyers. When she refused to do so, the grand jury indicted her for contempt. The appellate courts refused to dismiss the indictment, but one appellate judge, the dissenting judge, a self-proclaimed liberal, distorted the facts, criticized the shadow counsel concept, and made vicious personal remarks about my use of it, even though the concept of shadow counsel had long been accepted in federal courts. Because I had brought in the shadow counsel only at the request of the defendant and the district attorney's office—and not *sua sponte*, at my own instigation—people in the DA's office wanted and expected that office to take responsibility for its role in advocating the use of this procedure, particularly because the dissenting judge had misstated many facts in the case; but that did not happen. The attorney eventually pleaded guilty to a misdemeanor rather than a felony and went on with her career.*

I, too, went on with my career. In many ways, it was just a moment when expediency and politics overwhelmed the pursuit of justice. What prevented the DA's office from publicly admitting its role in pursuing shadow counsel for this defendant—or prevented a judge from recognizing what the federal courts had already determined to be acceptable? I viewed this experience as hypocrisy at its worst.

After I had been in the supreme court for several years, I had developed a reputation for running a tight courtroom, for being in control, and for not wasting time. So it was not a complete surprise when the chief administrative judge for the court system offered me a managerial position—either as administrative judge of all the criminal courts in New York City or as administrative judge of the supreme court, New York County, whichever I wanted. I was flattered by the offer, which was accompanied by the chief administrator's sincere attempts to induce me to accept this "promotion," but I turned it down for two reasons. First—as previously discussed—when years before I had accepted an administrative position as head of the consumer fraud bureau in the DA's office, I'd been bored to death and had learned a valuable lesson: not to take a position for its title if the work doesn't interest you, or you will obviously be unhappy and won't do a good job. I had no interest in being politic and political, which one necessarily has to be in order to fulfill the managerial duties of an administrative judge.

Second, I declined the offer because it would have taken me away from the job that I liked doing and would have severely

---

*This lawyer was recently indicted federally for conspiracy in another matter.

limited opportunities for creativity. Friends and colleagues importuned me to change my mind, saying that the administrative position could lead to a judgeship on a higher court and ostensibly to greater opportunities.

But the only court that really interested me was the trial court, where interaction with people and their legal issues occurs daily and can be intense. That's where the action is, and that's where, as a judge, you have to do the frontline work of seeing that justice is done.

MOB CONNECTIONS

One of my first interesting "connections" to the Mob began in 1992. I was routinely assigned a drug case. Its most unusual aspect was that it involved a "nice Jewish boy" from Columbia University—who was using his Ph.D. in pharmacology to aid a drug distribution operation run by a Mafia crime family. He was only one of the defendants. Another defendant was known by his street name of "Frankie Jaws"* and was believed to be a midlevel soldier in the crime family. A third defendant was Frankie's ex-wife. Because this was a large-scale drug operation alleged to cover several states and because it was a Mob case and Frankie also had a federal case pending, the Drug Enforcement Agency (DEA) was involved.

The defendants were brought in for arraignment. Bail had to be set. Frankie Jaws was represented by a sharp Mob lawyer, and a good one. (Mob lawyers are often smooth and charming but don't always know the law; this lawyer was expensively dressed, slick, but actually knew the law.) The prosecutors wanted remand for the defendants or at least very high bail. The defense, of course, wanted low bail, if not for Frankie, then for the ex-wife, so she could remain out of jail. Frankie seemed inordinately concerned about his ex-wife's freedom—but then, she was vital to their drug operation. Since the charges here were

*Not his real name.

A-1 felonies, with a lot of money involved, and Frankie had a federal case pending, I set high bail for both Frankie and his ex-wife.

Two weeks later, a bureau chief in the district attorney's office called and asked to see me. In chambers, he confided that "a defendant who was charged in another case gave us information that Frankie Jaws was so angry about you setting high bail on his ex-wife that he's put out a contract on you."*

"That's ludicrous."

"This is a very serious threat, Judge. It comes from a 'made' man who has the contacts, the money, and the habit of using violence to get what he wants. Also, we have evidence that the threat is credible: The confidential informant took a lie detector test and passed the part of it dealing with the threat to you."

I was bewildered: Why me? Yes, I'd set high bail, but I was sure that the threat was also connected to my being tough as a judge and with my being female. In the course of presiding over several drugs-and-violence cases, I had imposed some pretty stiff sentences. Word about these was out. Even more to the point, I was a woman: Many male defendants find it demeaning to be punished by a woman. This particular Mob guy apparently thought he could frighten me or, failing that, kill me.

I wasn't going to let the threat scare me off the case. But better safe than sorry: This time, at the insistence of law enforcement, the whole family got protection,† because it wasn't clear whether Frankie Jaws was trying to hurt me or, as a lesson to me, my family. Since the DEA was involved, they decided to take care of the kids, which led to quite a scene: When the kids were delivered to their schools, two DEA agents—who looked like typical undercover cops, dressed in street clothes, scruffy, and tough—would jump out and stand on the curb in on-guard position, looking up and down the street, with what appeared to be

*He apparently expected high bail to be set on his own case.
†This was two years before the Cowboys' threats.

machine guns at the ready, before they would let the kids out of the car to walk into school. The kids actually found this "kind of cool."

I didn't think it was cool. I thought the whole thing was unreal—could this really be *my* life? People were with us virtually all the time, several cops or DA's office investigators, except when we were inside our apartment or our offices or schools. Once again, our personal freedom and relatively carefree existence were under siege. And we couldn't tell anyone what we were facing or why. If I heard a loud noise on the street, I wondered if it was a gunshot. I had nightmares about DEA-Mafia shoot-outs with our children caught in the crossfire. I worried that Fred's nameplate was too visible on the exterior of his office.

My father had had a heart attack, and I was spending as much time as I could with my mother, taking her to visit him while he recuperated at a Manhattan hospital. I didn't want to alarm her, but I had to have an explanation as to why two detectives accompanied me everywhere. "I'm on a Mob case, Mother"—at least that part was true—"and the detectives are with me at all times because they need me to sign emergency updates to a wiretap that's ongoing." She seemed to believe me.

Fred and I had long had an unlisted phone number—pediatricians get tired of being phoned directly in the middle of the night and usually have a service that answers parents' calls before notifying the doctor. So our address and phone were not readily available. The police department asked employees and workmen at our apartment building to refuse to answer questions about us from anyone—and for the most part they complied, except for one who told an "investigator" that we did live in that building.

At one point, a threat was uncovered that was more specifically related to one of our kids and possibly to the case. Our son had gone to visit a college one weekend and was on his way back by bus. The detective was extremely concerned, because he himself had been the target of threats to "send his children back to him in a box," and a small bomb had actually been planted near his house, although no one was hurt by it. He and his partner met the bus and boarded it.

"Is there a Schnee-der on this bus?" they shouted.

Our son, traveling with some friends, was mortified and wanted to crawl under his seat.

"Schnee-der!"

Finally, "Schnee-der" 'fessed up; they hauled him off the bus like a criminal and didn't tell him the reason until they had him safely in their unmarked car. He was sure that his friends would never believe what had really happened—it looked so bad! The detectives accompanied him to our apartment; actually, before they'd let him enter, they went through the place with guns drawn. They then concluded that it was not safe for him to stay there through the rest of the weekend alone, so they drove him out to our summer home, where we were staying. He was extremely annoyed—he had to miss a good party that night.

I had no intention of recusing myself from the Frankie Jaws case since I knew I could be fair and there were incipient negotiations for plea bargains with several defendants, including Frankie and his ex-wife, which might have ended their part of the case before trial. But even though these negotiations had begun, the threat was still extant—as far as we knew, the contract had not been withdrawn—and the authorities were still very much concerned. You could never know when some goon would try to whack you and collect his money. So I was still in danger.

"I'm going to take care of this," a very good guy told me. "Mike,"* a retired NYPD detective, was one of the chief investigators for the DA's office, and he decided that enough was enough, he was going to end this threat. He wouldn't tell me ex-

*Not his real name.

227

actly how—law enforcement was trying to keep all the details from me, which was proper because I was the judge on the case and they didn't want me compromised, and, in general, they keep the target largely in the dark—but of course I found out eventually, after it was all over.

Just as in a Hollywood gangster movie, Mike picked up the phone and called a capo in the Frankie Jaws family. He and this capo went way back, to the days when Mike was an up-and-coming street cop and detective and the capo was an up-and-coming mobster, and they would run into each other in the neighborhood. Each knew what the other did for a living. Mike asked his old acquaintance for a "sit-down." And the capo agreed, not just for old times' sake, but because over the years Mike had developed a reputation for being fair as well as able in his dealings with the Mob.

They met in a restaurant at an odd hour. Mike told the capo about the threat from Frankie Jaws and then said, "You're going to end this, or you'll be sorry." The implications didn't have to be spelled out: If anything happens to the judge, we—the police department, the DEA, the DA's office, and everyone else in law enforcement—are going to hold you responsible. And we'll come down on you and your "family" with everything we've got.

"We're not gonna let this happen," the capo answered from the other side of the table and painted Frankie as a low-level fool. "Tell the judge she got nothin' to worry about. We'll take care of it." Again, the implications were crystal clear: We'll sit on Frankie because we won't let him do anything to ruin our business.

After the sit-down, the threat went away, I was told, and the protection was removed. Frankie Jaws and his ex-wife both pleaded guilty, and my family and I forgot about threats—for the time being.

A fascinating trial involved drugs, Mob defendants, and Mob attorney Bruce Cutler, who was making headlines by his constant and continuing defense of John Gotti. (Cutler's oft repeated statement "There is no Mafia" always amazed me.) Three defendants, including the nephew of Carmine "the Snake" Persico, were charged with selling drugs. All were represented by well-known lawyers, chief among them Cutler, who Alex and I assumed was representing the nephew out of respect for or at the request of the uncle. Moreover, his client and the others were out on bail, and they frequently brought their mobster friends into the courtroom, where it appeared that Cutler believed he had to put on a show for them.

Bruce Cutler can be a charming man, as well as a bully, and he demonstrated both aspects of his courtroom persona in this trial. He thoroughly intimidated the young and bright but relatively inexperienced assistant DA. Cutler is also quite histrionic and uses body language to underscore his points—and, frequently, to obliquely threaten witnesses, other lawyers, and the judge. He loves to stick his finger in your face like a gun and get too close for comfort or decorum during his questioning of witnesses and in bench conferences. Upon his return from lunch every day during this trial, he gargled with mouthwash in the courtroom, spat in a wastebasket, and then sprayed himself with a cologne that had a strong and—to my nose—very offputting smell.

One big concern in Mob cases is jury tampering. So in pretrial conferences, when Cutler showed up with a private investigator whose name had come up in one of the Gotti trials in connection with jury tampering, and whom Cutler wanted to have sit at the defense table during this trial, we had our first confrontation. I told Cutler that I'd read about this man and what he was suspected of doing in the earlier trial, and that if he was going to participate in this one, I'd be watching them both very closely. Cutler seemed startled, either because I knew this information or because I chose to confront him with it in open court and in the presence of the other attorneys. In any event, the investigator never appeared in the courtroom again.

Out of the presence of the jury, Cutler would frequently make up far-fetched stories, for instance, to explain why his client was late or could not have done something; while doing so, he would gesticulate wildly and look everywhere in the room but at me. One day I finally had had it with these antics and summoned him to the bench. "If you want to bullshit me," I said, "then look me in the eye and do it, so you know that I know exactly what you're doing." He laughed and didn't do it again—for a while. Every time he got near the bench, though, I could smell that awful cologne; so one day I went out and bought him some cologne whose aroma I liked better and gave it to him as a bit. I was never allowed to forget this gesture: He cleverly turned it into a story about my liking him so much that I had given him a gift! Ah, the male ego. . . .

In front of the jury, Cutler tried to promote confusion, make witnesses look bad, and obscure the evidence against his client, all quite effectively. But this was a courtroom trial, not a television drama, so when the inexperienced ADA, Peter,* would not rise to object to Cutler's more outrageous antics and tactics, I'd hint broadly to Peter that he ought to pay more attention; then I'd write less kind notes to Alex, asking, "Is Peter dead?" When hinting didn't work, I'd interrupt the cross-examination to ask a question or two on my own, either to elicit a clarifying answer or to prevent harassment of the witness. Of course, Cutler hated these interruptions.

Two legal issues arose during the trial, involving violations of rulings that I had made in pretrial conferences. The first had to

*Not his real name.

do with a wiretap that the government had decided not to rely on because it had not been productive; the defendant had found out about it and had been careful not to say anything incriminating on the telephone. I ruled that neither side could refer to the wiretap, since both the prosecution and the defense were concerned that the other would gain something unfair from its mention. Both sides agreed.

Partially to challenge me, and partially to stick a finger in the government's eye, in his opening Cutler mentioned the wiretap anyway, saying, "They had a wiretap and they got nothing from it."

I called a sidebar. Over the cautions of Alex—one of the few times we ever disagreed on a point of law—I ruled that since the defense had mentioned the wire, the prosecution could now refer to it and to the defendant knowing about it. Cutler had a tantrum, warning me that this ruling would certainly cause any conviction to be reversed on appeal. He pointed his finger at me like a gun and yelled in my face. I told him to stop threatening me and to get his finger out of my face. The prosecution was then allowed to make reference to the wiretap and why it had not been productive. Cutler had wanted to have his cake and eat it, too; but that was unfair and could not be allowed.

A second and potentially more serious difficulty also arose out of a pretrial ruling. The People had been directed not to mention at trial that Persico had made other drug dealers pay him "taxes" in exchange for their conducting drug business on turf he claimed as his. This idea of taxes was irrelevant to the drug sale charges under consideration and was highly prejudicial.

So during the trial, when the prosecutor violated my ruling— the information about taxes started to come in through a witness's answer to a prosecution question—the defense objected, and rightly so. There could have been a mistrial, and to prevent it I had to "make the defense whole" by doing something curative that would balance out the harm already done by the mention of taxes. I asked Cutler and the other defense counsel (out of the hearing of the jury, of course) what they wanted me to do of a curative nature, short of declaring a mistrial, and they made several totally outrageous requests.

Even though the requests were ludicrous, I granted one, which entailed giving a very strong instruction to the jury. I informed the jury that not only was the witness's evidence irrelevant and improperly elicited by the prosecutor, but it had nothing to do with the defendant. This was certainly curative, even if not accurate.

As the trial wend on, Cutler could not contain himself and began to yell at a witness during cross-examination. It was a regular feature of his intimidation routine and was also intended to score points with the jury—and, I suppose, with the mobsters watching the trial. I called a halt to the proceedings, cut off his cross-examination, and informed the jury, "He's having a problem." Then I sent the jury out of the room and told Cutler to stop yelling at witnesses or that each time he misbehaved I'd halt his cross and send the jury out. Not wanting to lose momentum—among other things—he apologized, assured me that it would not happen again, and was more polite to most of the witnesses from then on.

However, later, when I grinned when his questions did not elicit the answers he obviously wanted, Cutler yelled at me. "You liked that, dintcha?" He was unable to control himself. "You think that's pretty funny, doncha?" he continued, turning apoplectic purple.

"Okay, Mr. Cutler, that's enough. Jurors, please retire to the jury room—*again!*"

The jurors snickered and left the courtroom.

Cutler himself had a laugh, along with everyone else, when we had to listen to the diminutive but fearless undercover detective urinating while his microphone was still recording—he had forgotten to turn it off on the way to the bathroom. An unexpected peril of undercover work.

The case proceeded to the rather inevitable convictions and sentencing. When I handed down a stiff sentence for Persico, his mother yelled at me, "You have sons, too." It could have been a plea for sympathy or a threat. Or both.

The case was appealed and the conviction affirmed. The appellate court found, by the way, that allowing the prosecution to mention the wiretap after the defense did was not an error and that the strong instruction to the jury about the taxes testimony had been sufficiently curative to prevent a reversal.

I thought that was the end of the Persico case. But over the next couple of years, I met two different lawyers, separately, at social functions, and each conveyed a message—in a completely inappropriate manner—that Persico's sentence was too long and should be reconsidered. "If you think you have a motion," I'd say, "then bring it before me and I'll consider it." Each lawyer then intimated to me that before he could actually bring that motion, he needed an indication of whether I would look upon it favorably, implying that the mobster's family and friends would not look kindly upon an unfavorable result. That, of course, was even more improper, and I told each attorney to stop talking to me about the case or I'd have to stop talking to them altogether. The ex parte approaches at cocktail parties were offensive, but ultimately I did have to hold a hearing with all parties because of a technical sentencing issue. The defendant had to be resentenced, but his term of twenty years to life was not reduced. "Okay," the young mobster said to me, "I gave you your chance. I won't forget this."

Get on line.

The Persico matter was a warm-up for the largest and definitely most significant Mob-related case ever to be tried in my court. This was a case against the cartel of individuals, companies, and business associations that for forty years had controlled the private hauling of garbage in New York City—a case to be known to me forever as the "garbage" case.

The city's decision, in 1956, to let private haulers rather than the New York City Department of Sanitation pick up commercial waste was the start of an enormous expansion in private carting. More than fifty thousand new customers—restaurants, stores, office buildings—had to arrange for their trash to be hauled away, and this provided what one recent study called "a lucrative opportunity for racketeering."* By 1990, the private carting industry in New York was taking in more than $1.5 billion a year and was controlled by four major trade associations and a handful of large private firms such as Barretti Carting and V. Ponte & Sons. The conservative estimate of what customers were overpaying for these services was $400 million annually. Law enforcement had reason to believe that the carting business was Mob controlled and that the Genovese and Gambino crime families ran it in New York, just as the Lucchese crime family was believed to run it on Long Island. The chief mobster associated with the industry in the city was James "Jimmy Brown" Failla, a capo in the Gambino family who for thirty years had been president of the Association of Trade Waste Removers of Greater New York (GNY).†

In 1991, when the giant firm Browning-Ferris International (BFI), at the encouragement of the federal government, bought a route seized from an illegal carrier—refuse from the Columbia-Presbyterian Medical Center—a BFI spokesperson announced,

*Jacobs, James B., Coleen Friel, and Robert Rudick, *Gotham Unbound: How New York City Was Liberated from the Grip of Organized Crime* (New York: New York University Press, 1999); chap. 6, "Carting Away a Fortune."
†*Gotham Unbound*, pp. 83–85.

"We're sending a message to Cosa Nostra . . . we're not being run out of town." Shortly, a note and a package appeared at BFI in New York; the note said, "Welcome to New York," and the package contained the severed head of a German shepherd.* It was rumored that the head was that of the dog belonging to the owner of BFI and that his wife had gone into shock when she had opened the package at their home, where it had been sent (rather than to BFI headquarters)—but we were never sure of this. Certainly the story rivaled *The Godfather* stallion's head in the bed in its gruesome horror, no matter which version of the dog's head story one believed, and it was undoubtedly intended to do just that.

Since the cartel was Mob run, it was impossible for law enforcement to find potential informants inside its councils and inordinately difficult to insert an undercover agent into the business in a position from which to find out anything significant. But a once-in-a-lifetime opportunity unexpectedly came along on the morning of May 11, 1992. It was so unusual that if it were used in a Hollywood movie, audiences would snicker because it would seem so unrealistic.

A week before May 11, two men from Barretti Carting had appeared at the premises of Chambers Paper Fibres, a disposal company in Brooklyn, located at the foot of the Manhattan Bridge. In full view of the Chambers foreman—and with no attempt to disguise their identity—the two men set a new Chambers garbage truck on fire as a reprisal against Chambers having successfully weaned away a very lucrative customer, the building at One Wall Street. Chambers had won the contract by offering to pick up waste for $3,300 a month, versus Barretti's existing fee of $8,100 a month. Chambers was an old company, founded in 1897 by the grandfather of the current owner, Sal

---

*Quoted in *Gotham Unbound*, p. 195, and also discussed in pretrial motions in my court.

Benedetto—now a man of sixty and so vastly overweight that he could hardly move, but who ran a successful small business with thirty employees and a fleet of trucks.

On the morning of May 11, a week after the torching of Sal Benedetto's truck, two plain-clothed detectives from the NYPD were in the Chambers office, talking to Sal about the fire—which he had had to report to the police in order to obtain papers requested by his insurance carrier—when the two arsonists showed up. One of the detectives ran outside, where one of the intruders was holding his hand in his pocket as though he had a gun, while the other shouted, "Get out of One Wall!" and threatened "trouble" unless "we [get] our stop back."* As this detective tried to defuse the situation, Sal Benedetto came slowly out of his office, and the lead arsonist asked who the newcomer was.

"He's my cousin Dan Benedetto," Sal said without missing a beat.

The newcomer was in actuality Rick Cowan, a third-grade NYC detective, who had never been an undercover in his entire career. He had spent the majority of his years in the police department in the organized crime control bureau (OCCB), which meant that he knew a good deal about organized crime and the various crime families and some of their members, having conducted OC (organized crime) surveillances and manned OC wiretaps for years. He was at Chambers investigating this obviously OC-involved crime on the morning of May 11, to obtain information, file a report, and follow up on it.

If you have never worked with an undercover as a prosecutor, or as a judge presided over cases involving undercovers, you cannot appreciate how difficult and dangerous being an undercover is—it's a role fraught with peril at every moment. The undercover is always one step away from the possibility of death. And being a good undercover is an *art*, an art that can be perfected

---

*These quotes are from the later trial testimony of Richard Cowan.

only with experience. I have presided over many cases with undercovers, some short-term undercover buy-and-bust cases, some long-term undercover cases, where a cop may play a role for months—or more—and, as in the movies, go "deep," living as a member of a drug organization or the Mob. Each of these roles is dangerous, because if any drug dealer or mobster realizes who you are, you're not likely to survive. I had a young undercover shot in the chest at point-blank range in one case, a simple buy-and-bust. He had gone into the buy location alone; his backup team was outside, and the bad guys figured that out and decided to rip him off and kill him. Fortunately he lived, although his injuries forced him to leave "the Job." His near brush with death is another example of cops—good cops—as heroes. Who else would risk their lives for so little appreciation, and often so little respect, for $40,000 a year? I'd listen to the exploits of undercovers in my courtroom with incredulity: stories of guns pointed at their heads, demands that they snort drugs, threats and taunts of "We know you're the Man."

On May 11, 1992, the fact that Rick Cowan had zero experience as an undercover did not deter him for a moment. When Sal answered the arsonist's query by identifying Rick as "my cousin Dan Benedetto," Rick seized the opportunity of a lifetime and played along.

He told the arsonist that Chambers needed time to think about what to do about One Wall. The man handed him a card with a phone number and drove off in a Barretti Carting car.

In the afternoon, with Sal's permission, Cowan—still posing as Dan Benedetto—called the arsonist and arranged a meeting for two weeks later to resolve the issues; the man promised that until that meeting there would be no more truck fires or other harassment of Chambers equipment or employees.

While Cowan had never worked undercover, Sal Benedetto had never considered allowing his company to become the base for a major police operation that could break the cartel's grip on the garbage-hauling business in New York. It wouldn't be Rick alone who would be in danger; Sal would be placing himself, his family, and his company in mortal peril. Sal knew you didn't fool around with these guys—real movie-style gangsters—and survive. Nevertheless, he ultimately agreed to allow the police department to keep his "cousin Dan" working at Chambers and to cooperate with the NYPD investigation. Why? To this day, I'm still not certain of the answer, except that I know it is a complex one: I believe Sal felt that he and his company had been pushed around for too long, that his past protests of unfair treatment had been ignored, and, yes, that he even had some desire to do the right thing. Of course, if other companies were to be forced out of the carting business by law enforcement, his company would benefit financially, but his reasons for agreeing to work with the NYPD weren't that simple. In fact, Rick and Sal were an odd couple: Sal, a huge white whale of a man who had trouble just breathing; and Rick, short, stocky, with graying, wavy hair, very uncoplike in appearance and very likable.

So Cowan took on the role of Dan Benedetto—the long-lost black sheep cousin of the family, the illegitimate son of a hippie priest, rumor had it—and the NYPD bankrolled Chambers in its attempts to obtain new business by legitimate competitive bids from stops that "belonged" to carters known to be members of the cartel—and the Mob. The customers they pursued and won included the D'Agostino chain of supermarkets, the Fayva chain of shoe stores, the studios of Home Box Office, and many other large and medium-size businesses. As the NYPD had expected, these attempts ran into stiff resistance from the old-line carting companies and Mob-controlled trade associations, which did not hesitate to threaten Chambers (including Cowan as Dan Benedetto), subject the company to punishing economic sanctions, and on occasion use force—and other illegal acts—to try to push Chambers into either becoming a subservient member of the cartel or going out of business.

Rick played his undercover role intelligently; he never pushed too hard and slowly got to know the members of the various Mob trade waste associations. Many of them remained suspicious of him, because even though he was a "cousin" of one of their own, they really didn't know him and he had appeared out of nowhere. But gradually Dan Benedetto won over most of the defendants and some of the members of the trade waste association—but not all. He became good friends with Frank Giovinco, and Joseph Francolino liked him, but some of the "guys" never trusted him. For several years—an eventful and dangerous time—Cowan as Dan Benedetto wore a concealed tape recorder and recorded several hundred hours of conversations with many future defendants from the cartel as they tried to coerce Chambers into doing what they wanted.

As I listened to tapes at hearings and heard Rick testify at trial, with all the grilling he was subjected to on cross-examination by the various lawyers, my admiration for his courage grew. The grilling in the courtroom was child's play compared to the grilling he had gotten, and a number of other things that happened to him, during the investigation. Once he attended a trade waste association meeting filled with mobsters, including some of the ones who never came to trust him. One grabbed him and subjected him to a rigorous pat-down that included grabbing his crotch area and exploring it thoroughly, searching for any recording device that might be hidden there. The mobster, one of the Brooklyn guys, missed the recorder by about two inches. Rick was pretty shaken, but he persevered. Another close call, one of several, occurred in a restaurant and came out amusingly at trial—as I'll recount.

The real excitement of the case, based on the work of Cowan and Sal Benedetto and five years of work by the NYPD and the Manhattan District Attorney's Office, is hard to convey. It became the most significant case in numerous attempts by city, state, and federal government to rid the New York City area of

Mob control of the private carting industry. I was fascinated at being part of it, as I had been involved from the beginning with its wiretaps and, eventually, search warrants, subpoenas, and other legal issues. For those several years, it was unclear to me as the judge whether this long-term investigation would ever lead to any arrests or indictments. That point, of course, did finally arrive, after a video surveillance camera and a bug had recorded and eavesdropped upon key organized crime trade waste meetings and corrupt, anticompetitive, price-fixing plans. About thirty thousand pages of wiretaps had been accumulated when prosecutors came to me with an exhaustive warrant to search twenty-three target locations; I knew that at last the end of the preparation stage must be near. But my work had just begun.

The arraignment of the many defendants was a dramatic moment. Many defense counsel and a number of prosecutors vehemently argued immediate issues like bail. The prosecutors asked that enormous amounts of bail be set but, strangely, volunteered that they had no objection to the defendants' being released until they could raise that bail, which was something of a paradox. Ultimately I set substantial bail and agreed to the People's request to release the defendants for the time being; they all made bail, in any event.

A case like the "garbage" case is bound to be a long-term one that will never be resolved quickly. Complex motions of all kinds were filed constantly by each of the highly paid lawyers for the defendants, and these had to be responded to by the prosecutors and then decided by me. Alex, Teresa, and I adopted our usual team approach in deciding these motions, and we all had to work harder than ever to avoid drowning in the paperwork. High-priced lawyers love to drown everyone in paperwork, hoping to wear down their adversaries. Some of the motions were pro forma, some were frivolous, and some were of real legal significance. I decided to respond somewhat differently to one of the frivolous ones, in which the People and the defense had filed four sets of motions "to preclude further motions." I had Teresa consult a friend whose priest was fluent in Latin—since I had forgotten most of what I had studied—and we ended one decision with a quote in Latin from Cicero that translates to "What can I tell you about the value of horse manure?"—basically telling both sides to stop the BS. It took the defense a while to find someone to translate the phrase, and then we all had a good laugh.

Ultimately, we produced the longest pretrial decision ever rendered, to my knowledge, by any New York court of similar jurisdiction—so long that it was printed and bound. We were told that this was a first, which simply emphasized the significance of the carting case.

Among the most difficult aspects of the case was selecting a jury, a process that began in February 1997. Some five thousand people were interviewed over a period of three months before a panel and alternates were seated. It was an endless process. In most cases, I give out two-page questionnaires to prospective jurors to respond to orally as an aid to answering my questions quickly; in this case, the prosecution and defense both wanted a lengthy, written questionnaire. What we agreed to eventually was a forty-four-page one, which we gave to each prospective juror to fill out after an initial screening process.

Federal courts, unlike New York State courts, allow for anonymous juries. Such juries have been used in most organized crime cases out of fear of jury tampering, since that is a tactic that has been used with some frequency to obtain acquittals and hung juries (for example, in cases like those involving John Gotti).

Anonymous juries are also used in terrorist cases, more out of a concern for juror safety. When an anonymous jury is used, the jurors are identified only by numbers or sometimes by first names. Their identities are withheld from both prosecution and defense. In the carting case, the People argued that since the case involved organized crime ties, there was a substantial likelihood that there would be attempts to tamper with the jury. Since the anticipated length of the jury screening process was expected to be several months, the People believed that providing the jurors' names to the defense several months in advance of the voir dire would make jury tampering much more likely. Under New York law, both sides are entitled, once the actual voir dire or jury selection begins, to be given the jurors' names. As a judge, one of my goals is to maintain the integrity of the jury process and to provide both sides with a fair and impartial jury and a fair trial. In an attempt to lessen the possibility of jury tampering, we eventually worked out a compromise: For the screening process only, each juror would be assigned a number. Rocco and Teresa would have a master list that matched names and numbers. Once the screening process was over and voir dire was about to start, each side would be given the names that matched the numbers.

In practice, it was not that simple. The jurors would often provide too much identifying information in the questionnaires, such as naming their place of employment or their address, despite instructions to the contrary. Teresa had to spend countless hours reading the questionnaires and deleting all such information before the questionnaires could be copied and distributed to both sides. And there was a lot of detailed information. For example, jurors were asked to provide not only basic pedigree details such as their educational background, occupation, and marital status, but also what television shows they watched, what books and newspapers they liked, what their hobbies were. The questionnaire also asked for the jurors' thoughts about the police, the criminal justice system, and the use of undercovers and eavesdropping as investigative tools, as well as their opinions about organized crime.

I could not believe the parade of prospective jurors saying in open court, in front of the defendants, that they had either been victims of the Mob, or knew people who'd been hurt by the Mob, or were just flat-out afraid of the "people behind the carting business," did not want to serve on a jury in such a case, and could not be fair. One was a well-known actor who claimed that friends of his in the restaurant business had been victimized by the carters. In addition to those who did not think they could be fair when the defendants were alleged to be members of the Mob, there were those on the other side who had philosophical objections to evidence obtained from wiretaps and concealed tape recorders, although recognizing that these were legally authorized. Finally, there were thousands of people for whom a six-month trial would cause undue economic hardship.

When the group had been whittled down to a few hundred people who were willing and qualified to serve, I questioned groups of them at a time—large groups, with more than one hundred people in each—asking them, for instance, if they could follow some of the legal principles that were at issue in the case. The prosecution and defense each had the opportunity to ask questions as well—as the law permits—and, really, to try to brainwash the prospective jurors to their point of view. The defense objected to my questioning jurors in large groups; they wanted smaller groups, so that they could give their speeches over and over and, of course, make points. In the end, we seated a jury that was of much the same composition as the juries in all of our long cases, a jury such as I've described in an earlier chapter. I was later told that the defense spent over $200,000 on a jury selection expert, who apparently did no good whatsoever. The interminable jury selection process taught me a valuable lesson: Never do it this way again!

One defendant's attorney tragically dropped dead on the court-house steps on the way to court one morning, so his defendant had to be severed from the trial. And so, after numerous guilty pleas had been taken, remaining on trial before me, in May of 1997, were half a dozen individual leaders of the carting industry, several companies, and two associations, including the Association of Trade Waste Removers of Greater New York. The individuals were Phillip Barretti Sr. of Barretti Carting, the third largest in the city, with admitted assets of over $78 million; Louis and Paul Mongelli, owners of the Bronx-based carting company; Alphonse Malangone, a former business agent of the Kings County Trade Waste Association; Joseph Francolino, business agent of GNY; and Frank Giovinco, business agent of another association that was also a defendant, the Greater New York Waste Paper Association.

Malangone and Francolino were the standout defendants—and, in the courtroom, showed us two almost diametrically opposed personalities. Francolino, an alleged soldier in the Gambino family, was a surly character with a chip on his shoulder, full of machismo and so defiant of the system that he came to a bail hearing in a Sergio Tacchini suit that all but screamed he was a gangster. Malangone, an alleged capo in the Genovese family, was much more outgoing and charming and polite at all times: the "gentleman" gangster. Francolino had his family in court, day after day; Malangone would not permit his family to attend, not wanting—as he later told Teresa—to expose them to the bad things that would be discussed there. While Francolino demonstrated his antipathy to everyone in the criminal justice system, Malangone seemed to accept that the prosecutors, the court officials, and the judge were just doing our jobs and ought not to be resented for that.

During the trial, Malangone would frequently lunch at Forlini's, as I did. Most of the time, this presented no problem, as I eat there all the time, I know and love the entire Forlini family, and they knew not to place us near each other. But one day Malangone arrived earlier than I and was somehow seated at a table next to my booth (I have my own booth with my name on the wall adjacent to it). I came in and had to ask Joe Forlini, one of the owners and a friend, to either place me at another table or reseat Malangone, because it would have been unseemly to sit that close to him during the trial. Apprised of this, Malangone obligingly moved elsewhere in the restaurant.

Meanwhile, Francolino frequently came back from lunch apparently drunk and exuding belligerence; even his own lawyer was embarrassed.

At one point I called a recess in the trial so that a Lower East Side drug gang could be brought before me for arraignment. Malangone and Francolino remained in the courtroom as the twenty defendants, handcuffed, and shackled and chained together, were led into the courtroom, surrounded by cops—a dramatic sight. The chained gang defendants were members of Dead Men Walking and Gotti's Crew. Malangone remarked to Teresa that these defendants were monsters and asked, "How can you and the judge bear to deal with them?" Francolino appeared to be more offended, because the leader of one gang dared to call himself by the name of John Gotti, probably his hero as well as his boss.

The lawyers representing Francolino, Malangone, and the trade waste association were good lawyers. One had sat through much of the Cowboys' trial, learning that case because he represented El Feo, one of the men alleged to have been involved in the intended hit on me during that trial and ultimately convicted of multiple murders in federal court. This lawyer made it known that he had read up on almost every case I had ever handled so that he could "learn my style" and anticipate what I would do in this case.

Another liked to hear himself talk and conducted his cross-examinations as if he were on stage, remarking constantly on his own courtroom prowess. A third worked hard at being pleasant to everyone at all times, hoping this would lead to better treatment for his client. One liked to raise every single legal point he could think of—not a bad tactic when you know you're going to appeal if there is a conviction, and one that causes delays and confuses a jury. An additional time-honored tactic used by the defense in this case was to attempt to create reversible error by asking questions of witnesses that were deliberately inappropriate—and to which they knew I'd respond—or by asking questions of witnesses that elicited answers permitting the defense to get information in through the back door that I had ruled was not to be brought in at all.

I sometimes came down hard on these lawyers, and during the inevitable appeal, that was one of their issues—meriting, they felt, a thirty-seven-page diatribe in their brief. In those pages, they claimed that I "interjected [myself] in the proceedings seemingly to try to assure a victory" by the People. To respond, I can say nothing more succinct than the title of the reciprocal section in the DA's appellate brief: "Justice Snyder's Strict Supervision of the Lengthy Proceedings in This Case May Occasionally Have Bruised an Attorney's Ego but Did Not Deprive the Defendants of a Fair Trial." In a perverse way, it was flattering that they felt that I, rather than the evidence, was responsible for their clients' downfall.

One of the most difficult aspects of being the judge in this case was trying to balance, fairly, many of the issues. An outstanding one: How much evidence of organized crime should be allowed in general and as to each defendant? Despite asking questions myself and interrupting when I believed it necessary to clarify issues or control the lawyers—which as an active judge

I do in every case—I, like most judges, strive to be fair to both sides. The OC issue was complex. There was overwhelming evidence of all kinds that the garbage industry was run by the Mob and controlled by the Mob and that many of the defendants were members of a particular Mob crime family. The jury had to understand this basic fact to comprehend how the cartel, through the various trade associations, could maintain such an iron grip on an entire industry and frighten away outsiders over and over again. Thus this proof of OC connections was relevant and probative of the racketeering enterprise charged against the defendants, and I ruled that it would be admitted, balanced by a strong cautionary instruction to the jury as to the purpose of such evidence: to demonstrate how the enterprise could operate as it did, but not to convict anyone for just being in the Mob, which is not a crime.

The undercover, Detective Cowan, was the major prosecution witness; he testified on direct examination for eighteen days and on cross-examination for an additional nine days. Cowan's appearance had apparently made him believable to the defendants as Dan Benedetto, one of their own, even though he was actually of Irish descent. In fact, his unfamiliarity with matters Italian had placed him in jeopardy more than once. The most humorous incident occurred when he was having a meal with Francolino, who had taken a liking to him and had invited him to dinner at a favorite restaurant in Little Italy. Francolino took great care to discuss the menu and various recipes with both Dan and the waiter—an amusing conversation about lasagna recipes is immortalized on one of the tapes—while Francolino was also questioning Dan's true identity. Why should they believe he was who he said he was? How could they be sure he was really Sal's cousin? Francolino stressed that others were very suspicious and Dan had barely survived another frisk. Francolino had heard from a distant cousin of Sal Benedetto's that there was no such person as Dan Benedetto. Amazingly, in spite of all this, when

Cowan showed Francolino a fake driver's license bearing the name Dan Benedetto, this placated Francolino, and he seemed to forget the "problem." He liked Dan, who did not look like or act like a cop, and apparently wanted to believe him. However, Cowan almost blew the entire case when called upon to order his dinner. This "Italian" ordered buffalo mozzarella as a main course, thinking it was a kind of steak, assuring Francolino that it would be more than enough to eat. Francolino looked at him strangely, shrugged, and ordered several courses for himself, including the much discussed lasagna. Another close call. It is difficult to imagine what would have happened had Cowan blown his identity—and the case—due to lack of knowledge of an Italian cheese.

Cowan's testimony—for which he had spent almost two years in preparation, going over the hundreds of tapes—showed Chambers's continuing attempts to obtain new customers and the cartel's continuing attempts to force Chambers to either give back the stops to the individual carters to whom they "belonged" or pay the exorbitant sums demanded by those individual carters for the privilege of taking over the stops. By promising to make good, and then by paying in installments, Chambers (and the police department) kept the undercover arrangement going for a long enough time to amass the mountain of material that demonstrated illegal behavior by all the defendants. But nothing could prevent Sal Benedetto from suffering a beating himself and other violence to Chambers and its employees.

After Cowan's direct testimony, there was a three-day recess. I came back to court to learn that several more defendants had decided to change their pleas to guilty. They included Giovinco, the Mongellis, Barretti, the companies run by the Mongellis and Barretti, and one association. Now only Francolino, Malangone, three companies, and the GNY association remained as defendants.

Later on in the trial, there was a lot of complaining by the prosecution and defense attorneys about one another, and I spoke to them out of the hearing of the jury, chastising them. I told both prosecution and defense lawyers that I felt I was "running a kindergarten." I then called the jury back in and asked them to "ignore all this bickering" among the attorneys, if they could.

In an attempt to defuse the nastiness, at another point in the trial I asked the very theatrical lawyer—in front of the jury—whether "the television rights to your performance [have] been sold yet." "No, but I'm on the market," he said. The jury laughed, but such light interchanges, normal in most of my trials, were few and far between in this one.

Eventually the prosecution called its Mob expert, an FBI agent. His testimony, limited as it had been by my pretrial ruling, was fascinating and had the jury riveted—unlike much of the other trial testimony, which at various points had caused jurors to doze off. The expert detailed the structure of the Mob, discussed the Gambino and Genovese crime families, and explained what one had to do to be a "made" member. This was all relevant because some of the people Cowan had taped claimed only to be hangers-on, because of Francolino's and Malangone's membership in these families and because, on one tape, Francolino was recorded telling Cowan, "We're a cartel. We're the Mafia." From the mouths of mobsters.

Sal Benedetto was called as a witness six months into the trial. As I've said, Sal was an enormous man, so large that he had difficulty walking and could not climb stairs; we had to arrange for him to sit in a lowered chair rather than on the raised witness stand. He concluded direct examination and had begun answering questions on cross-examination from the first of the four attorneys for the defense when it came time for the weekend recess.

On Monday morning, we learned that over that weekend Sal

had been rushed to a hospital with multiple medical problems of an emergency nature and had been placed in intensive care; he suffered respiratory failure there and would have died had he not already been in the hospital. For two weeks thereafter, we proceeded with other prosecution witnesses. Sal got a bit better, was released from the hospital, but was not yet deemed well enough to testify. He then had a setback and had to be readmitted to the hospital. Ultimately, everybody recognized that Sal was not going to be able to return to court to testify in front of the jury. The defense, of course, was hoping that he would not be able to complete his testimony at all, because this would give them grounds for asking me to declare a mistrial—since the defendants would not have been able to conclude their cross-examination of a key witness against them, vitiating their constitutional right to confront the witnesses against them at trial. The People asked for a "conditional examination" of Sal, to be done on videotape in his hospital room—something that the law permits in just this situation, to memorialize the testimony of a witness who may become unavailable because of illness or death. The defense, of course, opposed this.

I ordered the conditional examination: Court personnel and the attorneys on both sides, but not the jury, trooped out to a hospital on Long Island, where we set up cameras and videotaped the rest of the cross-examination of Sal Benedetto. It was sad to see how sick he was, but he persevered in answering the questions for hours, until even the defense lawyers could think of no more. Why did he persevere, sick as he was? I'll never know. Perhaps his own need to do something right by honoring his commitment to come through? There was something admirable about his testifying when he had every right to be terrified. The tape was shown to the jury on the last day of testimony.

When it came time for me to give my "charge," or legal instructions, I joked with the jury that the attorneys had all been "boring" but that I was "going to win the most boring award hands down" with my charge on the law. Unfortunately, I probably did, as the charge lasted an entire day and was drier than sawdust.

Deliberations by the jury were relatively long, and the verdict that they returned, which convicted the defendants of most of the charges, reflected not only the seriousness and complexity of the case, but also the jury's ability to sift through the mountain of evidence and testimony and to think carefully about each count of the indictment. I was pleased with the process and felt that the verdict was reasonable and fair.

Sentencing day arrived. Francolino received an aggregate prison term of from ten to thirty years and a fine of $900,000; Malangone was sentenced to five to fifteen years and fined $200,000; and the trade waste association was fined $9 million and given a conditional discharge. The fourth defendant, a private company, was fined $2 million and also received a conditional discharge—it is hard, even for me, to put a corporation in jail.

The "garbage" case had taken eight months to try and had resulted in the conviction of the seventeen individuals, four trade associations, and twenty-three carting companies named in the initial indictment. Moreover, in conjunction with the freezing of the assets of the indicted companies and individuals—$268 million—New York City Local Law 42 was enacted. This law set standards for the issuance and revocation of waste-hauling licenses and established a watchdog commission that set minimum and maximum rates for garbage collection.

The "garbage" case was truly a landmark case and helped to finish removing the Mob from one of its major sources of income. It freed the garbage-hauling industry and its customers from the continuing fear of reprisals for any attempt to be legitimate. It also opened up that industry to the many small and medium-size garbage companies, most of them family owned, that had long wanted to compete openly for contracts to serve customers fairly. It saved those customers at least $400 million a year. I won't say that it is the end of the Mob in the garbage industry or that the prices charged by carters will never again be exorbitant. . . . In another ten or twenty years, if not sooner, city, state, and federal authorities will probably have to go after the industry again, to keep it clean. But at least for now, this case, coupled with the New York City Trade Waste Commission, has cleaned up an entire industry that—literally and figuratively—stank. A violent, illegal business has been brought under control.*

Although Francolino began to serve his sentence immediately, Malangone filed a notice of appeal and was permitted to remain out on bail by the appellate division. During that period, Teresa and I, my husband, and a friend went to a well-known Italian restaurant on Manhattan's Upper East Side. As we entered, Teresa and I gasped: There at the bar was Alphonse Malangone. My instinct was to turn around and walk out immediately, but I knew Malangone had seen us, and I was not going to be intimidated.

Malangone must have sensed our discomfort, but, ignoring the keen scrutiny of my security detail, he shamelessly walked up to my husband. "This is my favorite judge and my favorite law clerk," he told Fred as he bent over and kissed my cheek.

I wanted to pull away, but that would have been rude and might have been misinterpreted, so I permitted it and retorted instead, "And this is my favorite gangster!" He laughed.

"Do you think that was the kiss of death?" I whispered to Fred as we walked on.

*As in this industry, Rudy Giuliani probably did more to reduce crime in New York City than anyone ever has, along with people like former police commissioner Bill Bratton and the late Jack Maple.

He smiled in response and we sat down to dinner, wanting nothing more than to get through it and get out of there without further embarrassment. This was not meant to be. Malangone approached our table from the bar—with his wife. She looked distinctly hostile as he introduced her to us, and I was briefly at a loss as to what to say. Having been brought up to be polite, I finally murmured, "It's nice to meet you, Mrs. Malangone; your husband is a very nice man."

"I know that," she snapped back, then turned sharply and walked away to what was to be the Malangone table of relatives or friends in the back of the room. I was mortified. Why had I said he was a very nice man when he was, at best, a very nice gangster? And Mrs. Malangone clearly had no more desire to meet me—someone she obviously hated in theory—than vice versa. We went back to eating our food.

But the service was slow. In fact, it was almost nonexistent, because virtually every waiter in the place was attending the gentleman gangster and his party in the back, leaving almost no one to serve the other people in the restaurant.

The dinner seemed to take forever, and we were all grateful when it was over. We have never returned to that restaurant.

Sometime thereafter, all appeals in the case were denied, and Malangone began serving his sentence.

MURDERS
MOST FOUL:
CONFRONTING
PURE EVIL

Two eighty-year-old sisters survive the Holocaust only to be brutally robbed and beaten, one murdered and one left for dead in their ransacked apartment....

A crackhead disappears from the face of the earth; only her sister cares what happened to her. Years later, a skeleton is discovered, stuffed into a small refrigerator in a crack house....

A defendant wants people to believe he is a dog—at least sometimes—and that the dog or one of his other personalities viciously slashed and dismembered a lonely young woman....

A father is enraged when his daughter marries "beneath" her and without his permission, and he arranges for a drug dealer to hire a hit man to kill the undesirable son-in-law....

An evil, vicious man and his follower decide to rob a neighbor, kill him for no reason, and rape and sodomize the neighbor's innocent girlfriend, leaving her for dead and ruining her life....

These are but a few of the horrific cases over which I've presided during the last fifteen years—cases that make you wonder: Can you face the underbelly of humanity every day and escape with your own sensitivity intact? Confronted with the worst of human nature, can you continue to react "normally"—or react at all?

After I had been presiding over drug cases for several years, I asked my administrative judge to send me some murder cases as well. Some of those that I'll detail in this chapter, I received in the usual assigned way, and some came from the "capital wheel," established when the death penalty was reinstituted in 1995. I was selected as one of six judges who would handle murder cases in which the death penalty might be a sentencing option.

Terrell Martin:* pure evil. There is no other description possible for this man. What makes someone act like a monster? How does our society create someone like Martin, who ruins every life he touches? Here's what I recall as I relive this case. . . .

Anika is a beautiful, bright African American girl of nineteen. She is from a poor family, but her parents work hard and they learn of a school program outside the ghetto that will put her on the "fast track," remove her from the public school system, and give her a real chance at a better life. She is accepted into that program, does well in it, and receives a scholarship to attend a top college. Her life is on track, and things are going well—until she meets a young man on the subway.

John seems very nice. They talk; they have dinner; they begin to date. It is Christmas vacation, and she's home from college; Anika goes to John's apartment in Harlem to have dinner and spend the night.

Meanwhile, Terrell Martin is thinking about Christmas, too,

*All the names in this case have been changed to protect the victim.

255

but he's not imbued with the spirit of giving. He convinces his friend Mack that they need money. Neither Martin nor Mack has ever worked at a legitimate job, so for them the obvious way to obtain money is to rob someone. John is Mack's neighbor, and he becomes their target because Mack knows that John owns nice things like a Nintendo and stereo equipment. He knows this because Mack and John have been friendly neighbors and have never had any problems with each other.

It is evening and the lights are turned low in John's apartment. He is lying on the floor, half-dressed, with Anika, and they are listening to music when Mack knocks on the door. At first John tries to convince Mack to go away and leave them alone, but Mack is insistent and finally John opens the door.

Terrell Martin and Mack push in. Martin, the instigator and aggressor, demands money, pulls out a knife, and holds it to John's throat. Anika is told to avert her eyes and to stay on the floor in the semidarkness. She hears John tell the intruders to take whatever they want and go.

Martin is not satisfied with this offer. For no apparent reason, he stabs John—again and again. Mack joins him in the stabbing. Anika can see them both from the corner of her eye as they lean over John, making downward, stabbinglike motions. She hears John begging for his life: "Please don't hurt me! Please, take anything you want! Please!" The cries soon dissolve into a mumble . . . and then she can hear no sounds at all.

Anika doesn't know whether John is dead or alive. She is petrified, too much in fear to scream. And if she did scream, who would hear her? Anika believes she is going to die, but she is helpless. There is no one to help her, no place to go. She should have listened to her mother and broken off this relationship with a guy who her mother insisted was going nowhere. It's too late now.

Martin and Mack drag John's body into the bedroom, and

then Martin turns to Anika. "Get in the bathroom, you whore. Don't look at me; I'll kill you, bitch."

"Please don't . . . please don't!" she begs.

But he drags her into the bathroom, rapes her, sodomizes her, and then Mack comes in and does the same. After that they drag her into the bedroom and Martin throws her on the bed and sodomizes her again, while complaining that his feet are slipping on John's blood. Anika can see John's body nearby, can practically touch it, while she's being attacked, and now she knows for sure that he is dead.

Martin orders Mack to kill Anika, saying, "I killed him, you kill her. Don't leave no witness, asshole!"

Mack dutifully takes her into the bathroom and rapes her again. Now she not only knows she's going to die, she wants to die. She moans. But Mack says, "Shut up, bitch! Just stay here for two hours and don't leave. I'm not going to kill you."

The doors close, and she cannot believe that she is still alive. She is so distraught that she'd just as soon be dead.

She remains in the bathroom for what seems like forever but is only about twenty minutes; finally she gathers whatever willpower she has left and runs out, naked except for a blanket. A bloody mess herself, she doesn't know where to go or how to get help. In a daze, she makes it to a nearby bodega and dials 911.

These were the main facts of the case as I garnered them from conferences with the lawyers and from the grand jury minutes, before any hearings or trial. The assistant DA assigned to the case was an intense young woman from the sex crimes unit, whom I'll call Sarah. I liked her immediately because of her obvious concern for the victim and for the case; she was determined to prosecute both defendants successfully.

Over the course of the next year, I came to learn much more about the case: how the police initially bungled the investigation; how the defendants were not caught for several years and not until Martin had committed additional vicious crimes; the details of the surviving victim's background and her current state of despair.

In our criminal justice system, so much depends on luck and chance. Most defendants have assigned counsel, because whatever money they might have made or stolen has disappeared into the drugs they smoke, shoot up, or snort or into the purchase of clothes, jewelry, and women. Some assigned attorneys are mediocre, most are adequate, and—very occasionally— some are superb. Terrell Martin was very lucky: He was assigned a brilliant and wily attorney, whom I'll call Harry, who was arbitrarily selected from a group of "capital defenders." These are defense lawyers who attend what they call "death camp" and receive special training in handling death penalty cases. In capital cases, which are limited to certain serious felonies and extraordinary circumstances, the prosecution can seek the death penalty and has to decide whether to do so within 120 days of the defendant's arraignment on his or her indictment. In this case, Martin and Mack were charged with multiple counts of rape, sodomy, and murder and, as to Martin, murder in the first degree or capital murder, because of the prosecutor's view that his conduct fell within the capital murder statute.

Harry's first goal was to have the DA's office decline to seek the death penalty so that his client would then face *only* life without parole; if he were successful, Harry and Martin could then decide what tactic to pursue later on. Harry mounted a massive investigation into Martin's background, learning that he had purportedly been an abused child, passing from one foster home to the next and successively abused in each. Harry presented the facts he had accumulated to a panel established by the Manhattan District Attorney's Office to recommend to the DA himself whether or not to pursue the death penalty in each eligible case. I had been told, off the record, that almost everyone on this panel is opposed to the death penalty and that while the ostensible purpose of the panel is to consider the facts of each case, the primary purpose appears to be to insulate Morgenthau from personally making the decision on the death penalty and to assure that the death penalty—to which he is opposed—will never be sought by his office, regardless of the nature of the case. I have no proof of this, of course, but the fact is that since 1995 the Manhattan District Attorney's Office has never sought the death penalty for any defendant. I was hardly surprised when the panel ruled, once again, that in the Martin case the prosecution would not seek the death penalty.

One could spend hundreds of pages discussing the pros and cons of capital punishment. Suffice it to say, I believe it is no panacea and should be used only sparingly, for the most heinous cases, and with appropriate safeguards in place to assure that there is no miscarriage of justice. In my view, Terrell Martin was the perfect candidate for the death penalty. The man was gratuitously evil, vicious, violent, and dangerous, and if his guilt could be proven beyond a reasonable doubt, I would not lose a moment's sleep if a jury decided that death was the only appropriate sentence. In our system, only a jury can decide such a penalty, in a separate sentencing proceeding conducted after a verdict of guilty has been rendered; moreover, the jury must be unanimous in its decision for the death penalty or the defendant will receive some other, lesser sentence, life without parole or twenty years to life as a minimum under New York law. I believe that the jury, not the Manhattan District Attorney's Office, should have had to decide whether or not Terrell Martin should have been put to death for his crimes. Sarah, who had spent time with Anika and had seen up close what had happened to that lovely young victim's life—and who had also learned a great deal about Martin and Mack—appeared to agree with my view and to be disgusted by the decision not to seek the death penalty.

Because Mack was not facing death, because there were different legal issues regarding him, and because there were "interlocking confessions" (a special consideration under the law), it became necessary to give each defendant a separate trial.

The Martin matter was considered first. In pretrial conferences, more facts emerged about the night of the awful events. While raping Anika, Martin boasted of his prowess, even asking her, among other endearing questions, "Who do you like better? I'm bigger, right?" Despite her trauma, Anika had definite impressions of who had done what to her and in what room, but she had not actually seen the defendants' faces clearly because she had been too frightened to open her eyes during most of her ordeal. There was the possibility that she might be confused as to the role of each defendant. Fortunately for the prosecution, at the outset of the events she had indeed seen both men stabbing her boyfriend, and she also knew that both had brutalized her sexually. And both defendants were charged on the theory of "acting in concert," even if they were to be tried separately.

The concept of acting in concert, which has to do with accomplice liability, was central to every one of the multidefendant cases tried in my court and made it possible to convict minor players as well as major ones. In this case, the concept was such that it made no difference in the eyes of the law which defendant had a major or minor role in committing the crimes in John's apartment, as long as each of them intended to commit the crime and either ordered it or intentionally aided the other in its commission.

Additional facts emerged in pretrial hearings about Anika's ordeal—at the hands of the 911 operator, whom she called as she stood in the bodega, bloodied, near hysteria, and covered only with a blanket on a cold December night. The female civilian operator had put her through a new hell by asking such questions as "Where are you calling from?" "Give me the exact address." "Where did this happen?" "What apartment?" "What floor?" "I can't help you unless you give me the specific information I want, and if you don't, I'll have to hang up." This insensitive inquisition continued on until the bodega owner interceded and spoke to the 911 operator and Anika calmed down enough to give the basic information. I was sufficiently outraged that I resolved to send a copy of the 911 tape to the police commissioner after the proceedings were completed. By the time they were, I learned that the operator had been fired, apparently for unrelated but—I would suspect—similar offenses.

Martin had finally been arrested for these crimes while in North Carolina in 1997. Harry convinced Martin that he should pursue a particular strategy. First Harry would conduct a "Huntley-Dunaway" hearing. At that type of hearing, I would have to determine whether there had been probable cause for Martin's arrest and whether any confession made was voluntary and admissible. Martin, through Harry, was raising a variety of legal obstacles to its admissions, characterizing the statement as the tainted fruit of an illegal arrest. Harry told Martin that if he lost at the hearing and the motion to suppress was denied, Martin should then plead guilty and attempt to bargain to receive some lesser penalty than life without parole so that he might someday "see the light of day."

I was adamantly opposed to any plea bargain. Sarah had informed Harry and me that Anika had tried to commit suicide more than once since the murder and rapes, had dropped out of college, and could not seem to put her life back together. With such consequences, why should the man who caused them ever see the light of day again? My blood boiled, but I did not have to decide anything until after the suppression hearing, to which the defendant was of course entitled.

I then had to decide a number of legal issues that judges have to deal with all the time, but which never show up on television programs dealing with the law; they involve "technical" issues of the sort that TV producers evidently believe no commercial sponsor would want to pay for. In this instance, the legal issues required extensive hearings, arguments by both sides, and a lot of careful research. The facts were that Martin had been caught in North Carolina, where he was terrorizing a housing project, abusing his "wife" and children, and dealing drugs. Before moving there but well after killing John and leaving Anika for dead, Martin had dealt drugs and guns elsewhere, was alleged to have shot another gun and drug dealer and left him for dead, and had generally conducted a rampage of crime across several states. Was his arrest lawful; had his confession been obtained properly pursuant to a lawful arrest and without violating his right to counsel? I denied his motion to suppress, ruling in favor of the prosecution, finding all law enforcement conduct to have been lawful. His confession would be admitted at his trial.

Harry now begged for any plea for his client. I turned a deaf ear and made my position clear to the DA's office. But the ADA understandably wanted to spare Anika from having to testify at a trial, so she agreed to a plea for Martin of forty-five years to life. If Martin lived until the end of the minimum, he would be around seventy, and I doubted that someone as violent as he was would survive that long in prison. I reluctantly agreed to accept his plea.

Throughout all these proceedings, Martin had exhibited no emotion, no affect. When I sentenced him, I had difficulty controlling my own emotions; after hearing again from ADA Sarah about what had happened to the victim Anika, I wanted to weep and could not prevent tears from welling in my eyes, which was a very unusual thing for me in the courtroom. In a moment of anger, I actually told Martin that he should have received the death penalty and that I would have been willing to give him the lethal injection myself. He could not have cared less.

We now all expected the co-defendant, Mack, to plead guilty

as well, to receive a similar but slightly lower sentence because he was not facing the murder one charge. But he was a very strange man who insisted on going to trial and did so clutching a Bible, having convinced his mother and aunt to believe in his innocence. He admitted only one rape to the police, which, sadly, made it necessary for Anika to testify after all. Fortunately, she was treated quite gently on the witness stand.

Mack was convicted and sentenced to a lengthy prison term of seventy-five years to life. While Martin, as part of his plea bargain, had waived his right to appeal, Mack did not. His case is still on appeal, so I cannot discuss anything more about his trial.

In August 1982, the sisters Rose Jacobs and Ida Kass are in their late eighties. They grew up in Nazi Germany and were interned in the death camps; surviving the Holocaust, they came to New York and took up residence in one of the nicer housing projects in upper Manhattan. By 1982, the housing project in which they share an apartment is no longer such a nice one. They've also endured crime in New York, a push-in robbery and burglary at the apartment a few months before.

This day, two people push their way into the sister's apartment, brutally beat them, rob them, and leave them for dead. By the time the assault is over, Rose is lying dead in the bedroom, her hands bound, her head bashed in. Ida, brutally beaten, has survived and she calls 911—once, and then again after a few minutes when there has been no response. Two minutes later, the emergency response team arrives; they hear from Ida some of what happened, and they take her to a local hospital; on their charts they list her as "likely," police shorthand for likely to die.

When the police come, they dust the various surfaces of the apartment for fingerprints and they lift, from among the many prints of Rose and Ida, half a dozen other latent prints, most significantly from inside the bedroom in which Rose has been killed. Ida, almost miraculously and after a lengthy hospital stay, emerges to live for another five years. But the people who broke into her apartment are not identified or arrested.

For many years, no matches to the set of latent prints lifted from Ida and Rose's apartment were found. Before 1990, the NYPD had no automated means of comparing fingerprints; all comparisons had to be done by hand, a lengthy and laborious process somewhat reminiscent of the use of quill pens by court reporters to record entire trials (instead of today's computerized machinery).

In 1990, however, the NYPD acquired a new, computerized fingerprint-matching machine known by the acronym SAFIS, which allowed thousands of prints to be fed into the computer's data bank and identified. Gradually, prints from all old, unsolved cases were fed into the new system. So in 1991, even though both victims were now deceased, the NYPD fortuitously decided to run the 1982 prints from their apartment against the two million then on file in SAFIS. Two possible matches were found—those belonging to an emergency medical technician and those belonging to Anthony Jackson. Since 1982, Jackson had been a busy man. He had committed numerous crimes, including serious felonies, and was about to be sentenced for violating his parole in a robbery case.

In June 1991, two detectives went to the jail and detention center on Riker's Island in Queens, to interview Jackson, who was being held there on the parole violation. Jackson agreed to speak to them, and they read him his *Miranda* warnings and then interviewed him very carefully. The lead detective deliberately did not specifically say he was investigating the murder of Rose Jacobs and the attempted murder of Ida Kass, and just as deliberately did not let Jackson know that his prints had been found in the sisters' apartment. Rather, he asked Jackson if he had ever been in that section of Manhattan or in that housing project. Jackson not only denied knowledge of the building, but also stated vehemently that he had never even been in the area of Manhattan in which it was located. He also denied knowing the victims. The lead detective wrote out what Jackson said and showed it to him; Jackson asked that the sentence that said he had never been in the housing project be amended. He would not sign the statement until it reflected his insistence that he had "never been in that area" of New York City—never in his entire life. Then he signed the statement.

This document was what we call a "false exculpatory statement": It was a denial of the defendant's presence in the apartment, when that presence could be proved by other evidence—namely, his fingerprints and palm print on the inside of the bedroom door in the bedroom in which Rose had been murdered. With the fingerprints and his denials, the detectives believed they had a case against Jackson for the murder and attempted murder of the Holocaust survivors. But the DA's office evidently thought the case still had legal problems—such as the delay between the lifting of the prints and their identification—and did not immediately order an arrest.

Six months later, one of the detectives realized that Jackson was due to be released from an upstate prison on New Year's Eve 1991 and that he would then likely disappear from view; he argued strenuously enough to obtain permission to go to the prison and, as Jackson walked out, to rearrest him for the murder of Rose Jacobs and for various other charges stemming from the break-in of Rose and Ida's apartment in 1982.

At an initial speedy-trial hearing, I asked the fingerprint expert to clarify various points—for instance, how he had happened to compare the prints from this old case with those in the new SAFIS system. It turned out to have been almost random: When the experts had extra time, they ran groups of prints from old cases through the computer. At the end of the hearing, I ruled that since the computerized fingerprint match system had not existed in 1982, the fact that it had taken nine years to match Jackson's prints to those from the scene of the crime did not constitute a violation of the defendant's constitutional right to a speedy trial.

This issue is, to laymen, one of the most boring aspects of a case, but being guaranteed a speedy trial is one of the most important rights that every defendant has, and it is covered both by state statutes and by the U.S. Constitution. You'll probably never see on TV programs that pretend to accuracy (like *Law & Order*) the tedious process of counting up what days have been "consented" to—that is, are not to be counted toward the state's requirement for a speedy trial—and which have not. Or how we analyze the requirements for the constitutional right to a speedy trial, for instance, by evaluating whether the delay was intentional, avoidable, or prejudiced the defendant. In the Jackson case, the delay was clearly unavoidable, because the technology to solve the crime, or at least to point to a likely suspect, had become available only eight years after the crime.

Anthony Jackson was by then a thirty-year-old man with a long criminal history. While prior to the Jacobs-Kass incident— which took place when he was nineteen—Jackson's arrests had been mostly for misdemeanors, in the interim between 1982 and 1991, he had twice been convicted of felonies involving robberies, which made him a "predicate felon." He now faced an A-1 felony, with the maximum sentence of twenty-five years to life. He was represented by an experienced, state-assigned attorney, Harold Schwartz, who had appeared before me many times and with whom I enjoyed a relationship of mutual respect. Schwartz tried hard to talk Jackson into accepting a plea with a minimum of ten years, but Jackson insisted it was not his signature on the statement from Riker's Island and that he was innocent and would not plead guilty. This stance appeared particularly irrational, for several reasons. The DA's offer was, in my view, very generous when measured against the enormity of the crime being charged. The "defense" of a forged signature on the document also appeared ill-advised, because Schwartz informed Jackson that if a handwriting expert—engaged by the defense—decided that the signature was indeed Jackson's (as seemed likely), he would be in an even worse position at trial. Jackson seemed not to care about that.

Nor did he seem to care whether his case was decided by a jury or a judge. I had called for a jury panel and was screening the panel when the defendant made an unusual application. In New York State, as in some other jurisdictions, only the defendant can waive a jury trial and opt to be tried by a judge.* Often the trial judge is, as I had been, the same judge who has already heard evidence that a jury would not be permitted to hear because it would be considered too prejudicial, such as evidence about the defendant's background and his numerous convictions for violent crimes. The jury might hear about some of these, but only if the defendant actually took the witness stand in his own defense—a rare event in our system. In this instance, I knew a great deal about Jackson's background and prior convictions. So imagine my surprise when he suddenly told Harold Schwartz that he wanted to waive a jury. Most defense lawyers believe that I know the law and will apply it fairly but will come down hard on violent criminals whose credibility is suspect. So they advise their clients to take their chances with a jury, not with me.

I asked Harold Schwartz to explain clearly to his client that due to the nasty facts alleged, waiving a jury was not a good idea; while I, as the judge, knew I could keep an open mind

*In federal court, both the prosecution and the defense must consent to the defendant's request for a jury waiver.

about the case, since I had not yet heard all the evidence, I advised against it. Harold explained this to Jackson. I explained it to him, too—at length and on the record. Perhaps he reasoned that the jury would have too much sympathy for the murder and near murder of two lovely old ladies whose lives had almost been snuffed out decades earlier in the most massive, barbaric, and brutal killings known to mankind in all of history. Who knows? In any event, after I questioned him to insure that he knew what he was doing and was doing it of his own free will, he still insisted on waiving a jury trial, and we proceeded to trial without a jury.

Oddly, from time to time during the trial, Jackson would suggest that he might well take the stand—and then he would indicate just the opposite. Ultimately, he did not testify. And he also would not take a plea with a minimum of seven years, the absurdly lenient offer tendered in midtrial by the DA.

Jackson was one of those people who had been in and out of the criminal justice system so many times and had received such relatively lenient treatment—dismissal because of his age, probation, deferred sentences, time served, plea bargains that got him out in six months—that he may have believed he could beat the rap this time, too.

The ADA in charge of the case had had to drop all charges except the murder because the statute of limitations had run out on the others and they could no longer be prosecuted. The trial proceeded quickly because there was no jury present, but even so I occasionally became impatient at the pace and had to ask questions of witnesses to cut through some repetitive material and to obtain clarification. How many different ways do you have to ask (and have answered) the question of what the police witness "really" means when he says the apartment was "ransacked"? Or inquire as to why the EMT witness checked only some of Rose Jacobs's vital signs to ascertain she was dead and not others? "I heard it; I'm not a jury," I said to defense counsel after one such repeated interchange, meaning that I didn't require as much explanation as a jury might. "All right, I give up," Schwartz retorted.

At another juncture, the court reporter recorded the following interchange:

> *The Court:* You're acting as if there's a jury here. I get your point; you make the same point six times over, Mr. Schwartz. I get it. I get it.
> *Mr. Schwartz:* Judge, I understand. It's a tough thing.
> *The Court:* You know—[the ADA], he's got more patience than I do.
> *Mr. Schwartz:* Well, teaching an old dog new tricks—
> *The Court:* You're talking to an old dog!

Once, when Schwartz had finished with a witness and had tried to leave a somewhat inaccurate impression, I jumped in and asked the witness questions whose answers served to dispel the lingering ambiguities (something I end up doing in many cases, I must admit). Evidence—and the record—should be crystal clear.

But it was really the assistant district attorney who disturbed me the most. While his murder case was not overwhelming, he had the fingerprints and palm print and the signed Jackson statement—which the handwriting expert did conclude was actually signed by Jackson, despite his protests that it was not. It was a strong circumstantial case. Of course, there could be doubts raised on certain substantive points: One could not say exactly when the fingerprints had been put on the door or wall; they could have been there for some time before the crimes took place. Similarly, one could argue that because Jackson had not been apprised of the specific crime the police were investigating, he had made a broad, blanket denial, whereas if he had been apprised that they were looking into the murder, he might have said, for example, that he had earlier burglarized that apartment but hadn't killed anyone—a statement that could have provided a reason, however implausible, for the prints on the bedroom wall. The question was whether any of these doubts were *reasonable* doubts.

These potential doubts were why, when, partway through the trial, the tape recordings of two 911 calls relating to the incident finally turned up, the tapes were such likely bombshells. On them, Ida Kass calls for help, describes some of the injuries, and provides a partial description of the attackers. Even after the existence of these tapes became known, the ADA did not want to introduce them into evidence. He had various legal reasons for not doing so—for instance, there was no one who could verify that the voice on the tape was Ida Kass's, and the precedents relating to introducing such tapes were not *crystal* clear—but he did not want to try. In between moans and groans, Kass had described a tall black man (and his "wife") as her assailants, and she had also said that the perpetrators had previously robbed the sisters in that apartment. Anthony Jackson was black, six feet three inches tall, and he had a history of arrests for robberies and break-ins. I was apoplectic at the DA's position—the case needed these tapes, and while the precedents were not overwhelming, they were sufficient—certainly sufficient in a case where anyone, especially the prosecutor, ought to have had enough outrage about the facts to want to pursue the case aggressively. Finally, the ADA decided to introduce the 911 tapes.

Of course, an appellate court might later toss out a conviction if it determined that the tapes were wrongly introduced, but that did not seem probable. In fact, I thought that if the tapes were not introduced, there might be a greater chance of reversal on appeal: The 911 tapes would not become part of the evidence on which I would have to rule, and were I to find the defendant guilty, the case would be more likely to be found legally insufficient. Putting in the tapes would allow me to rule based on all the evidence and would allow an appellate court to rule on the sufficiency of all the evidence and, if it found the admission of the tapes to have been error, to assess the sufficiency of the evidence without them. It seemed obvious to me, therefore, that the prosecution had to offer the tapes.

In his summation, the ADA explained what he thought Kass had implied on the 911 tapes: Jackson beat the sisters in an attempt to get them to reveal where they had hidden the treasures that he had not found and taken during the previous robbery.

At the end of the case, I reserved decision and later delivered my verdict in writing. In a lengthy decision, I found Jackson guilty of felony murder. Sentencing came still later.* Jackson told the probation authorities involved in preparing a presentence report that he might have been in the apartment prior to the break-in, delivering groceries. "I suppose that would explain why his fingerprints were found on the inside of the murder victim's bedroom door," I commented sarcastically.

Because of the utter viciousness of the crime, the defendant's long history of violent criminal behavior, and his refusal to accept any responsibility for his actions, I sentenced him to the maximum, twenty-five years to life. And I hoped that removing him from society for this long a period brought some measure of justice to the memory of the two elderly women who had survived the Holocaust but had not been able to escape this vicious predator.

It is 1985. Veroah Turner is an eighteen-year-old crack-addicted mother of two small children when Tom Crawford lures her into an abandoned building that is being used as a crack house. He

---

*The verdict and sentence came after months of submissions by both sides and a lengthy written opinion by me. On appeal, the defendant's sole claim was that the verdict was unduly delayed. He never denied his guilt.

believes she has stolen $300 from him and has used it to buy crack and smoke it. In the crack house, Crawford accuses her of stealing the money, and Turner pleads with him to be allowed to pay him back, but he decides to kill her anyway. He strangles her to death using an electrical wire, a cloth belt, and a scrub brush to tighten the ligature. Crawford then stuffs her body into a plastic bag, puts it in an unused refrigerator, seals the refrigerator with putty, and flees. Her sister reports Veroah missing, but no one knows she had gone to that crack house, so no traces of her are found—and other than her children and her sister, no one on earth cares.

More than a year later, a desiccated body was discovered inside a refrigerator in an abandoned building. The skull had fallen off, but the body was clothed and had been folded into a fetal-type position. It took additional time and some innovative forensic techniques to figure out the body's identity and to find ways to make a match between the skeleton and what was known of Veroah Turner.

You might wonder why the police would expend time and energy on such a case. Aside from the requirements of justice— that any murder ought to be thoroughly investigated and the perpetrator brought to trial—there was the sense that the person who had strangled this vulnerable woman was surely capable of killing other people and that unless the perpetrator was found, he or she would very likely go on to commit more murders. But what was important to this case were a determined, able prosecutor and dedicated and caring detectives.

In 1987, a man known to be a friend of Veroah Turner's, Gregory Capers, was arrested for assault in New Jersey, and the New York detective assigned to the Turner case questioned him about her murder. Capers thought, based on remarks that his childhood friend Tom "Slick" Crawford had previously made to him, that the murder was probably committed by Crawford, who Capers knew was then in jail in Georgia for manslaughter.

As with many cases, including some that we have discussed, it became obvious that the only way to solve the crime would be to enlist Capers's assistance—for which, of course, he would want more lenient treatment. Another deal would have to be made. But in this instance, someone charged with a lesser crime would receive a benefit for bringing a murderer to justice, and that was a deal that in no way shocked anyone's conscience.

At the detectives' request, Capers contacted the defendant's family in Georgia to determine in which prison Crawford was serving time. Capers wrote Crawford, saying he would like to visit him, and the defendant readily agreed. Since prison visits were restricted to relatives, the defendant placed the name Dennis Crawford on his visitors list.

With the assistance of the authorities, Capers spoke with Crawford in prison while wearing two concealed tape recorders, both controlled by the detectives who accompanied him. Crawford started the conversation by asking if the police had found "out about that girl yet" and gave a chilling account of how he had "croaked the shit out of that whore" and "crunched her body up," providing details of the crime (and its concealment) that only the killer could have known. He also conveyed his attitude by such statements as [that he] "ain't lost a near drop of sleep over that shit there" and felt no remorse because the "bitch dead, that's all."

Five years after the murder—and after Gregory Capers himself had died—the Crawford case was assigned to me. The immediate issue in a pretrial hearing was whether the Capers-Crawford taped conversation was admissible, an issue made more complicated since Capers was no longer around to provide the normal basis for its introduction. But the defense's most significant contention was that because Crawford had not been read his *Miranda* rights before talking with Capers, the confession should be excluded.

As a general rule, after a suspect has been taken into custody, *Miranda* warnings must precede any interrogation by law enforcement officers. However, this was not an "interrogation" by law enforcement, and there was some precedent for not reading the defendant any *Miranda* warnings in this situation; after all, this was a conversation between two friends, and the fact that Crawford was unaware it was being taped was irrelevant to whether his "rights" were or should have been preserved. While legally the position that Crawford should have been read his rights was one that the defense had to advance, it seemed so absurd to me that I could not restrain myself in addressing it. Can anyone seriously believe that the police should arrive at a prison, advise an incarcerated defendant of his *Miranda* rights, and then tell him an old friend of his wants to talk to him? To place such a restraint on law enforcement would be to gag it: No inmate would hold a conversation with an old friend and possibly incriminate himself after such warnings—and the interests of justice would not be served.

Any such requirement would defeat the entire purpose of the questioning; the police might as well take a defendant out of jail and bring him or her to a police station. Unless an incarcerated defendant's confession is actually coerced, being in jail alone should never, in and of itself, be considered coercive per se. Although the issue had not yet been addressed in liberal New York State, the U.S. Supreme Court had recently addressed a similar issue, holding in relevant part that the ingredients of a "police-dominated atmosphere and compulsion are not present when an incarcerated person speaks freely to someone whom he believes" to be—in that case—a fellow inmate; the coercive element is lacking. Our case was even stronger. Adopting the Supreme Court's reasoning and building on it, I also found that when a friend, real or feigned, speaks with an incarcerated defendant while assisting the police, this is not the functional equivalent of interrogation as envisioned by *Miranda*. The defendant was free to terminate the conversation at any time and to leave, albeit to return to his jail cell.

Since Capers was acting as an agent of the police, it had been critical that Crawford incriminate himself voluntarily and that Capers not put any words into Crawford's mouth. But Capers had not had to say anything about the murder, because even before pleasantries had been exchanged between Capers and Crawford, the defendant himself had brought up the murder, boasting about it in vivid detail—and on tape. Since no charges had been filed against the defendant as to Veroah's murder, the only subject of legal inquiry, the defendant's Sixth Amendment right to counsel had not attached. Moreover, because officers had observed the conversation between the two men and had taken custody of the tape right after it was made (and had never thereafter breached the chain of custody), it was admissible.

Another issue at trial was whether and how the People could prove that the skeletal remains in the refrigerator were those of Veroah Turner. Crawford had assisted the police in this regard by corroborating that identification in his conversation with Capers—but another key to the proof was the testimony of a forensic anthropologist called by the prosecution as an expert witness. She was an expert in the reconstruction of faces and features from skeletal remains by means of painstaking physical reconstruction aided by photographs of the victim and computer projections. Using those techniques, she was able to conclude that the victim had been a black or Negroid female, slim, from twenty-five to twenty-eight years old but appearing older than she was either by reason of childbirth or drug use. In an ingenious videotape that was played for the jury, the forensic anthropologist took video images of both the victim's exhumed skull and an actual photograph of Veroah provided by her sister and superimposed the images. It was an electric moment in the courtroom as the images came together and the forensic anthropologist gave us her conclusion that the skull was indeed that of Veroah Turner.

Another point raised by the defense in a presummation conference was a request to charge the jury with manslaughter as a "lesser included" crime, and with the defense of intoxication, on the ground that—and here the evidence they cited was from the tape—Crawford had been, in his own words, "fucked up" on crack at the time of the murder and that "if I wasn't high off that crack, I probably wouldn't have croaked her, probably would have whupped her ass." These charges, if given by me, would have allowed Crawford's counsel to argue to the jury that Crawford was not guilty of the murder because he had been high on crack and would have allowed the jury to find Crawford guilty of the lesser crime of manslaughter.

The defense argued that the defendant's own words manifested sufficient evidence of intoxication, but the prosecution pointed out that most of the defendant's own words, including his clear and vivid account of holding the wire around Veroah's neck for a full five minutes as well as his description of the procedure of folding her into a bag, stuffing the bag into the refrigerator, and sealing it, demonstrated that Crawford knew exactly what he was doing. The prosecutor argued that to do all this, Crawford could not have been intoxicated, that he did have the specific intent to kill Veroah, and that no impairment from crack was involved in forming that intent—despite the existence on the tape of one self-serving remark that he had been high at the time of the murder. I refused to submit the manslaughter charge and the intoxication defense to the jury, since, as the appellate court later ruled, "There was insufficient proof of intoxication to allow a reasonable person to entertain a doubt as to the element of intent on that basis." It also ruled that "contrary to defendant's contentions, the record demonstrates that he lured the victim to the site of the crime, was coherent at that time and strangled the victim for some five minutes until he was sure she was dead. The nature and brutality of the crime also negate defendant's argument that he formed an intent other than to kill the victim," thereby making a manslaughter and intoxication charge inappropriate.

Crawford was convicted of murder in the second degree. I sentenced him to the maximum, twenty-five years to life—to be served after he concluded his twenty-year sentence in Georgia for the unrelated manslaughter conviction. A man who had no conscience, no concern about right or wrong, who did whatever he wanted to advance his own interests, had been brought to justice. Veroah's children and sister had some degree of closure at last.

One day in September 1994, Fogarty George, a Guyanese by birth, comes back to Manhattan from vacation to find a message from a fellow Guyanese, Rohee Sibadan. Returning the call, George is interested and perhaps a bit surprised to learn of his old friend's somewhat unusual request: "I want someone killed!"

Rohee Sibadan knows that Fogarty George had once upon a time been on a relatively straight and narrow path as the owner of Fogarty's Sportswear store in upper Manhattan but has since strayed from that path. To garner more business, George relocated his store right into the heart of a crack-selling district in Manhattan Valley and cultivated customers among the dealers. Soon he allegedly began to sell kilogram quantities of cocaine, as well as fancy jackets, sweatshirts, and sneakers. Because Sibadan knows this, he has telephoned George.

When they speak together, Sibadan gives George some of the back story: It seems that Sibadan's daughter Sara has fallen in love with another Guyanese, a man named Fizul Khan, who has previously worked with Sibadan in his shipping business but is now holding down two jobs, one at a nursing home and a second as a driver for a car service. Over the summer, Sara and

Fizul have gotten married in a secret civil ceremony—secret in part because the Sibadan family practices the Hindu religion, and Khan is a Muslim, and the young people know that Rohee Sibadan would not approve. They also know that Sibadan would never approve because he considered Fizul "beneath" his family and wants to select an appropriate husband for Sara himself. After Sibadan finds out about the marriage, he attempts to have Khan send his daughter back home. Confrontations with each of the young lovers do not bring about that result; in fact, at one point, Sibadan is so angry that he nearly chokes his daughter to death. Sibadan then decides to pay someone to kill Khan so that his daughter will return home, without the undesirable spouse.

Fogarty George takes in all this information and agrees to find a hit man. Sibadan gives George a photo of Khan, the phone number of the taxi service, and the license plate of the taxi that Khan usually drives; he also instructs George on how to accomplish the murder—have the hit man hire Khan's taxi, drive to a deserted location in Queens, and execute him there.

But George decides to give the job to Raymond "Dilly" (for Dillinger) Rivera, a sometime drug dealer who accepts the hit and then immediately reports it to the New York City District Attorney's Office, for whom he is already working as an informant in an unrelated case—something that Fogarty George obviously does not know.

Now, under the guidance of the DA's office, Rivera holds several taped phone calls with George and wears a wire to a meeting in which he and George discuss the hit. George is arrested, and incriminating pieces of evidence including a loaded nine-millimeter gun, $1,700 in cash, and a piece of paper in Sibadan's handwriting containing information about Khan are recovered. Realizing his situation, George rolls over. He agrees to plead guilty to the lowest offense and to accept a sentence of one to three years on the condition that he give up Sibadan and testify truthfully against him at trial.

Sibadan was arrested. After waiving his *Miranda* rights at the station house, Sibadan admitted to having wanted someone to give Khan a "good beating" but did not confess to hiring anyone to commit murder. He was charged with two counts of conspiracy to commit murder, the only legally available charge, since he had planned and ordered the murder but no murder had occurred. After failing to have his statement to the police suppressed, along with the evidence that had been seized at his home, Sibadan went to trial before me. His attorney was an obnoxious, aggressive man who, in my opinion, totally alienated almost everyone. He was convinced he knew more than everyone about everything; he also had no defense. In contrast, ADA Deborah Hickey did her usual excellent job. The trial was short but not always sweet. A typical interchange at the bench between the defense counsel and me, early on in the case, went something like this. Counsel: "If you make that ruling, Judge, I'll get you reversed . . . but then, I'm going to do that anyway, this will just make it easier." I looked at him incredulously and just shook my head. He obviously didn't want me to like him and succeeded admirably in that goal.

Within two weeks of the start date, the jury found Sibadan guilty. I sentenced him five to fifteen years. Incredibly, at the sentencing hearing, his entire family begged for mercy for this despicable man, who despite his crimes was still the husband and father of the family. Because of their pleas, I refrained from giving him the maximum.

Almost every case that results in a conviction is appealed, if for no other reason than that the defendants are going to be sitting in jail, often for long periods of time, and have little to lose by bringing such appeals. (Of course, many convince themselves that they have been wrongly convicted as well.) In Sibadan's appeal, the basic charge against him—that he had hired someone to murder his son-in-law—was not contested at all. In other words, his guilt was not at issue.

I had made many rulings during the course of the short trial. For instance, I had ruled that it was permissible for Sara Sibadan to testify that her father had previously tried to choke her to death, because even though he was not charged with that particular crime, the action was part of the narrative about the crime and demonstrated the defendant's intent to commit the crimes with which he was charged. This ruling conformed to a well-recognized legal doctrine permitting such "uncharged crimes" evidence in certain situations. I still recall my "discussion" with defense counsel. He argued against my ruling rudely and vociferously; I finally had to dress him down, saying something like "You just don't understand the law, Counselor. I suggest you stop arguing and read the case law; you obviously aren't familiar with it. Numerous cases have extended the law to more than cover this situation. . . . So read the law and stop embarrassing yourself!" All of this was said out of the jury's presence but in no way improved our opinion of each other.

Many other points were raised, most frivolous. The public should understand that for every one or two valid issues raised in most appeals, there are many spurious ones as well. While some cases involve difficult and close legal issues that warrant careful appellate attention, many do not. At times it is tempting to ask whether our criminal justice system is being drowned in unnecessary paperwork. Sibadan raised a number of points on appeal. The Court of Appeals affirmed his conviction.

No discussion of murder cases could be complete without considering one in which the defense asserted an "insanity" defense—technically, a lack of mental responsibility. Here is one, the case of Hubert Eric Napier, in which the facts, allegations, and legal issues were even more complex and bizarre than I had initially expected them to be and more so than in most insanity defense cases.

It is December 1990. Twenty-eight-year-old horse groomer and ex-con Hubert Eric Napier has cadged a room in Elmont, New York, near Belmont Racetrack, from another young trainer, Arthur Amaya, whom he has met earlier in the year when both worked at a Florida racetrack. Napier needs the room because he has recently been fired by his employer and had to move out of the racetrack dormitory. To Amaya and his mother, who owns the house, Napier says he is David Applegate. In mid-December, Napier/Applegate makes the acquaintance of a woman named Deborah Garcia and they make a date to go sight-seeing around New York City.

On the evening of December 17, at the end of that sight-seeing date, an unusual pickup occurs. Napier and Garcia are at a Manhattan bar, and after a few moments of conversation with a woman on a nearby stool who is wearing a full-length mink coat, Napier buys her a drink. Kim Nicholls is a lonely young professional. She offers to cook dinner for both Napier and Garcia at her apartment on Roosevelt Island. They accept. During the late evening hours, at Nicholls's apartment, all are quite intoxicated. Napier pulls out a joint and offers it to the women; they refuse it, and he smokes it alone. Angered at the turn of events, Garcia soon leaves.

The next morning, Napier telephones Garcia from Nicholls's apartment to apologize and eventually convinces her to deliver to him in the parking lot of Nicholls's building some suitcases that he had left at her apartment. She does this. Kim Nicholls works at a temporary Christmas season job at Saks Fifth Avenue on December 19, and on December 20, one of Kim Nicholls's sisters phones her apartment and the phone is answered by a male voice. When the sister calls back, she speaks with Kim about a family matter.

These are the last times anyone hears or sees Kim Nicholls alive.

On December 23, alerted by the Nicholls family, who had not heard from Kim, the police found Kim Nicholls's body on the bed in her apartment. She was horribly mutilated; her neck was almost severed from her body, and she had multiple knife wounds, including a gaping opening in the abdomen. Her face and body were covered with pillows, and the room was, as the investigator characterized it, "totally wrecked" and "quite a gory scene." On the bedsheet under the body, the legend "George #138" was written in Nicholls's blood, and on the mirror was another legend, "Zigor 623," also written in her blood, with an "8" underneath the letters, the top of the eight looking like a heart. As the medical examiner later testified, Nicholls had "put up a tremendous amount of struggle" in defending herself from her assailant, and some of her wounds had been inflicted after death, probably in an attempt to dismember the body. Even the detectives and medical examiner found the crime scene more repelling than most of the countless others they had seen. The cause of death was later determined to be sixty-one stab wounds and slashes to Nicholls's chest, abdomen, and extremities, with a huge slash wound to her neck, which severed the carotid arteries, jugular vein, and larynx. It was also reported by the medical examiner that attempts had been made to dismember the body by removing the head.

Deborah Garcia's business card was found in Nicholls's bathroom, and questioning of Garcia soon led toward Applegate/Napier. But Napier was not immediately found. During the period from December 21 to 26, he was staying in a hotel in Manhattan and using credit cards that he had stolen from Kim Nicholls and from Arthur Amaya to buy luggage, an attaché case, two money pouches that could be attached to the body, champagne, and a Greyhound bus ticket to Atlantic City. He had also cashed checks from Nicholls's bank account. On Christmas night, he "ordered" a woman from an escort service to his hotel room, had champagne and food brought up by room service, and claimed to the woman that he was Arthur Amaya from Kentucky, in New York to sell some Arabian horses. That night he ran up a bill of $675 on Amaya's Diners Club card.

On December 26, Napier's blatant use of Amaya's credit card caught up to him. Amaya's mother told the hotel employees that her son was in Florida and that the card was probably stolen. The Holiday Inn Crowne Plaza security personnel held Napier until the police could come and arrest him. Searching his belongings, the cops found property belonging to both Amaya and Nicholls. After opening a pouch strapped to his leg, the officers found receipts from the use of the Amaya credit card as well as jewelry, Nicholls's Saks credit card, and various other cards that bore her name, including her Social Security card. In another concealed pouch, police found several checks from Nicholls's account, made out to Arthur Amaya but in handwriting later established as Napier's.

Since on December 26 the arresting officer had no knowledge of who Kim Nicholls was, Napier was investigated only on the Amaya credit card counts. Mrs. Amaya was brought into the station house and identified him as David Applegate—whereupon Napier cried out, "Mom, please don't do this to me. You know I love you," and claimed that she had Alzheimer's. The detectives who questioned him asked about Kim Nicholls's cards and property, not knowing that Nicholls was dead, accepted Napier's explanation that she had loaned these things to him. Napier was charged and arraigned on December 28 only on the Amaya credit card counts. He was released on his own recognizance until his next court date, on January 22, 1991.

On January 6, 1991, the detectives looking into the Nicholls murder made two connections. They took Deborah Garcia to Elmont, where she pointed out the house from which she had picked up David Applegate for their sight-seeing date; and they learned that some of the prints in the Nicholls apartment matched those taken from the man who had been arrested, arraigned, and given an ROR ("release on his own recognizance") in the Amaya fraud case. The chase led quickly to the Holiday Inn Crowne Plaza, where the manager showed the police luggage he had confiscated from the man who had registered as Amaya; in the bags, the cops found items belonging to Nicholls and to Amaya, as well as documents referring to Hubert or Eric Napier from Ohio and others referring to David Applegate. They also found a U-shaped spike that had probably been used in making holes in the wall in Nicholls's bedroom.

When Napier/Applegate did not show up for court on January 22, 1991, a bench warrant was issued for his arrest—on the fraud charges. Alerted by the NYPD to the likelihood that Napier might be in Atlantic City, the New Jersey police picked up the trail and found and arrested Napier (on the bench warrant) at Bally's Hotel on January 27. After reading him his *Miranda* warnings, the New Jersey detectives questioned Napier, who said he was David Applegate and that the fraud charges probably had to do with names that the CIA had given him in connection with some of his secret work.

Detectives from New York City made their way down to Atlantic City and, after receiving instructions from a Manhattan

ADA to question him only about the homicide, interviewed Napier on videotape on January 28–29 and also obtained a written statement from him. In the interview and statement, Napier admitted killing Kim Nicholls.

He told the detectives that "a voice inside of him," named George, told him to "get" Nicholls, yelling, "Cut her like a pig." He stabbed her in the leg, pulled her to the floor, and kept stabbing her; then "Zigor" told him to cut off her head. As he started to do that, George returned and told him, "No, I want her gutted like a pig," so Napier sliced open Nicholls's abdomen. He took a piece of her clothing, dipped it in her blood, and wrote "George #138" on the sheet; then, putting blood on a cloth, he wrote "Zigor 6238" on the mirror. He placed her body on top of the sheet, put a pillow under her head "to make her comfortable," and covered her with a blanket "because George doesn't like people watching." Then he went to sleep and the next morning left the apartment, taking much of Nicholls's property.

Napier informed the detectives that he had first heard George's voice at a New Year's Eve party in 1979, after he had drunk beer spiked with PCP and had to be hospitalized. He estimated that George had "come out" about fifteen times since then. As for Zigor, a girl he had met in a bar had told him about this god of witchcraft. The numbers he had written on the bedsheet and mirror were "command codes" that forced him to act. The heart-shaped eight referred to the time when he was eight years old and had been raped by his uncle.

At the conclusion of the interview with the detectives, Napier asked what would happen to him and was told he would be arrested. He asked to go to a hospital and receive treatment for his problem with George and Zigor. He waived extradition and agreed to come to New York. Further investigation uncovered the murder weapon in Napier's motel room and, in luggage that he had cached at the Port Authority Bus Terminal, the bloody clothes worn during the murder.

When in late January 1991 Napier was arrested and arraigned in New York on the murder charge, it had already become apparent that he was a seriously strange person who needed psychiatric evaluation and treatment. He had spent some time in a Veterans Administration Hospital in Cincinnati for severe psychotic behavior, as well as in prison in Connecticut for using a name and Social Security number that were not his. He had had a terrible childhood that (according to him and to one witness) had included physical, emotional, and sexual abuse. Observers at Bellevue Hospital in New York in mid-1991 described him as mentally unfit to stand trial at that time. Some psychiatrists who examined him concluded that he had "multiple personality disorder" (MPD), that Applegate, George, Zigor, and other personalities, including that of a dog, existed within him and had, in effect, driven him to murder Kim Nicholls. Other psychiatrists who also examined Napier at length had an opposite impression: that although he was clearly a deeply disturbed man, he was not suffering from MPD—rather, in their view, Napier was a malingerer, one quite skilled at faking this particular illness. What with psychiatric examinations, long periods of time set aside for observation, and the usual delays of the criminal justice system, it was late 1993 before this case went to trial.

Some of the most important legal issues in the case came up in pretrial proceedings, as they always do. One of the legal issues central to the Napier matter was of the sort that you almost never see on television but that arises periodically in the criminal justice system: an accusation by the defense that the defendant's right to counsel was violated by the police. The defense contended that because Napier had had counsel in the fraud case at the time of his arraignment and had been arrested and detained on a bench warrant relating to that charge, the New York police had violated his rights by not notifying counsel to be present during his questioning in New Jersey on the murder charge. Therefore, the argument by his able Legal Aid lawyer went, his confession and the fruits of that confession, including the murder weapon and other items associated with the murder turned up by searches of Napier's belongings, should be suppressed by the court. The prosecution, of course, contended that the fraud and murder cases were separate, that there was no "derivative" right to counsel for Napier flowing from the Amaya case to the Nicholls murder investigation, and that Napier's confession had been obtained lawfully.

I had to rule on this complex matter, on which legal precedents could be cited by both sides as appearing to favor them. Ultimately—and to make a long story shorter—I found on this issue that there had been no violation of Napier's right to counsel as to the homicide charge. On instructions from the DA's office, the New York detectives had deliberately not spoken to Napier about the Amaya matter but had informed him that they wanted to talk about the Nicholls murder. They had followed proper procedure in obtaining a waiver of his right to counsel and his confession.

After a jury trial, Napier was convicted of intentionally murdering Kim Nicholls and of thirty-four other crimes, including grand larceny and forgery. The defendant made no effort to defend himself against any charge other than the murder. In summation, his lawyer conceded most of the other crimes, telling the jury that he, the lawyer, was "not here to waste anyone's time." Nor did the defendant deny killing Kim Nicholls intentionally. Rather, he relied on what is known as the affirmative defense of "lack of criminal responsibility due to mental disease or defect"—what everyone calls the "insanity defense." Since in New York this is an "affirmative" defense, the defense must prove it by a preponderance of the evidence, which is a lesser standard than reasonable doubt but is nonetheless something that the *defense* must prove.

The issue of the defendant's insanity, or lack of criminal responsibility, was critical to the case and unusual in its specific claim—that Napier was suffering from multiple personality disorder. The defense presented two experts, experts who could not agree on a diagnosis. One, Dr. Drob, was the chief forensic psychologist at Bellevue Hospital. The other, Dr. Levin, was a psychiatrist and chief of a private hospital that handled some patients with "dissociative disorders," but he had no experience with MPD in a murder case. Each interviewed Napier several times. Drob, who was not a specialist in dissociative disorders or in testing a person for MPD, performed a battery of tests on Napier and concluded that on one important test, the defendant had scored very high on the section that measured the feigning of mental illness.

While Drob never met any of Napier's personalities other than George, Napier claimed to Levin that he felt he was schizophrenic and that he was an eight-year-old named Eric whom George had to protect. When Napier was informed that his final interview with Levin was to be videotaped, he became David Applegate and claimed that what George had done was wrong and that George should be punished for it, but that if George was punished, Applegate would have to be punished, too, even though he had done nothing wrong.

Also while showing off for this videotape, Napier made his most amusing claim: He was a dog in one of his alternate personalities, "Demolition Dog." In order to demonstrate that "personality," Napier got down on all fours, barked, licked the floor, and claimed that his mind was inhabited by the dog—something that did not appear to unduly distress him. He also put forth (on the tape) numerous other far-fetched claims, all of which the jury had trouble listening to with a straight face—as did I.

The defense wanted to offer into evidence that videotape of Napier as he became some of his "alternate" personalities. The first time we viewed the tape in the courtroom, no jury had yet been picked, and I had to decide whether the tape was admissible at trial. When there is no jury present, the courtroom is much more relaxed and sometimes we let our guard down.

That's what happened here. As Napier transformed himself into a dog and proceeded to bark and to lick boots and shoes, everyone in the courtroom began to laugh. And while laughing, I forgot that there was a class of high school students in the courtroom. After the tape was finished and the lawyers had left the room, one of the students asked me what I thought of the videotape. I said it was "utter baloney"—and this remark was picked up by a reporter from the *New York Post*, who apparently was in the courtroom as well. It appeared in that newspaper the next day, to my chagrin. Fortunately, defense counsel did not try to use that offhand remark against me. In any event, I agreed with the defense that the videotape of the defendant acting like a dog (as well as "inhabiting" other personalities) could come in at the trial, though I warned the defendant's lawyer that it might well make the jury laugh harder than I had. In fact, that is exactly what occurred, although the jury attempted to hide its obvious giggles and guffaws.

Ultimately, both Dr. Drob and Dr. Levin concluded that when the defendant killed Kim Nicholls, he was in a psychotic, delusional state as a result of his disorder and did not know and appreciate the nature of his acts or their consequences *and* did not know that his acts were wrong. Neither doctor had an opinion as to whether Napier was criminally responsible for any of the charges other than murder.

The People's rebuttal case was a strong one and included witness evidence that Napier had boasted that he had almost fooled the leader of the treatment team into believing his mental illness. The prosecution also called a third psychiatrist, one who supported its position and who concluded that Napier was malingering, voluntarily feigning illness to avoid conviction. This shrink also concluded that having an antisocial personality disorder was in no way indicative of being unable to know or appreciate the nature of one's own conduct. These assertions helped the jury convict Napier.

During the inevitable appeal of the conviction, the defense objected to my instructions to the jury on the insanity defense, in particular on the point that the defendant wanted to blame the murder on one of his alleged alternate personalities— George or Zigor. Defense counsel argued that if an alternate personality was in control of the defendant at the time he committed the murder, then the defendant was not guilty by reason of insanity. What I made clear to the jury was that the defendant and any alternate personalities were still one person in the eyes of the law, and that the law could not apportion criminal responsibility between personalities. We do not allocate guilt, I told the jury, by "dividing it among personalities," since "it is still this defendant, regardless of any alter personalities," with whom we are dealing.

The jury appeared to understand this rather complex legal point because they convicted Napier of murder as well as the many counts of forgery and fraud. I sentenced Napier to forty-five years to life. I was glad to have him put away, because of the extreme viciousness of the murder. On appeal, the several legal points that had been raised during the proceedings regarding Napier's right to counsel, the insanity defense, and my charge to the jury were all considered by the appeals courts and rejected. His conviction and sentence were affirmed.

The Napier/Applegate case highlights the critical problem with insanity defense cases: The trial always becomes a battle of the experts. If one side finds an expert to say A, the other side will always find one to say, no, B. And since the expert testimony is often quite technical, the jury is frequently confused. The expert who is more articulate and who stands his or her ground is the "winner" and the one more likely to be believed, all other things being equal. (In the Napier case, testimony from other witnesses somewhat balanced out that of the experts.)

The question that must be raised is whether this aspect of a case should be decided by a jury at all. Perhaps judges are better equipped to resolve dispassionately the issue of sanity or insanity—after having asked the right questions and, one hopes, without being swayed merely by the appearance or demeanor of the experts. However, such procedure would have to pass legal and constitutional muster and almost definitely could not, since it is considered to be an issue of fact, which the fact finder (generally a jury) must determine.

Unfortunately for this discussion of murders most foul, one of the most fascinating—and repelling—insanity defense cases that was decided in my courtroom is still on appeal, that of John Royster. This defendant was charged with striking terror in the hearts of women all over New York City and Westchester by brutally raping, assaulting, and leaving for dead a number of women and murdering a respectable businesswoman. A jury convicted him of all charges and he received the maximum sentence, his insanity defense having been rejected. Again, as with other cases on appeal, that is all that can be said about the case until all appeals are resolved.

After presiding over so many horrible cases of unbearable brutality, I often ask myself the Shadow's famous question—seriously: What evil lurks in the hearts of men (and women)? I am afraid that the only answer is incomprehensible evil, pure evil.

IN A
DIFFERENT ROLE: VICTIM

On August 8, 2000, I was preparing for two matters—a thirty-three-defendant trial in a convoluted stock fraud case; and my vacation—when I received a call from a supervisor in the district attorney's office who insisted on seeing me right away.

"I just wanted to let you know," the supervisor said after entering my chambers, "that tomorrow we're going to announce the indictment of Stuart Winkler for conspiring to murder you."

My mouth fell open. "Not again!" I groaned.

Once more a defendant in a case in my court was making threats against my life. And, for the first time, the threats had risen to the level of an actual indictment. The supervisor said that Stuart Winkler, the chief financial officer of the company involved in the stock fraud case and the lead defendant, had been taped in jail by an inmate as he made plans to pay $30,000–$50,000 to have me "assassinated." One scenario discussed on the tape, I later learned, was to throw a hand grenade at me and my police detail as I emerged from my usual lunchtime spot, Forlini's.

The supervisor provided a few more bits of information about the threat but would not reveal the details—"too sordid," he said, "and they might prejudice you." He assured me that the DA's office was going to bring the indictment in a "low-key way," but he added that the DA was as yet uncertain as to whether it would be necessary to ask that I be removed from presiding over the stock fraud case.

Then he left me to contemplate all this.

Stunned, I reached for the phone to call Fred. I was particularly concerned that my aged parents would receive the news from the media before I could alert them. I told my mother that she might see something in the next day's paper about a threat to me, but that the danger had passed because the person making the threats was in jail and the authorities had thwarted his plans. This was something of an exaggeration, because the danger was real and continuing, since Winkler had the resources to keep trying to "get" me even though he remained in jail. My security was beefed up yet again.

But I was still unprepared for what happened next. It wasn't low-key. In reaction to the press release, which provided news organizations with copies of the indictment and edited transcripts of the taped jailhouse conversations, reporters jammed the courtroom as Winkler was brought in and arraigned, obviously before another judge. (He pleaded not guilty to the charges.) Front-page headlines in the *New York Daily News* and the *New York Post* were identical—KILL THE JUDGE!—and were each accompanied by an enormous, full-page photograph of me. Television news channels started broadcasting the news at seven that morning. All the reports featured excerpts from the taped conversations—lines like "Do it. It's a done deal. Don't worry about it. Just don't get [expletive deleted] caught." The tapes—recorded during June and July—were laced, I was told, with an unbelievable amount of profanity, and included Winkler devising a code to communicate to the hit man, who was shortly to have been released from prison, information on my courtroom security arrangements and details of my vacation plans.

My phone rang nonstop with reporters calling me for comment, but I refused to say anything about the indictment or the threat except that I was doing well and expected to continue doing my job as I had always done. A spokesman for the Office of Court Administration told a reporter, "Unfortunately, this [threat] is not something that is new to Judge Snyder, and it will certainly not deter her from doing her job in the future." That was nice for me to read, as were positive comments to reporters from my old friend Bernard Kerik, then the corrections commissioner, and from my colleague Judge Edwin Torres, whom I respect and admire. But I was *not* gratified to learn that although the DA's office had requested that Winkler be returned to prison and not permitted to phone anyone but his lawyer, he was going to be permitted—by the other judge—to make and receive calls from his wife and children—calls that, as I had learned in other cases, often permit defendants through these family members to threaten witnesses or give orders to carry out reprisals against witnesses, cooperators, prosecuting attorneys, or the judge.

How had we gotten to this point? Winkler and his co-defendants, most of them associated as he was with the A. S. Goldmen stock brokerage firm headquartered in Florida and New Jersey, had been arrested in July 1999 and charged with bilking $100 million from investors. At the arraignment, the prosecutor played an audiotape of Winkler telling associates, in so many words, "I've been fucking the system all my life, and I'll keep on fucking it—I'll hire the best fucking lawyers. . . ." After these words had been heard in the court, the tape actually exploded in the tape recorder—as it always did in *Mission: Impossible*. Winkler was then represented by a well-known defense attorney. Despite having just heard his client's raving on the tape, this attorney actually asked me not to impose one of the legal requirements for posting a bond, which entailed posting property equal in value to twice the amount of the bail bond. "Don't you think that's asking a bit much? Do you actually expect me to help your client f— the system?" I inquired of the defense attorney as Winkler sat at the defense table with contempt visible on his face.

I set a reasonable bail, $1 million—after all, this was a case in which the defendants were alleged to have stolen $100 million—and decreed that the usual bail conditions would apply— that is, that any property pledged would have to equal twice the face amount of the bond. He met those conditions after several days in jail and was released.

Then, around the turn of the year, and during the time when Winkler's assets were frozen and he was constrained by the bail bond arrangement not to leave the country, he managed to charter a private jet to the Cayman Islands, a trip on which he took along over a dozen of his friends. After that, and for only the second time in my career on the bench, the bail bond company appeared in court and said that the bond had to be withdrawn, in this instance because Winkler was not meeting the conditions set for the bail. The prosecutor asked me to remand Winkler, but I wasn't ready to do that yet. Rather, I placed him under house arrest and raised the bail to $1.5 million. After Winkler made several unsuccessful attempts to raise his bail, I lowered bail back to the original $1 million.

By March, it had become clear to the DA's office and to me that he was not going to meet the conditions I had set. At that point, the DA asked once again that Winkler be remanded, and although I refused to remand him, I agreed that he should finally be put in jail pending the trial, unless and until he could raise the $1 million. It was then, apparently, that Winkler began to fashion his sinister plot to have me killed.

Later, I would look back and recall that Winkler had been remanded at his arraignment on the same day that the "gentleman gangster," Alphonse Malangone, had come into my courtroom to surrender in order to begin his jail sentence. The two of them had spent time together in the holding pen, and I have often wondered if it was at that moment that Malangone had discussed the details of my routine, such as my frequent lunches at Forlini's, with the man who soon hired someone to have me killed.

In jail, Winkler must have mouthed off about this desire, because a fellow inmate, who was scheduled to be released in early summer, told Winkler that for the right price he could possibly arrange a hit when he got out. Then the inmate told this to the authorities—in exchange, of course, for promises to benefit himself—and went back to jail wearing a wire.

By the time the news of Winkler's indictment for attempting to have me killed came out, Winkler had changed his lawyer and was now represented by another well-known defense attorney.

I felt that the appearance of justice required me to recuse myself from the portion of the A. S. Goldmen stock fraud case that involved Winkler, because of the massive publicity surrounding his indictment for conspiring to kill me. His case was severed from that of his co-defendants and was then scheduled for separate trial before another judge. I agreed to retain the rest of the case and its many defendants. Before the stock fraud trial began, Winkler went to trial on the charges stemming from the threat to me—conspiracy and criminal solicitation.

Almost every defendant has a "story," or an excuse for his conduct, I've learned from experience. Almost none take responsibility; it's always someone else who committed the crime, or someone else's fault. Some actually convince themselves of this. Winkler's eventual "story," well orchestrated by his lawyers and trumpeted to the press, was no exception. It went like this: Since I was an unreasonably tough judge, his fate was unfairly preordained, and he had no choice but to hire someone to kill me. The logic of this escaped me; I thought it so ludicrous as to be unworthy of comment, but the media still gave it some attention.

I was informed at the last minute before the trial that I would be called to testify for the prosecution. I had hoped this would not be necessary and had deliberately not listened to the tapes of Winkler's conversations in the jail cell or read the transcripts. Everyone connected to the case had suggested that that would be upsetting and serve no constructive purpose, and I had taken their advice.

As the moment approached when I was to take the stand, I realized that for the first time in my career of dealing with criminal matters, after having been a prosecutor, a defense attorney, and a judge, I was now the victim of a crime—a very different role. And I had a victim's sense of powerlessness about the proceedings. I began to relive my experiences in the sex crimes unit. As in so many rape cases, the defense strategy in this case was to put me, the victim, on trial. Since most of the trial was being held in the media, I couldn't do much about it, either. Judges are not allowed to comment on pending cases.

I was on the stand, testifying, for only a short while, perhaps fifteen minutes. The ADA asked me questions designed to elicit a few facts to reinforce the material on the tapes. Yes, I ate regularly at Forlini's; yes, I had a son. My appearance was important, the ADA had told me, so that the jury could see who I was, the very real person whom Winkler had plotted to assassinate. I certainly wasn't going to cry or fall apart, but I was upset and angry. I could not let any of this show, and as a result, I believe that I appeared to the jury and onlookers as somewhat cold and businesslike. I could not let my guard down. If I had, I don't know what would have happened; my outrage and frustration at the defense attempt to make me the "bad guy" was great. However, the defense chose not to cross-examine me, which was a smart move, because I would probably have been able to elicit more empathy for myself had I been on the stand longer or if they appeared as malicious in confronting me as they had been in the media. They continued to attempt to denigrate me in the press when they wouldn't confront me on the witness stand—the cowardly approach.

It soon became apparent to the defense that the tactic of putting me on trial, in the courtroom and in the media, was not working, so they switched to the defense that Winkler had been entrapped by the dastardly inmate. Winkler himself was on the stand for two days. I did not attend his testimony, but I was told that he was quite the con man.

The four or five days when the jury was out, deliberating, were unbelievably stressful. I had always known this was a difficult time for participants in a trial to endure, but now, in my role as victim, I could hardly bear the wait. Christmas was approaching, and the jury wanted very much to go home and was annoyed at being sequestered. I later learned that during the deliberations, one juror had to be replaced and the defense agreed to that; this was unusual, as the defense does not usually agree in such circumstances, and it can't be done without their consent. And after that juror was replaced, the jury rendered its verdict—guilty on both counts. After all the money Winkler had paid to his lawyers, a sum close to $2 million—money that had been taken from his innocent victims—he had not, in his words, "fucked the system."

I was relieved that the only possible, rational verdict had been reached.

Winkler was sentenced to a long term in jail for attempting to have me killed and he also pleaded guilty to reduced charges in the stock fraud case, the sentences to run consecutively. He waived all rights to appeal. So, was the threat over? Unfortunately, I have heard that Winkler would still like to harm me, so who knows?

The stock fraud case involving the other defendants went forward in my courtroom and in the summer of 2001 resulted in convictions on most of the charges. It was the most boring case I have ever tried, and it lasted seven painful months. Winkler was blamed for everything by his co-defendants, since he was not there—a not unusual course of events. However, I am constrained from discussing the case further, as it is on appeal.

The unwanted publicity that I received because of the Winkler threat was one of the matters that led to a *60 Minutes* profile of me in the spring of 2001, although the producers claimed they had wanted to do it for some time. In many ways, this was the culmination of my "television career." I had been appearing with some regularity on the morning shows and serious broadcasts during the years I had spent doing the many drug gang cases. Then came the O. J. Simpson trial and the rebirth of the public's awareness of the importance of criminal proceedings. I was frequently asked to comment on the trial by various television programs, including the *Today* show.

Roger Ailes, then head of a cable network (and now chief of the Fox News network), did two one-on-one interviews with me, and I appeared a number of times on an early Chris Matthews program. On these broadcasts, I would try—as I had been doing since an appearance on *Face the Nation* in 1990—to talk about drug treatment and alternative sentencing, as well as about my belief in lengthy sentences for violent criminals. I would also discuss the subjects that, according to the media, were in the forefront of the public's mind, such as the Rockefeller drug laws, the "war" on drugs, and other issues of current interest.

But appearing on these programs, and others, which credibly addressed serious legal issues, did not change my view of the media as largely sensationalist. While there are some excellent television programs involving the law, the real interest in portraying law appears to be to seek out areas that will titillate or appeal to the prurient interest and thus entertain. Lawyers are portrayed in variations of ruthless, opportunistic, brilliant, eccentric, or corrupt—all caricatures.

And no one can dispute the effect that television and other media have had on the public's perception of the legal system. Jurors have come to expect, even in ordinary cases, fingerprints, DNA evidence, and scientific tests, because of high-profile cases like O. J. Simpson's and fictionalized law shows. In fact, most cases consist simply of witness testimony, with perhaps a diagram or some photographs. For example, in real life the hundreds of thousands of crack vials and glassine envelopes of crack or heroin confiscated each year on New York City streets alone are never tested for fingerprints. To do so would not be practical or legally necessary. But juries are led to expect this kind of evidence, as well as drama, excitement, and sensational endings. They also expect things to go smoothly and quickly in the courtroom, expect the lawyers to be as theatrical and polished as actors . . . and on and on. Thanks to the media, they are sometimes even ready to believe the total fiction the lawyers may attempt to dish out in a particular case. And, certainly, the media's interest in covering a case is to seek the headline that will sell the newspaper or keep the viewer glued to that channel. These motivations are understandable, but the portrayals of the criminal justice system do not often reveal the complexity of the case covered or the reality of the courtroom.

Many Americans watch vast amounts of television every week. Since law and crime shows abound—with only occasional, reasonably accurate ones—I believe one can conclude that many Americans derive their concept of our criminal justice system from these sensationalized and inaccurate fictional programs. This is a frightening thought!

These points were reinforced by my own experience. The Winkler case was never analyzed; it was sensationalized. There was no media interest in Winkler's real victims, only in Winkler trying to kill the judge before whom he was to be tried. And when he, via his attorneys, attempted to make himself appear to be the victim, the media found that intriguing and gave it substantial play. Had they analyzed the case and his claims, they would have sneered.

No matter how many times I had dealt with victims and witnessed firsthand what they endured, I had never expected to be a victim myself. But compared to most victims, how fortunate I had been. I had not had to endure the vicious pillorying on the witness stand that so many crime victims have had to endure—that feeling of being victimized all over again. Nevertheless, the helplessness and frustration, the total lack of control over an irrational situation in which you, the victim, are placed on trial, all that will not soon be forgotten.

BREAKING THE MOLD: SENTENCING REFORM

One day, a not-so-young defendant with a wooden leg was brought into my courtroom on an A-1 drug possession charge. His lawyer was an able attorney known around the courthouse for having, almost exclusively, Dominican drug clients. A fellow judge had been heard to joke that every Dominican has a constitutional right to be represented by this lawyer. Another lawyer told me that this man keeps a list of fees posted in his office—and for "cases to be tried by Snyder" he charges double.

After months of stalling and of dancing around the system, the one-legged defendant finally reached the point of "plea or trial"—the ultimate bottom line in the criminal justice system—and had been offered a plea of four years to life. It was a very reasonable offer for a man with a long rap sheet who seemed to have no defense. He had been picked up on a minor charge but, in the holding pen at the station house, had been caught unscrewing his wooden leg, in which the cops had found cocaine. His lawyer begged him to take the plea and explained his lack of a defense, but the defendant insisted on going to trial.

A jury soon found him guilty. Now I was going to have to sentence him to the mandatory minimum, fifteen years to life. I balked. This was a minor criminal with a disability. I didn't want to send him away for that long. I called a conference with his attorney and the ADA and appealed to the young prosecutor. "This is not right and you know it," I said, and told him that if he agreed, I could set aside the verdict, have the defendant plead guilty, and give him a lesser sentence. "It's unusual, and should not be done very often, but we ought to do it here," I argued. To my surprise, the young prosecutor agreed but said he'd have to clear it with his boss, Special Narcotics Prosecutor Sterling Johnson. A truly nice person, Sterling is today a federal judge and has always been a man interested in being fair. He agreed to my solution, on condition that the defendant receive six years to life. He did, and everyone was satisfied, including the defendant. We had averted a real injustice, despite initial irrational behavior by the defendant, because everyone concerned with the case, from the lawyer to the young prosecutor to the judge, really cared about the fairness of the outcome.

A few days after the September 11 attacks on the World Trade Center, I ran into a plea-pushing judge in the elevator of 100 Centre Street. Several court officers had lost their lives in the WTC disaster, because they had run over from our building to help with rescues; the courthouse's phones were out, and most court business had been suspended. In the elevator, without even saying "hello" or commenting on the disaster that had devastated me and virtually everyone else I knew, he asked, "Well, have you been able to move your calendar? Get any pleas? I'm trying to dispose of cases; I'm not going to let the lawyers off the hook. What about you?" Incredulous, I wasn't very polite. I told him I didn't give a [expletive deleted] about his calendar or mine just then, because there were a few more important things in life going on—and I stormed off the elevator.

Is it necessary to push pleas and avoid trials in order to get around mandatory sentencing laws? Because I've been a "drug judge," I've handled many high-profile drug gang cases and have frequently handed down heavy sentences. So I am often asked my views on New York State's Rockefeller laws (tough mandatory pleas and jail sentences) and on mandatory sentencing in general.

Basically, the Rockefeller laws' mandatory sentencing requirements come into play when someone is charged with possessing four or more ounces of a narcotic drug like cocaine or heroin or with selling two ounces or more—an A-1 felony punishable by a minimum of 15 years to life and a maximum of 25 years to life; or when someone is charged with possessing two ounces or more of narcotic drugs or with selling half an ounce or more—an A-2 felony punishable by a minimum of 3 years to life and a maximum of 8⅓ years to life (more for those with prior felony convictions).

But in our penal system, the "life" part of the sentence has no meaning. No one stays in jail for life or on parole for life in drug cases in New York. And even if you are first charged with an A-1 felony, you can, with the consent of the DA, have the charge reduced and plead guilty to an A-2 felony and receive as little as three years to life. Since most defendants who receive this sentence are eligible for the boot camp program known as "shock incarceration," which lasts all of six months . . . well, in practice the Rockefeller laws are not necessarily as draconian as their opponents describe them. Moreover, their harshness can be mitigated if the DA is willing to knock down the charge. I am sometimes amazed at the leniency of the plea bargains offered to midlevel drug dealers, undoubtedly either because the DA wishes to avoid a trial in which the identity of informants would have to be disclosed or because the case has legal problems.

Sometimes, press coverage of the Rockefeller drug laws tends to play up the "unfairness" of the mandatory sentences by presenting human interest stories that are so favorable to the drug dealer and his or her family that it seems their poignant tragedy is worthy of being a soap opera. The press rarely bother to explain that this darling defendant is getting a harsh sentence because he is a predicate felon (one previously convicted of a felony) with prior felony convictions for dealing drugs. It is important to remember that by the time someone becomes a predicate felon in a major urban criminal justice system, he or she may well have been arrested a dozen or more times and convicted on half those occasions. Another point: I am tired of having the crime of selling drugs referred to as a "nonviolent crime." As has been detailed throughout this book, drug dealing and violence are inextricably interwoven.

The Rockefeller laws do hamper a judge in certain situations. The first is the one referred to with the peg-leg defendant—when the defendant chooses to go to trial, is convicted, and then faces a minimum sentence of fifteen years to life even though it may not be an appropriate sentence. In such cases, I believe the sentence ought to be subject to judicial review for revision downward, say, to eight or ten years to life or even lower, if there are dramatically extenuating circumstances. The second instance arises if the defendant is a predicate felon. For a second conviction, this defendant faces a mandatory minimum of six years to life, even if the second offense is bargained down to an A-2 felony. For a real drug dealer, six to life is hardly inappropriate, but what if the defendant is a junkie who deals in small quantities of drugs to support his or her habit, is unable to kick that habit, and keeps getting arrested and convicted because of it? Then six to life may not only be too severe, it may also be a sentence that does nothing to address the defendant's underlying drug addiction. We now have the possibility of a state-run drug program in lieu of jail for certain second-time drug offenders, but the problem of underlying drug addiction still needs further attention.

Because everyone seems to want changes in the Rockefeller drug laws, I'm sure there will be some—but I'm also sure that these changes will be too liberal for some and too conservative for others. I feel that way because in the two decades before the election of Governor George Pataki, virtually no criminal justice legislation was passed by the New York State Legislature. Every criminal justice bill was blocked either by the assembly as "too conservative" or by the senate as "too liberal." During those years, I was a member of the Chief Judge's Advisory Committee on Criminal Law and Procedure, which writes and recommends legislation in the criminal justice/criminal procedure area; and for six years (until very recently), I was the chair of that committee. My colleagues on the committee were distinguished prosecutors, defense attorneys, judges, and academics. We seethed in frustration when, after years of trying to achieve reform in critical areas such as discovery (that is, exchanging information and documents about a case, in advance of trial), we would have a bill introduced in the legislature only to have it die in committee. Governor Pataki has been the first politician willing and able to move criminal justice legislation—sometimes very important and controversial legislation.

Many judges decry any mandatory sentencing provisions and especially the severe provisions, complaining that these laws undermine their judgment and discretion. Theoretically I agree, but I have been able to work around those provisions, when necessary, and have been able to convince most ADAs to give a break to a defendant when one is warranted. I also fear that increased discretion would be abused—by the "plea pushers" who count their dispositions every day and assess their effectiveness by the total number they obtain.

"It's up to you to decide what to do with your life," I tell every defendant. "If there is an offer, *you* must decide about it. If you have a good defense, go to trial; if not, perhaps you should seriously consider this offer. Consult with your attorney and let me know." If a defendant is hesitant about deciding instantly, I give him or her time to think—hours, days, even weeks, depending on the case. There is no question that knowing about the mandatory sentences will factor into a defendant's decision.

If judges were to have unbridled discretion as to the sentencing of drug dealers or violent criminals, it would be critical also to have some mechanism for appellate review of those sentences, a review process neither too cumbersome nor too lengthy. Sentences claimed to be inappropriately harsh or lenient would have to be subject to this appellate review, so that both sides would have an appropriate remedy.

While many of my cases have involved violent drug dealers and murderers—some prisons, I am told, have what they refer to as a "Snyder wing" for the violent offenders that I have sentenced to very long terms there—I have also dealt with quite a few "white collar" crime cases that have sometimes allowed me to design interesting sentences. Stock fraud, insurance fraud, and crooked lawyer fraud are serious matters, too. They cost taxpayers a lot of money: Insurance premiums for individuals and businesses spiral upward because of these crimes that bring higher costs to the insurance industry, which it passes on to consumers; maintenance payments increase for co-op apartment owners in any buildings that suffer inflated costs based on collusion between contractors and real estate management companies.

In these cases, my concern was not with removing a vicious felon from society; rather, it was with deciding on proper punishment and restitution. In one group of insurance fraud cases, the defendants were all either in the handbag business or in the construction industry. Through the agency of one corrupt insurance broker, several dozen defendants had set fire to their own goods and submitted claims for these, or for other fraudulent losses, and had collected on their false claims.

These men had agreed to negotiated guilty pleas, but they had to pay their "debt to society." Since they were working men with families, and first-time, nonviolent offenders, I saw no benefit to society in sending them to jail. On the other hand, I was not willing to sentence them to straight probation, as that would not have been sufficient punishment. I looked for a way to have them avoid jail but also to make restitution, and I found it in the Andrew Glover Program.

Over the years, as a prosecutor, defense attorney, and judge, I had come to know and to work sporadically with this wonderful program, run by an amazing man named Angel Rodriguez. Originally established to deal with Lower East Side problem youths who came in contact with the criminal justice system, it provided both sufficient supervision and opportunities to permit these youths to avoid having to go to jail. Due to Angel's intense personal involvement and his extraordinary ability to relate to these youths on many levels, the Andrew Glover Program had become widely respected and used throughout the criminal justice system. What judges like about Angel and his program is that he will not accept a defendant he doesn't think he can help or one who might not succeed in the program—and he unfailingly turns in the defendants or immediately reports them if they leave school, leave their jobs, or get into any further difficulties.

On this insurance fraud case, Alex, Teresa, and I had a brainstorming session and came up with an idea that was innovative and that worked—all too rare a combination. After consultation with Assistant District Attorney Pat Dugan, a man who really cares about justice and who proved to be very flexible in his thinking, I suggested to some of the handbag and construction defendants that if each was to employ a minority youth recommended by the Andrew Glover Program for a minimum of one year at a decent wage, then that would be my condition for probation; in addition, the arrangement would meet the DA's requirement for restitution. I could not have forced any defendant to accept this idea, and it would not have worked had I tried to, but the defendants' lawyers understood the benefits to their clients from the plan and convinced their clients that this was a very reasonable way for them to avoid jail. The pleas and sentences were structured so that the defendants agreed to return before me in a year for reconsideration of their probation. They could also come to me at any time earlier to report problems associated with the Glover program youth they employed.

The fraud defendants kept their part of the bargain—there would have been severe sanctions if they had not—and some even ended up retaining the Glover program youth in their employ. Frankly, I could hardly believe that my solution had worked so well; and its success reinforced my belief that in certain cases, one should always look for creative sentencing solutions.

In the co-op apartment case, where the kickback schemes had affected many of the co-op buildings in the city, the district attorney's office had threatened the top defendants with long jail terms. For many months, the ADA had ranted and raved to me about how "bad" these defendants were, how many people had been victimized, and so on. While they certainly had done bad things, I could not consider these defendants evil in the sense that the violent drug dealers and murderers I faced every day were evil. But the DA's office had finally convinced me that these white-collar criminals should go to jail. So I was bowled over one day when the ADA came in and told me that his recommendation for them was "no jail, just restitution." I never obtained a satisfactory explanation for this shift in position but wondered if it might be part of a pattern of behavior that I had seen before: ADAs in charge of white-collar cases trying to make points with the high-profile defense lawyers who appear opposite them. There was nothing venal in the practice, it was just a way of accumulating goodwill toward the day when the ADA might want to go into private practice.

In any event, after the radical shift, I indicated to defense counsel that restitution was expected but that it would be insufficient punishment by itself and that something else would also have to happen. The defense lawyers expressed outrage when I then suggested that if their clients were quite happy to "buy their way out" of the charges, as the DA's office was permitting, I would make it possible for them to do something worthwhile for the society they had so casually ripped off; in fact, I would insist on it. They would have to create a large fund to aid minority youth. After some huffing and puffing, they agreed. I was truly pleased with this sentence because it was a constructive one for society.

Later, I learned that the manner in which I had structured my sentence was technically not permissible, and I was told that I would never be able to do it that way again. Who complained? I am convinced that it was the high-profile defense attorneys, perhaps because the solution could have caused them to lose some of their enormous fees. But the sentence had helped a segment of society that needed help, so it is unfortunate that this kind of sentence cannot be replicated as a solution in other appropriate cases.

Even in some drugs-and-violence cases, alternative sentences are possible and appropriate, depending on the defendant's background and the extent of his or her involvement in the particular crime. All of this is relative, of course; none of these lesser defendants are the sort of people who should be guests of honor at testimonial dinners—but sometimes they deserve a break.

One woman, whom we'll call "Mira,"* had been an outstanding student at a top university—until she met and began dating "Jorge," who not only sold drugs and guns but also hooked Mira on cocaine and lured her into dealing drugs and guns with him. When she first appeared before me in court, she was a physical and mental mess, looked like a slob and a junkie, and was facing life in prison rather than a Phi Beta Kappa key. It was difficult for me to believe that she had once been an outstanding student, but her defense attorney tendered proof of that fact, emphasized that this was her first arrest, albeit on a most serious A-1 felony charge, pointed out that she had not personally hurt anyone, and argued that she could and should be rehabilitated.

Mira's story (as related by her able defense attorney) struck a chord with me, as it echoed those of the many young women sucked into the drug world by men who use them in every way possible—giving them drug habits and illegitimate children, then making them dependent on these men to provide money and a place to live. Frequently, the women are forced into working in the drug trade, sometimes even into prostitution, to support their habits, and they eventually suffer every sort of degradation. In their own minds, they are locked into this world through the men who are their providers. When I see such women, because I understand how they became involved in the drug world, I am frequently sympathetic and willing to try alternatives to incarceration if the defendant seems motivated to rehabilitate herself. Some lawyers have said I'm "soft" on women defendants. More accurately, I'm soft on any criminal, male or female, who I think is not violent, not already a preda-

---

*All names in this section have been changed to protect individuals who are rehabilitating themselves.

tor, and might eventually become a law-abiding member of society—with help. Assisting such a person in escaping the drug world and in becoming a productive citizen is the most rewarding part of being a judge—and positive reinforcement of doing something worthwhile. I only wish the opportunity for it occurred more often. But when it does, I go to bat for such defendants, acting as an advocate for an alternative sentence.

Because of Mira's background as a good student with no prior criminal record of any kind, and because of her path into the drug world and her role in it, I agreed (and the DA's office agreed) to place her in a lengthy residential drug treatment program and to give her what I call my own "deferred sentence," in which she had to come before me at specified intervals to report her progress, in the expectation that later on, the DA's office would allow her to replead to a lesser offense. Two years down the line, and after numerous interim updates and progress reports, there appeared before me in court a wonderful young woman whom I barely recognized—Mira, now totally drug-free and ready to get on with her life. She continued to make court appearances for the next several years, because of the serious nature of the crimes to which she had originally pleaded guilty, while she enrolled in another university and eventually earned that Phi Beta Kappa key. Her progress had been so extraordinary that several years later, the prosecution agreed to dismiss all the charges against her. Now she could really get on with her life. She found a job in the media, assisting in the production of documentaries and other television programs. We kept in touch, and last year—ten years after her first court appearance—we had lunch together. I continue to be proud of her success.

Mira was lucky, of course, because there was a drug treatment program that was appropriate for her as well as available when she needed it and because her family could afford it. There are very few good programs for people who have become defendants in criminal cases, especially if they are poor. The best ones target more than the person's drug problem, they also offer job training, educational components, counseling, and long-term emotional support. There are even fewer such programs for women, fewer than that for Spanish-speaking women, and still fewer for women with children. The situation cries out for improvement.

"John," a young Latino male, was charged with A-1 cocaine possession—he was driving a car whose trunk contained seven hundred kilos. His situation looked even more bleak when the police discovered that this cocaine belonged to a large-scale Colombian drug cartel, the Caliche organization. The Caliche cell was particularly violent, and its MO included numerous drug-related kidnappings and torture as well as the importation of thousands of kilos of cocaine.

John's attorneys made a strong argument that he was basically a good kid who had made one mistake, that he had only been trying to make some money and was not a dealer and was certainly not a violent person. He had known he was doing something wrong when he agreed to drive the car and deliver the drugs, but, his attorneys said, he was someone on whom a judge could take a chance. The DA's evidence made it pretty clear that John was not a member of the Caliche organization and had been hired only to drive for this one occasion.

Fortunately, I had an excellent alternative program that seemed just right for John: Abraham House, run by Sister Simone Ponnet in the South Bronx. Founded in 1993, it provides a range of assistance and services to defendants and their families, with extensive personal and family counseling at the center of its program. It includes residential and nonresidential components, drug treatment, job training, and educational opportunities. Sister Simone is as much a realist as Angel Rodriguez: She accepts candidates only after careful screening and takes only those who she feels are likely to succeed at Abraham House. John was one of those. He pleaded guilty to the top charge and was sent to Sister Simone's program; he had to report to court every month, and his progress was monitored. His progress reports became better and better, and eventually he became a role model for Sister Simone's program. After two years, the top count was dismissed and he pleaded guilty to a lesser charge and no jail time. John continues to do well and to keep in touch with Sister Simone.

One reason that many of these alternative sentencing arrangements worked out was that a smart and flexible man whom I'd known for years, Bob Silbering, was then the special narcotics prosecutor for the city of New York. I would receive permission from a defendant's attorney to speak to Silbering ex parte, without them present, and would ask for special treatment for their client. Silbering would listen and ask good questions, and if my request was reasonable, he would almost always accede to it, after first checking with the ADA handling the case. Some prosecutors suffer from rigidity and even, sometimes, lack of guts—unwilling to face down the criticism they think they might incur if they do anything that is "outside the box." Not Silbering.

And, of course, every time you try to rehabilitate a defendant, you are sticking your neck out. In one recent case, the candidate for alternative sentencing was "Mary," a lovely woman in her thirties with two daughters. She and her male co-defendant were both on methadone. Mary's drug problem was more severe than her boyfriend's; she had a long history of drug abuse and possession, many misdemeanors and felonies, and was already a predicate felon. Her present case involved selling methadone to support her habit—an offense that was far from the most serious crime but was serious for her because of her prior record. But she was a charming woman who captivated all of us by her personality, and even the ADA agreed to the idea of putting her in a drug treatment program. Eventually, and at my insistence, he agreed to three or four different ones because she kept flunking out of them and seemed to deserve another chance—until, after more than a year of trying to help, we all had to conclude that Mary just could not make it in treatment. Addicts often need more than one chance, but there must be some limit. The ADA and I gave up, and as I had warned Mary from the beginning, I had to sentence her to jail. We all felt discouraged that Mary could not help herself, could not kick her habit, but at least we had tried . . . and tried . . . and tried.

The "skankiest"-looking bunch of defendants that we ever saw in my courtroom were the pitchers for the "No Fear" drug organization based on 112th Street in Manhattan. In most drug gangs, some of the pitchers are crackheads or addicts willing to work for a fix; in this gang, they all seemed to be in their thirties (older than the norm). About ten of these pitchers had been in and out of jail, the revolving door of the criminal justice system, but were still addicted to crack. I was able to get them into alternative treatment programs. Some time later, one of the former female defendants saw the prosecutor on the street and stopped to talk, even though she had already completed her program and her case was over. She remembered precisely the short lecture that I always give to defendants about to enter alternative programs, as well as to skels whom I'm going to put away for the rest of their lives. She told the prosecutor, "When I pleaded guilty, the judge told me how much she believed that I could succeed in this program and that it was my last chance to turn my life around. That inspired me to succeed, because somebody finally seemed to care about what happened to me." She is now employed at a clerical job in a small company, and I'm very happy for her.

There were even successes with the worst of the worst, the Wild Cowboys. Two of the pitchers were Nikki and Smiley. The fact that Smiley had actually been a New York City police officer was at first hard for us to believe. After her husband abandoned her and took their children, she lost her NYPD job and moved to the Bronx with her sister, Nikki, a crack-addicted pitcher and prostitute for the Cowboys. Soon Smiley entered Nikki's world, and the next time this former NYPD officer entered a courtroom it was as a defendant handcuffed to her chair because she was suffering the aftereffects of withdrawal. She no longer smiled.

Her attorney, arguing that she had been a good person before personal tragedy had accelerated her into the arms of the Cowboys and drug addiction, suggested that an alternative treatment program was appropriate. She entered Hopper House—today no longer in existence—and spent the next two years in it. Within months, her appearance underwent a significant change, and by the time six months had gone by, I could see why she had once been known as Smiley; eyes that had looked empty and haunted on her first appearance in my courtroom were now full of light. Nikki, who (unlike Smiley) had always been involved with drugs, entered another program, and both sisters eventually completed their programs and emerged successfully to begin new lives. So today, when I think of the Wild Cowboys, in addition to visualizing Lenny, Nelson, Paqualito, and the other leaders, violent men who will be in jail for decades to come, I can also take some satisfaction in visualizing Smiley and Nikki and their rehabilitated lives.

In the past decade, we have built a lot of prisons. This has been a boost to employment, and it's hard to object to having enough prisons . . . unless they are simply a replacement for thoughtful sentencing, sentencing of the sort that might produce more positive results for society.

As I have already discussed, some people cannot be rehabilitated—ever. This group includes those who have committed such heinous and violent crimes that society can have no interest in rehabilitating them. Only a small percentage of defendants convicted of serious violent crimes—at least, non-drug-related crimes—are probably even capable of being rehabilitated. Our jail system makes minimal effort and devotes only minimal resources to rehabilitation: The percentage of prison budgets devoted to training, the teaching of technical skills and basic literacy, counseling, follow-through, and support is low in most states; only a small percentage of prisoners is affected.

Eventually, though, most prisoners are paroled, and parole is another major problem in our penal system. In the 1990s, trying to fix that problem, fifteen states abolished parole and substituted "truth in sentencing" laws so that a sentence of six years means just that, with time off for good behavior and no other provision for early release. In states with a parole system, parole continues to be a problem. Rather than serving their entire sentence, prisoners are dumped back into exactly the same environment from which they came and in which they lived while committing their crimes—often high-crime, high-drug neighborhoods—and without being given the sort of intensive "after care" that was intended and is needed in order to make parole work: help in finding jobs, drug treatment, family counseling. Parole has no possibility of accomplishing its goals unless it is given sufficient resources. Currently, caseloads per parole officer are incredibly high, at least in urban areas, and parole officers have few resources. Moreover, four of the states that in the early 1990s abolished parole have since reinstated it because the absence of parole has brought about severe overcrowding in prisons, with the result that some prisoners have to be released early anyway.*

The same problems undercut the effectiveness of probation, which could be our most important alternative to incarceration

---

*Butterfield, Fox, "States Ease Laws on Time in Prison," *The New York Times*, September 2, 2001. The states that rolled back earlier no-parole laws are Connecticut, Louisiana, Indiana, and North Dakota.

if it were properly funded and had adequate resources. It is not and does not. Currently, 3.7 million adults are on probation, nationwide; almost 2 million of these had been convicted of one or more felonies but received probation rather than jail time. On average, the states spend only about $200 per year for each person on probation, and on average each probation officer in a major city has to supervise more than five hundred probationers—an impossible task. But where probation has been taken seriously, even in major cities, in jurisdictions from Texas to Massachusetts to Pennsylvania, strict supervision, arrests of probation violators, and drug treatment and job-counseling services have made probation more effective and have cut down on crime.* A meaningful probation system, with varying levels of supervision, escalating up to highly intensive supervision for the most difficult cases,† would not only be far less expensive than prison but, far more important, would probably help many young people and afford them a real opportunity to complete their education or obtain a GED (high school equivalency diploma), undergo drug treatment, find a job. To date, we have been unwilling to commit our resources to probation or parole but are all too willing to say that these programs have failed.

In my view, a key to probation and parole may be to focus resources on the rehabilitation of the youngest offenders, for whom a return to society as law-abiding citizens can still be a goal.

Every state makes its own determination of the age at which someone is transformed from being a "juvenile" to being either—at least potentially—a "youthful offender" (a New York

---

*DiIulio, John J., and Joseph P. Tierney, "An Easy Ride for Felons on Probation," *The New York Times,* August 29, 2000.
†A report by the Reinventing Probation Council, a group of probation officials from around the country, recommends graduated sanctions, beginning with curfews and house arrest, to more intensive supervision or monitoring, mandatory drug treatment, a brief period of confinement in jail, or placement in a closely watched residential facility, to make probation work better. Cited in DiIulio, *op. cit.*

category covering sixteen-to-nineteen-year-olds and affording them the possibility of no criminal record for many crimes) or an adult felon.

States like Colorado have embarked on experimental programs aimed at rehabilitating violent youthful offenders who have been charged as adults with violent and/or weapons crimes. Those who have committed murder or sex crimes are not included, but most of the offenders have been convicted of such serious crimes as assault and robbery. Colorado's intensive, well-resourced program, known as the Youthful Offender System (YOS), prepares these young offenders for reintegration back into society by offering each one a specially designed program that includes education, counseling, and vocational training. Its purpose is to give youngsters a second chance—a stark contrast to most departments of correction, whose philosophy is to warehouse inmates in a secure environment.

The YOS program is somewhere between the juvenile system and adult prison and lasts two to six years per offender, always with the threat of adult prison hanging over him or her. It begins with an intensive "boot camp," with strict physical demands but with no physical abuse tolerated. This thirty-day program is designed to break down gang ties and establish discipline; it also involves diagnostics and orientation. It is followed by successive stages of peer group sessions and education; school is held from 8:30 A.M. to 3:00 P.M., with full academic subjects, computer lab, and vocational training. Slowly and gradually, after ongoing drug testing and supervision, freedoms are increased. Misbehavior brings severe sanctions and, at worst, the imposition of the offender's full prison sentence, which can mean up to forty years in a real prison as contrasted with spending six years at YOS. While the results thus far are mixed, the program has been extended to 2004. And while Colorado's program may be too extreme for some, this or other progressive-type programs should be attempted, at least on an experimental basis, in every jurisdiction.

In the process of dealing with many drug cases, I became acquainted with supervisors and agents of the federal Drug Enforcement Agency. These included the then head of the DEA's New York operation, Bob Stuttman, and Bob Strang, who was then the agent in charge of its press and public relations. After lecturing on the drug laws at a regional meeting, I met Strang and discussed with him an idea that Alex and I had been mulling over for some time. "Let's try to bring drug education to public schools," I suggested to Strang in the late 1980s. "We'll offer out services to the board of education and put together antidrug panels or instruction that the DEA can help with." Strang, a personable and able young man, was very enthusiastic, and the three of us mapped out some specific agendas—panels and lectures, mock trials and interactive programs.

But when we went to the board of education, we were stunned to be rebuffed with the refrain "You'll have to sell yourselves to each local school board; we won't help sell you to them—it's your problem." I could not really understand this reaction; it was outrageous. Did the board of ed not acknowledge that there was a drug problem in New York's schools? And very little drug education? Didn't they care? Here we were offering drug experts, the DEA, a judge, a law clerk—at no cost—and the board wasn't willing to do anything about it. We had hit a stone wall.

Fortuitously, I had a friend who had worked with me in the DA's office in administrative capacities while completing advanced degrees in education, and she had become the principal of an elementary school in the city. Anna Carillo is an exceptional woman who runs one of the best and most desirable schools in New York, P.S. 116. I discussed with her what we wanted to do in terms of drug education, and she invited me to "adopt" her fifth and sixth grades and become active in her school.

I've been doing that for the past ten years and have loved every minute of it.

"Active" means that I go there every month, and every month the kids come to my courtroom to watch a trial; we discuss the criminal justice system and concepts of justice, fairness, right, and wrong. When the sixth grade was joined to the junior high, I changed to the fourth and fifth grades. The students are inquisitive, interested, and not yet cynical about life, so interacting with them is always uplifting. I introduce them to cops, agents, and lawyers who speak to them about police work, prosecution and defense advocacy, and the like. There are always a few silly comments,* but the kids also ask lots of good questions. Each month, the day I go to school and the day they come to my court are total uppers; I understand why people love teaching young kids—although I don't think I could do it full-time.

In the same spirit of getting more drug education into the schools, a few years ago I became involved in DARE, the only nationally recognized program that trains police officers to go into the schools to teach drug awareness and educate the young about drugs and violence. DARE has been criticized—unfairly, in my view—for not having a permanent effect on the children, but any failing is due in large measure to insufficient funding that does not allow the message to be pounded in, repeatedly, from kindergarten through twelfth grade. Limited resources keep the program available only in some schools and in the

---

*The kids write me individual letters at the end of each school year. Some are very serious, some short "bread and butter" thank-yous. My favorite read, in part, as follows: "I have learned so much from being in your courtroom; I have learned how hard the seats are. . . ."

lower grades. DARE is studying possible changes in its curriculum and is hoping to expand its reach. Having observed the program in action, I can say that the police who are involved do a wonderful job of capturing the interest of the kids, and the kids respond enthusiastically to them. Many success stories have resulted from the DARE program. Being part of the program is one of the most rewarding things I do, as is being involved with the Kips Bay Boys and Girls Club, which assists underprivileged youngsters in many ways.

All in all, in our system there is a place for tough sentencing, a place for leniency, and a place for rehabilitation. Any sentencing reform must allow for each of these possibilities in the appropriate case and must try to ensure that none will be misused or abused.

WHERE
DO WE GO
FROM HERE?

At some point, one begins to wonder about the pluses and minuses of the criminal justice system, where it fits into society, what it—and we—can do about society's problems.

To start with a small but central difficulty: We have a serious disparity in levels of *courtroom* experience between the prosecutors and the defense attorneys. It is a matter of concern in complex cases and is particularly visible in white-collar cases. There, sadly, the defense team (often experienced, high-priced lawyers with flair) so frequently overwhelms the prosecution team in terms of courtroom savvy and ability to manipulate the jury that it sometimes seems almost surprising when the People win. I am convinced that the People do win, most of the time, because of good trial preparation and hard work by investigators and the police and because the prosecutors are good lawyers. But the People's victories are rarely attributable to their *courtroom* skills. They simply do not try enough cases. Not blind to the prosecution's general inexperience and lack of courtroom savvy, jurors in my major white-collar cases have regularly remarked to me—after the trials, of course—on this disparity in courtroom abilities. Fortunately, most jurors base their verdict on the evidence, not the lawyers' wiles or charm. But making jurors like you as a lawyer is an important courtroom skill, because trials are theater.

While many ADAs have charming, warm personalities and a great sense of humor when you speak with them off the bench, too often they display none of these characteristics before juries, unlike their more experienced adversaries. I think of the late William Kunstler in this regard. The famous radical defense lawyer may not always have shown mastery of the law or been terribly well prepared, but he was charming and used his personality well. In one high-profile case, part of which I attended as an observer, the ADA was bright, experienced, and had put together a good case. But Kunstler ran circles around him because the ADA was a stiff. Kunstler had the jury eating out of his hand, and as a result, an apparently dangerous individual was acquitted of serious charges.

As I've illustrated earlier in this book, sometimes ADAs on trial are too timid, especially in high-profile cases. At the other extreme, some ADAs are too aggressive, with a self-righteous "God gave me my mission and I am always right" attitude that presumes that every defendant is guilty and that the ADA must seek the maximum penalty for each and every one.

These observations underscore the existence of a larger question for the criminal justice system: How can we obtain and retain good prosecutors? Or any good public servants?

In the decades before I became a prosecutor, and even into the mid-1960s, spending your entire working life being a "career" prosecutor in as well-known and highly regarded an office as that of the District Attorney of New York County was not unusual. The pay was miserable and the working conditions were poor, but the importance of the work done by a prosecutor and the prestige attached to doing that work were considered a fit balance to the negatives. In fact, in 1980, three-quarters of Americans graduating from Harvard's John F. Kennedy School of Government, and other schools like it, entered the public area; now only one-third choose public service,* although this may have changed since September 11.

The climate had already begun to deteriorate by the time I joined the DA's office in 1968. Almost all the career prosecutors in Hogan's office had left; only a handful remained, and they were very good ones—John Keenan, Mel Glass, Al Scotti, and Peter Andreoli, for instance. But we young lawyers understood that the continued presence of Keenan, Glass, Scotti, and Andreoli, and others in the office, was unusual.

Today there are also some terrific and seasoned lawyers scattered throughout the various units of the DA's office. Interestingly, over 50 percent of the prosecutors in many DA's offices, like New York County's, are women. They apparently recognize the greater likelihood of balancing family and career successfully in public service. But the total number of good *trial* prosecutors—male or female—is low and will continue to decrease as the financial incentive for the good ones to leave and take positions in the private sector increases exponentially.

Good people have always found it necessary to leave public service for financial reasons, and they were doing so in 1968, but back then the disparity between the incomes of a lawyer on the public payroll and one in private practice was not so huge. I took a cut in salary when I became an assistant DA. But today's young assistant DA starts with a salary of $48,000, while his or her counterpart at a big firm in New York City will make $125,000 in the first year out of law school, with a sizable bonus on top of that. Lawyers for the poor fare even worse.

Moreover, fewer people coming out of law school can now afford to choose public service over private work. This is because many law students, perhaps even the majority of them, gradu-

---

*Nye, Joseph S. Jr., "The Best and Brightest Now Shun Public Service," *International Herald Tribune*, August 24, 2001.

ate from law school encumbered by tens and even hundreds of thousands of dollars of debt incurred to pay for their tuition.

Throughout the criminal justice system, the disparity with private sector salaries is glaring. My salary as a supreme court judge with over nineteen years on the bench is $136,000 a year. Now, for the man and woman in the street, that certainly seems like a lot of money; but it is actually less than that earned by that typical first-year associate at a big law firm. My senior counterparts in the private sector, and some of the defense lawyers who appear before me in court, make several times that amount annually. While I love what I do despite the lack of high financial reward, the relatively low salary of a judge is not exactly an incentive for attracting people to the position. It has also engendered a lack of respect for the bench from attorneys who earn far more.

The public rails at the inadequacy of parole, too lenient judges, incompetent prosecutors, and "bleeding heart" public defenders but won't do anything to alleviate these problems, and not only because fixing them requires money. We in the system have to contend with attitudes like that of a former governor of New York State, who, while in office, frequently declared that his state's judges did not need their salaries raised.* If a judge did not like the salary, the governor suggested, he or she ought to leave the system, because there were "many people waiting in line for the job."

Yes, Governor, there are always people who want to be judges, but are they the ones the system really needs to attract? Are they the best and the brightest lawyers? I guess that governor didn't care much about the quality of judicial applicants.

Let's be frank: The criminal justice system is one of society's stepchildren. And everyone who works in it is treated equally badly—parole officers, probation officers, court officers, police of-

---

*In fact, judges' salaries, in my experience, are grudgingly raised about every eight years, in what amounts to barely a cost-of-living adjustment.

ficers, public defenders, prosecutors, assigned counsel, law clerks, court clerks, judges. We are all underpaid and under-respected.

To encourage the best people to become career prosecutors, public defenders, or judges, we have to begin by altering the underlying remuneration structure. Then there are other things that can be done—that *must* be done—to attract good young professionals to public service, to keep them in public service once they have become experienced, and also to bring them back to public service when they have made enough money in the private area to afford to return. For the fledglings, certainly, incentives and subsidies can be offered. Several law schools now pay off a new lawyer's law school tuition loans if he or she chooses public service. In September 2001, the New York State Bar Association announced that it was drafting a plan to help relieve law school tuition loans for attorneys providing legal services to the poor, with funding expected from both public and private sources. The government could make that kind of offer to more law school graduates, which would make it more attractive for young people to consider working for a lower salary in the public sector and to do so for a longer time before transferring out. In return for loan forgiveness, young lawyers would be required to work for four or five years in some area of public service. We could—and should—begin a criminal justice system "Peace Corps." We could seek private sector subsidies for the ADAs and Legal Aid lawyers. There are many things that we as a society could do—and should do, as soon as possible.

To interest young people in public service, I've taken a very small step in my courtroom with an internship program. It began some years ago with a few people from law school who had asked to intern with me during the summer and now includes some undergraduate students and even an occasional high school student, as well, during the school year. Some years we have had as many as sixteen interns. Teresa and I work out a program where the students attend court sessions and write drafts of opinions. I speak to them regularly about legal issues and the criminal justice system, and Teresa sets up weekly lectures given by our friends in the DA's office, the defense bar, corrections, the police, and so on. I enjoy having young, enthusiastic people around me; the interns love Teresa, who is their "mother hen" and guide to the criminal justice system; and they are fascinated with their brief view of the underbelly of humanity. I think the program is both meaningful and fun for all involved, and I am pleased that some graduates of this internship have become ADAs and public defenders or have gone into some other are of public service. Each of us should try to inspire that interest wherever we can.

Another aspect of concern about the system was highlighted for me when I recently came across some of my old court calendars. Each supreme court judge designates one day a week as a "calendar day," meaning a day on which our primary task is to handle the cases that have been assigned to us, which usually total over 100 at a time and generally for me have numbered more than 250. Each case is not called for a hearing each week, of course, but each week a judge may call 60 to 100 of them to hear bail arguments, discuss legal issues, engage in plea bargaining, and set trial dates.

1986 CALENDAR DAY:
    —100 Drug cases, lower level
    Pitchers, dealers, drug possession, stash houses, car stops.

1990 CALENDAR DAY:
    —100 Drug cases, higher level
    Drug dealers, gang members, drug-related murders; other murders.

1994 CALENDAR DAY:
—100 Cases.
Major violent drug gangs; drug-related murders; other murders.

1998 CALENDAR DAY:
—65 Cases. (After cleanup of NYC, there are fewer indictments.)
Major violent drug gangs; drug-related murders; capital cases (murder); sex crimes.

2001 CALENDAR DAY:
—100 Cases.
Major violent drug gangs; drug-related murders; other capital cases; sex crimes, etc.

In other words, we're very busy, and my 2002 calendar is not very different from what it was in 1986, except that now all of its cases are very serious ones. The unchanging calendar also spurs some philosophical rumination: Are we in the criminal justice system accomplishing anything? Am I as an individual judge accomplishing anything?

I continue to believe that the answer to the second question is yes. I feel I have accomplished something, having presided over many serious trials involving incredibly violent people, almost all of which have ended in juries—appropriately—convicting the defendants of the highest-level felonies. This has permitted me to send these violent criminals to jail for many, many years—not infrequently for one hundred to two hundred years—which has removed many gang members and killers from society forever. Few convictions in my court have been reversed. And I have been able to make new law.

As to the first question: I don't know anymore how much the criminal justice system is actually accomplishing. The endless repetition and sameness of my calendar from year to year is truly discouraging. The faces of the defendants change; their antisocial behavior does not. And we have to wonder why. Yes, crime is down—for now—and that is a good thing. But we know it will rise again. Without realistic, long-term solutions to the "root causes," the problems of homelessness, joblessness, inadequate education, substandard living conditions—let alone the drug problem itself—the dip in crime will almost certainly prove to be temporary. And we will have to resign ourselves to the understanding that the rise in the cyclical curve will begin to kick in all too soon.*

Society expects the criminal justice system to clean up its mess, its major problems. We can't do it, and we shouldn't be expected to. My courtroom is merely the last stop in a system that has many steps, with problems at each one. It is a truism that few defendants ever show up before me without a long prior history of difficulties and run-ins with the law (unless he or she has recently—and almost always illegally—arrived in our country). Prior to defendants' reaching my courtroom, how many chances to have prevented their antisocial acts have already been squandered?

We in the court system are now attempting to wade into the fray earlier in the process, before a young person becomes too difficult for society to handle. Modern court reform has led to experiments like the one in Brooklyn headed by Judge Alex Calabrese, my former law clerk. The Red Hook Community Court is an extraordinarily progressive concept in modern jurisprudence: It combines criminal, family, and housing court cases in an attempt to bring a broad, holistic approach to resolving issues, and it incorporates counseling, drug treatment, and rehabilitation as essential ingredients in finding solutions. There are also many drug treatment courts now, of course. Red Hook and the other innovative courts around the country are

---

*In fact, early 2002 has seen an unreported rise in shootings and street crimes, although the court system is less busy than 2001, in part because of September 11.

trying hard to solve basic societal problems like drug addiction, domestic violence, dropping out of school, and problems of dysfunctional families, in addition to administering justice in minor criminal matters. They aim to rehabilitate the offender if possible and to use jail only as a last resort. But such courts deal only with lower-level crimes, not with A-1 felonies, which carry automatic jail time. Moreover, Red Hook and similar courts are able to deal only with limited caseloads and not with every type of defendant.

Unfortunately, as previously discussed, the vast majority of cases, and especially the serious and violent felonies, are rarely amenable to "alternative treatment" solutions. Most of these defendants must be sent to jail either because of mandatory sentencing requirements or because they are too violent and antisocial to be permitted to remain in society—they are no longer candidates for any attempts at rehabilitation, and society must be protected from them. A recent study by the Bureau of Justice Statistics, the statistical branch of the Department of Justice, found that prison populations nationally had increased from 1.1 million people in 1990 to 1.725 million people in 1997. (Violent offenses account for the largest increase in the male prison population—52 percent—while drug offenses accounted for the largest increase in the female prison population.)* It is important to point out that a full 80 percent of the inmates nationally have either violated drug or alcohol laws and/or been high when they committed their crimes.†

We have to recognize that sending criminals to jail is only a partial, if important, solution to crime and violence.

Now, it may seem strange for a judge who is viewed by almost everyone else in the criminal justice system as a conservative to

*Butterfield, Fox, "Prison Population Growing Although Crime Rate Drops," *The New York Times*, August 9, 1998.
†Wren, Christopher S., "Drugs or Alcohol Linked to 80% of Inmates," *The New York Times*, January 9, 1998.

be concerned about the root causes of crime. But in order to solve America's drug problem, far more than better enforcement and prosecution is required. Treatment on demand, mandatory drug education from the lowest through the highest levels of our schools, and many other basic changes are needed to eliminate the source of the problem and the demand for drugs—as all but the most unenlightened criminal justice and law enforcement professionals agree. And if we improve in these areas, we will surely eliminate at least some of the racial disparities decried by so many, which are too complex to be addressed here.

Perhaps the most tragic casualties of the drug trade are the women and children. I have seen so many of them: huge numbers of single mothers lost to crack addiction during the 1980s and 1990s. With their loss, we also lose the kids, the rest of their families, and what might be left of family values. Crack nearly completed the destruction of the family in many areas of every city, and we have yet to recover from it. The young people I see before me do not know the difference between right and wrong; they have no values and no ability to relate to these concepts. They look at me with utterly blank eyes—and minds—at any mention of these ideas.

Let us hope that we fight the war on terrorism more successfully than we have fought the so-called war on drugs. Even though in the aftermath of September 11, 2001, the war on drugs seems a lot less important than it did prior to the tragedies of that day, we cannot forget the drug problem.

A number of people have begun to discuss the very certain link between terrorism and drugs. Terrorism is fueled, at least in significant part, by drug money. Selling drugs results in an enormous amount of money, and that money must be "laundered," or cleaned. It is often passed on to terrorists like al-Qaeda, all over the world, channeled through many foreign countries and banking institutions. We need to strengthen and then vigorously enforce our money-laundering laws and convince other countries to do so as well: This will help to thwart both terrorism and narcotics trafficking.

Will it take a cataclysmic event, a national disaster, to force this country to finally agree to fight the war on drugs? To reach beyond our disagreements, fashion bipartisan proposals, and get to work on the problem? We have had a general in charge of the drug war, but he has been a general without an army and without the funds to implement significant policies. In the war on terrorism, we have come to understand that it will not be enough to eliminate Osama Bin Laden; we have to get to the underlying causes of terrorism. In the war on drugs, we must also get beyond the obvious target of the drug dealers.

When people feel hopeless, we all know they may turn to drugs to combat that hopelessness, a feeling that springs from not having an education or job training and therefore not having a job or adequate housing or money to pay the bills.

Ordinary, law-abiding citizens sometimes say that people who become lost to drugs have brought disaster on themselves. But what about the eight-year-olds sucked into drug gangs—and into drug use—by the lure of money that they have *no hope* of making legitimately? Did these vulnerable children really have a choice? They couldn't just say no to drugs, because to do so they would have had to have opportunities to say yes to real education and a chance at a better life in legitimate enterprises—all of which hardly exist in their environments. Drugs undermine our civilization in more insidious and less overt ways than bombs, hijacked airplanes, or letters filled with anthrax, yet drugs are no less vicious and deadly. Fortunately, we are filled with moral outrage at what terrorism is doing to our great country; but where is our sense of moral outrage at the national tragedy of drugs? Any war on drugs will require a long-term commitment by us as a nation, as well as international cooperation. Too many countries now make money from our enormous demand for drugs, money that is more important to them than participating in any coalition to eliminate the supply of illegal narcotics. There are no quick fixes. Unfortunately, politicians don't like long-term solutions: Their push to get elected isn't helped by a twenty-year plan, however sound it might be. Legalization or decriminalization of drugs? Those are nonsolutions and, in my opinion, ones that would set an unacceptable moral example.

Years ago, when I was a participant in the Fred Friendly public television series on the Bill of Rights, another panelist was William F. Buckley, Jr. I still vividly recall him describing his concept of the "federal drugstore," where all adults over eighteen or twenty-one could obtain whatever narcotic drug they needed, with no legal prohibition. Just ask for cocaine? Heroin? PCP? Meth? Ecstasy? In my opinion, the concept was absurd in 1990 and is more absurd now. Buckley had no answer to my objection that the black market that would appear in order to serve those under the legal age would produce the same conditions that the federal drugstore concept aimed to ameliorate.

Our one legalized intoxicant, alcohol, is responsible for more crime—spousal murders, deaths by drunk driving (now reaching twenty thousand a year), child abuse, and the like—than the forces pushing legalization of drugs will ever admit, as well as for more illness and damage to individuals (heart disease, cirrhosis of the liver, and more) and to unborn fetuses. It is one of the largest contributors to suicide, which is the eighth leading cause of death in the United States and to divorce. Currently, 54 percent of eighth-graders, 72 percent of tenth-graders, and 82 percent of twelfth-graders admit to using alcohol.* Why legalize more intoxicants?

Part of the difficulty is that we lump together different drugs, like heroin, cocaine, and marijuana, when experts agree that

*Brody, Jane, "Coping with Cold, Hard Facts about Teen-Age Drinking," *The New York Times*, April 6, 1999, and other articles, citing statistics from the DOJ and the National Center on Addiction and Substance Abuse.

heroin and cocaine are the most violence inducing and result in more crime than do most other drugs. Or we get hung up on issues like "medical marijuana" for the terminally ill, needle exchange programs, and whether or not to legalize the possession of small amounts of marijuana. These issues may be of some significance, but too often knee-jerk popular positions fuel politicians' campaigns and substitute for real concerns about the core issues.

Some people also blame the current drug laws. In poor areas, drug laws do little to deter drug distribution or drug use and abuse. And although some decry the cost of drug enforcement, according to criminal justice experts, only 4 percent of our tax dollar goes to the police, the courts, and all of law enforcement—a concrete example of how the criminal justice system is indeed a stepchild of society. While 75–80 percent of all crime is in some way drug related, and at least 50 percent of those on parole and probation are drug users, we simply have not addressed the underlying addiction problems of these offenders. As prison populations have been growing, the amount of drug treatment offered to the prisoners is shrinking.* An estimated 840,000 of the 1.7 million people in prison are in need of treatment, reports the National Center on Addiction and Substance Abuse, but only 150,000 of them will have received any drug treatment before they are released.†

As a result, I see in my courtroom people who at the ages of eight, eleven, or thirteen were sucked insidiously and perniciously into drugs. By the time they are eighteen or twenty-one—appearing before me in court as career criminals facing multiple charges ranging from selling drugs to assault, robbery, and murder—they deserve the sentences that remove them from society for the rest of their natural lives. There are also

*Butterfield, Fox, "Drug Treatment in Prisons Drops As Use Rises, Study Finds," *The New York Times*, January 6, 1999, based on DOJ Statistics.
†Wren article, *op. cit.*

people who began using drugs when young whom I never saw in court, people who died before they reached twenty-one, by overdoses, by suicide, or by being murdered by the drug dealer from whom they stole a crack vial or two. The cumulative toll from drugs is in the hundreds of thousands. How many more must die before our nation mounts a genuine war, with the backing of a genuine national commitment and substantial resources, intelligently allocated against the drug problem, with the zeal and intensity that we are now demonstrating in the war against terrorism?

Recently, I was invited to give the commencement speech at my alma mater, the Bryn Mawr School in Baltimore, Maryland, now a progressive, modern institution. In preparing my remarks, I thought a lot about my own life and what I wanted to say to these young women about the future. I tried to paint a picture for these mostly privileged high school graduates about someone a world away—Little Marvin, the four-year-old son of Shabazz, the drug dealer and murderer, a boy whom I could not save from what was likely to be a life of drugs, violence, and despair.

To have any hope of breaking the cycle of drugs, crime, and violence in our society, to save other Little Marvins—and Miras—and Smileys—the commitment of our young people is critical. Almost anyone can mentor a kid in need, adopt a class, get involved, make a difference—and still have a career of one's own.

My central message to these young women: "You can do anything you want, be anything you want to be—*but do something and be somebody.*" By this I mean: Do something that is worthwhile for society and be somebody who gives back to the world. Find out what gives you pleasure, what makes you feel good, what makes you look forward to each day—and do it!—while helping others.

Two paths will lead to accomplishing these goals: finding ways to devote a portion of your life, every day or every week, to helping other people in a meaningful way and devoting at least part of your working career to public service. Past generations understood the value, the glory, and the importance of working in the public sector, but in recent decades, far more Americans have built lives that never had anything to do with public service and reflected the cynicism and contempt for government that suffused the last third of the twentieth century. After the events of September 11, 2001, we need more than ever to reverse that trend, to spend at least a chunk of our lives working for the common good. Work in the public sector offers great rewards—not as much money as the private sector, to be sure—but the satisfaction of knowing that as a teacher, a prosecutor, a public defender, a public health doctor, a judge, you are doing something worthwhile, of benefit to society. And it is doing those worthwhile things that makes our lives worthwhile.

EPILOGUE
Winter 2002

I am sitting in my robing room, trying to write a decision, when the intercom buzzes. It's Rocco.

"Judge, it's Intell on the phone. Inspector McGuiness."*

"Okay, thanks." I pick up the phone. "Hi, Inspector, how've you been?"

We exchange pleasantries for a moment, but then McGuiness says, "Judge, I'm sorry to tell you I'm calling on serious business. We just got word that there are two guys on the street holding a contract on you. We're not sure who they are, and we haven't confirmed anything yet, but we're concerned. We think the contract probably comes from a Lower East Side drug dealer you put away—a really bad guy. The information sounds credible, so I'm sending Sergeant Harley right over. Don't go anywhere. Stay in your office. You know the drill."

*This and Harley are not their real names.